SMART INVESTING

SMART INVESTING

A Step-By-Step Guide
to Financial Security

ANDREW J. SENCHACK, Ph.D.

An Invest Publishers Inc. Book

TAYLOR PUBLISHING COMPANY
Dallas, Texas

Library of Congress Cataloging in Publication Data
Senchack, A. J. (Andrew J.)
    Smart investing.

    Includes index.
    1. Investments—United States—Handbooks, manuals, etc. I. Title.
HG4921.S45 1987   332.6'78   87-1923
ISBN 0-87833-575-7

Printed in the United States of America

0 9 8 7 6 5 4 3 2 1

This book is dedicated to my real personal wealth:

My Family
Ginny, Alesha and Lauren

My Parents
Bernice and Andy

Acknowledgment

I want to acknowledge my appreciation to those individuals that gave so freely of their time and efforts to make this book possible: Vic Arnold, Jo Anne Buress, Bo Byers, Michael Clendennen, Yvonne Guajardo, Steve Koomar, Michael Steele and Bob Witt. My family, especially my wife Ginny, also deserves special recognition for their constant patience and encouragement. My sincere thanks to you all!

PREFACE

A recent survey found that 95 out of 100 Americans aged 65 or over do not feel they have adequate assets to be comfortable in their retirement years. This is despite a major shift from individual to government/corporate benefits: Social Security, pension plans, unemployment compensation, and group life insurance. But a comfortable retirement is only one financial goal that you have; others may include

- a higher standard of living for you and your family
- protection for your family in the event of your untimely death
- lower taxes
- a college fund for your children

This list could go on and on, but the point is that you need to put your money to work today in a way that will help you *realize* these goals and not to let them continue to be just a dream.

Americans are becoming more sophisticated in money matters, and are now bringing their consumer cunning to bear on their savings and investment decisions. At the same time, the opportunities for money to make money are growing at a phenomenal rate. For example, take

1966: The average investor had few investment alternatives; most investments remained in the domain of institutions and the very rich. Savings accounts paid 4%; checking accounts paid 0%; a full-service broker had to be used to buy stocks, bonds and mutual funds.

1976: Certain types of checking accounts began paying interest; the first money market funds came on the scene but money market deposit accounts, Super NOWs and many types of mutual funds were yet to appear--the investment choices for individuals were still limited.

1986: An explosion of *new* investment alternatives has occurred: zero-coupon and put bonds, GNMAs, specialty mutual funds, real estate CDs, call options, IRAs, . . . You now have many more ways to profit. But this new-found freedom also means you need to know about more types of investments--and to make more *choices* than ever before.

More importantly, every phase of your financial planning and nearly every financial decision you make--from buying a stock to buying a home--is affected by the TAX REFORM ACT OF 1986, signed into law by President Reagan on October 22, 1986. This far-reaching legislation lowered individual tax rates and limited many familiar deductions. The result: A new world of choices and a need to take a fresh look at your *existing* investments and to develop new strategies to reap the greatest rewards. In sum, more potential reward for extra effort.

So, what will tax reform do to investments? Over the long run, it favors *financial* assets such as stocks and bonds over *real* or *hard* assets such as real estate. There's less need for investments that produce losses to offset your paycheck and greater emphasis on investments that generate income. It should force investors to spend more time on the real economic issues and stop worrying about how to beat the tax law.

Despite this, no one has all the answers. Even those experts that studied the day-to-day developments as the tax bill worked its way through Congress are still puzzling over its many implications. But let's take a brief look at some of them, which, along with others, are more fully discussed later in the book:

- **SAVINGS**--Perhaps the most significant change is the dramatic reduction or flattening in individual tax rates. Few taxpayers will find their tax rates unchanged. Because of this, look for old-fashioned savings to become more respectable. In general, the ability to save more should be improved because you'll keep more of your hard-earned income after taxes. Also, the after-tax "value" of interest earned should encourage you to set aside more of your income.

- **INSURANCE**--Whole life insurance is one of the few tax-advantaged investments left unscathed. The "cash buildup" in such policies still go untaxed until you tap them. Watch for the insurance industry to push products such as single-premium policies and annuities as a way to reduce the I.R.S. bite.

- **STOCKS** – High-yielding stocks gained at the expense of growth stocks. For the first time since 1921, capital gains have no edge over dividends. Both are taxed at the same rate. However, don't overly fixate on dividends--the really big money in stocks will continue to be capital appreciation. In addition, investors no longer benefit from holding a stock for 6 months because of a more favorable tax treatment. This means stock trading volume will increase. Maybe tax reform will become better known as the "Stock Broker's Act of 1986."

- **BONDS** – With capital gains now taxed as ordinary income and tax rates slashed, bonds with their high current yields are more attractive. Moreover, tax-exempt municipal bonds become one of the few tax shelters retained under tax reform. But, as Chapter 8 will indicate, there are alot of exceptions that you'll need to keep in mind.

- **MUTUAL FUNDS** – Sweeping changes are in store for mutual funds under the new tax law-- and some aren't pleasing for investors. Many, for example, may find that they have to pay taxes on "phantom income" from mutual funds and that "tax-free" funds may yield income that, in some cases, is taxable.

- **REAL ESTATE** – Tax reform hits real estate the hardest. Forget using a real estate limited partnership to shelter your income from the tax man. These tax-motivated investments will all but vanish. Instead, investments such as real estate investment trusts and master limited partnerships will come to the forefront. Partnerships structured with an income- rather than a tax-orientation will also become more prominent.

- **INDIVIDUAL RETIREMENT ACCOUNTS** – The 14 million taxpayers with IRAs may have to rethink their pension strategies. Tax-deductible contributions to IRAs are still allowable, BUT only if you or your spouse are not covered by a company-sponsored pension plan and/or if your adjusted gross income doesn't exceed certain limits. A *non-deductible* IRA can still be funded that enjoys a tax-deferred buildup of income.

As you can see, the investment world continues to grow more complicated and challenging. This means you need current, concise and unbiased information and advice about today's investments and their tax consequences. This is what motivated me to write this book--to provide you with a basic understanding of different investments and, in some way, to serve as your "personal advisor" in helping you make sound investment decisions.

In one fell swoop, tax reform has made all personal investing books *obsolete*. Soon, bookstores will be hit with numerous new books and tax guides with "instant wisdom" to capitalize on the public's thirst for knowledge. So what makes this book so special? First of all, this is a *revised* edition in which each chapter has been carefully rewritten to reflect changes brought about by the new tax laws, as well as the latest developments in the financial markets. On the former, we have even devoted a full chapter (Chapter 19) to help you understand the basics of tax reform and to estimate your taxes under the new rules (Worksheet No. 9). This same chapter also summarizes how different investments may be impacted by tax reform and provides tax tips on ways to reduce your taxes.

In addition, this book is written with the average investor as well as the novice in mind. It recognizes that, while most of us are hardworking and often ingenious at earning money, we don't necessarily know *how to best make money earn money*--or we're too busy to learn how.

With this in mind, each chapter has been designed to be an easy-to-read, easy-to-use reference on an individual topic. Each contains timely, definitive information and advice to help you build your personal wealth. Each chapter is also written so as to eliminate the "go-go" or "rah-rah" style found in most investments books. We're not offering you a way to make $1,000,000 in 10 easy lessons-- such a book hasn't been written yet and never will be. Life's not that simple.

But what *is* offered is my extensive experience as a teacher, scholar and personal investor for more than 20 years. In part, this experience includes the knowledge learned from studying the ideas and methods of successful investors. Each chapter has been carefully developed to not only provide you with a basic knowledge and understanding of investments, their operation and terminology, but also to give you helpful tips, suggestions and checkpoints that you can easily refer to when you are making your decisions. Moreover, charts, tables, examples, suggested references and an extensive glossary of investment terms should help answer the questions most often asked by investors. A number of personal worksheets have also been included to give you "hands on" experience with such things as estimating your personal wealth and investable funds, and selecting individual stocks. What we want to do is provide a direction for your personal investing which will ultimately lead you to financial independence and security.

Finally, another unique feature of this book is that each chapter is short, self-contained and shouldn't take more than 30 minutes to digest.

The book is organized into seven major sections. (You may want to refer to the Table of Contents.) The introductory section begins with how to determine where you are now financially and where you want to be. This will help to establish exactly what your financial goals are--the first step toward financial security. Therefore, we encourage you to complete the two worksheets associated with Chapter 1 before continuing with the book.

Try to read Chapters 2 and 3 together. These chapters contain a description of the different types of investments you can use to accomplish your goals, as well as the inherent risk and return that distinguishes each investment. In addition, you'll learn how to measure risk and return. The next two chapters can be read on their own. In Chapter 4, we'll examine the personal attributes of a successful investor and learn some important "Do's" and "Don'ts" of investing. Chapter 5 presents the mechanics of how securities markets operate. If you're comfortable with this material, it can be safely skipped over.

The next four major sections contain information, suggestions and advice on the different investments covered in this book. If you have an immediate need concerning a specific type of investment, you can go to that chapter(s) first because Chapters 6-15 do not have to be read in any particular order. (However, it is suggested that you cover all these chapters before reading Chapter 16 on mutual funds.)

Specifically, though, Section II focuses on low-risk investments that involve your cash reserves and life insurance. While these topics may appear to be too mundane to many readers, it's important to recognize that everything you do with money is an investment. Buying stocks and bonds are obviously investments. But building a cash reserve or buying insurance are also investing--investing for future security. There should be something for everyone in these two chapters.

Sections III and IV take up fixed-income and equity-type securities. You'll notice that, while only one chapter is devoted to debt, preferred stock and stock options, there are *four* chapters on common stocks. This is because stocks are the most complex security. Therefore, we suggest you read Chapter 10 by itself and digest its contents first. Then, try to read Chapters 11 and 12 together because they are closely related. Finally, after Chapter 13, you will have covered stock investing from basic considerations through time-proven methods for choosing what stocks to purchase and when.

Section V covers two other investments that are popular with investors--real estate and mutual funds. The two chapters in this section can be read on their own, as time permits. As you'll learn, there are many ways to participate in these two investments, and we try to provide suggestions that will help you select the right ones for you.

In Section VI, a number of other important investment considerations are presented--how to select a broker or investment advisor, what to do with IRAs, how tax reform affects you and your investments, etc. Each in its own right needs to be carefully analyzed if you expect to be a successful investor.

Finally, six appendices have been included to supplement the rest of the book. They contain personal worksheets, suggested model portfolios to help you construct an overall portfolio strategy that fits your needs, how to read an (often ignored) annual report as well as references for further study of a particular topic and an extensive list of investment terms and definitions.

Whether you're 18 or 80, or have $1,000 or $100,000 to invest, this book can help you manage your investments better and help you build your personal wealth for financial security. If you get just one useful idea from each chapter, then I will have accomplished my goal in writing this book, *and* your purchase (investment) will have paid off handsomely. Good reading and good investing!

TABLE OF CONTENTS

INTRODUCTION

1 PLANNING FOR FINANCIAL SECURITY

Chapter Objectives

1. Taking a Financial Inventory of Where You are Now
2. Assessing Your Personal and Financial Objectives to Determine Where You Want to Be
3. Budgeting Cash for Investing in Order to Get Where You Want to Be
4. Choosing Investments that Meet Your Investment Objectives

In a world of perfect certainty, very little planning is necessary. It's the uncertainty about the future that makes financial planning essential—to provide financial security and a certain standard of living for yourself and your dependents. Most people know how to make money but few know how best to *make money make money*. Often they're too busy to find out. Moreover, the increasing variety of financial products constantly being introduced makes this task even more difficult and somewhat frustrating. There are no magic formulas that fit every individual under all circumstances. Yet, there *are* basic considerations and steps that are common to us all. In this chapter, we present a general approach to personal investing that will help you to evaluate where you are financially, where you want to be and how to get there. This evaluation is necessary before you start developing a sound investment program. In the following chapters we then focus on the various elements of this program.

STAGE 1: WHERE YOU ARE NOW— TAKING A FINANCIAL INVENTORY

If you're like most people, you have little idea what you're worth, or you may be worth more than you think. Calculating your net worth is the *first* step toward developing a sound plan that will provide future financial security. Once you've done this, you can set objectives and develop ways to realize them. In other words, *you need to know where you are before you decide where you want to go.*

This will take a little work because you need to construct a *personal balance sheet* such as the one we have provided in Worksheet No. 1 (*see* Appendix). A balance sheet lists your assets ("what you own") and liabilities ("what you owe"). Subtracting your liabilities from your assets indicates how much you're worth.

So, what does your net worth tell you? If it's *negative*, you're in debt (perhaps deeply). That's acceptable (to some degree) if you're young. But, if you're over 40, you need to forget about investing for a while because *paying off some debts* should be given top priority. If what you own is just balanced by what you owe, you're not much better off. Why? Because there are no *extra* assets to cover an emergency such as illness, accident or loss of job, and to work toward your long-term objectives.

Most people, though, have a *positive* net worth, the size of which depends on such factors as age, income and family status. Is there any rule-of-thumb as to what the appropriate amount of net worth should be? Not really because individual circumstances vary so widely.

One guideline, however, is the results of a recent marketing survey which found that the *average* net worth of high-income households ranges from $105,000 for those earning at least $25,000 annually to $676,000 for those with annual incomes of at least $100,000. *By age*, it showed that the net worth of high-income household heads between the ages 25-29 averages $57,000. It increases to $189,000 in the 45-49 age group and to $466,000 for household heads 70-74 years of age.

Knowing your net worth is also important because it's a *financial inventory* of where you are at a specific point in time. It can answer such questions as:

- Are there any potential problems, e.g., too much debt or too little savings for emergencies?
- Are your assets consistent with your objectives?
- How close are you to achieving these objectives?
- Do the realities of your financial life match up with your goals for saving and investing?
- Are you "overinvested" in a single type of investment?

Moreover, you need to monitor your progress through a periodic review and analysis of your balance sheet. (Unfortunately, few people do this.) A good time to redo your balance sheet is at tax time when all the information is handy.

SUGGESTION: Before reading on, take time to fill out Worksheet No. 1, especially if you've never done a personal balance sheet. The best time is *now!*

STAGE 2: WHERE YOU WANT TO BE—ASSESSING YOUR PERSONAL AND FINANCIAL OBJECTIVES

Assessing Your Personal Objectives *

What would you do if you suddenly had $10,000 more in income a year? Spend it? Pay off the home mortgage? Take a long vacation? Or save it, perhaps to fund your retirement years.

Playing such a game is actually a good way to assess your personal objectives. In a sense, you're creating a "wish list," and yet at the same time you're helping to set what your objectives are and their order of importance to you.

But you can't stop with ranking your objectives as to their relative importance. You also need to *set deadlines for reaching your objectives.* Take a minute and rank your personal objectives by filling out Worksheet No. 2.

---

*Reprinted from the 1984 Money Guide: Personal Finance, by special permission, copyright 1984, Time Inc., all rights reserved.

REMEMBER: The relative importance you attach to a particular objective and the time you allow yourself to achieve it affect the types of investments to consider.

For instance, what if a college fund for your children is extremely important. This means you'll want to take less risk with the money you set aside for this objective. But, low risk implies low returns and that means you'll need to start working toward this objective sooner. Similarly, if you want to buy a car soon, you'll need to set aside a large amount now and place it in a safe, liquid investment—you don't want to end up with less than you started.

Assessing Your Investment Objectives

Given your personal objectives, the next step is to balance your needs among three investment objectives: *safety of principal, current income and capital growth.*

1. *Safety of Principal.* No one wants to lose his investment. Safety of principal is most important when there is a specific future financial need. For example, you may want to set up a fund for old age or sickness. At least some part of the money saved for such purposes should be in investments which will not lose value if economic conditions turn for the worse. *EXAMPLES:* Savings or money market accounts in financial institutions and short-term government securities.

Unfortunately, there's an inverse relationship between safety of principal and the other two investment objectives—income and potential growth. Higher income or growth can be obtained only by incurring risk. If safety is of utmost importance, then expect a lower yield, with little prospect for capital growth. Remember also, safe investments return a fixed dollar income which means the purchasing power of this income decreases in times of inflation. That is, as prices rise, the dollars earned buy less.

2. *Current Income.* If you are largely interested in supplementing your present wages or in providing income if you are retired or widowed, then income earned

is the primary concern. You want to focus on how much an investment returns or yields in current income. *EXAMPLES:* Any investment that pays a regular, fixed income such as interest-bearing securities, savings or money-market accounts, loans, preferred stock, and rental property.

Return is expressed in *dollars* while *yield* is a *percent.* Yield is calculated by dividing the annual return (e.g., dividends on stock, interest on a savings account or bond) by the value of the investment. Examples are the annual interest paid on a bond divided by the market price of the bond, or the stated (compounded) interest rate on a saving account's principal amount. If a $1,000 bond pays a return of $100 in interest per year, its current yield is $100 ÷ $1,000 = 10 percent.

    3. *Capital Growth.* Growth of capital or capital gains is probably the most popular objective among investors. A capital gain is achieved whenever the investment is sold for more than its original cost. *EXAMPLES:* Common stocks, options and real estate.

A capital growth objective implies increased risk and a reduced level of current income. Common stock of companies which offers good growth potential will provide little immediate yield because such companies reinvest their profits to produce future growth and only pay a small amount in the form of dividends. Result: Good growth prospects but low yield. In some cases, you may have a zero yield but have the prospect of future price appreciation, e.g., raw land.

If you can afford to forfeit current income for a potential increase in value, then capital growth investments should be considered.

What can we conclude? There is no investment that can provide *maximum* safety, *maximum* income and *maximum* growth of capital. You must decide what mix or tradeoff among these investment objectives best suits your needs. This, in turn, will dictate what *type* of investments to consider.

For instance, the low yield on a money market account is offset by the fact that principal is extremely safe; however there's no growth potential. The low yields on common stocks are offset by the potential for future *(but highly uncertain)* appreciation in value.

Another critical consideration in setting your objectives is the relative differences in the timing (regularity) and uncertainty (risk) of the desired returns. The choice of specific investments will be a matter of *emphasis* on the tradeoffs between safety, income and growth. Most securities will offer you a combination of two of these while deemphasizing the third.

Since alternative investments involve differing degrees of safety, income and growth, a useful way to think of an investment is in terms of its total return. *Total percentage return* is the sum of the current (income) yield and the capital gains yield. For example, if a security pays current income equal to 8% of its value or price and its price appreciates at a 5% rate, its total return is 13%. If you are less concerned about which type of return you receive, then you can simply focus on *maximizing your total return,* given a certain degree of safety.

STAGE 3: GETTING WHERE YOU WANT TO BE—BUDGETING CASH FOR INVESTMENTS

Once you've established where you are and where you want to be, the next step is getting there. First, you need to figure out where your money has gone recently. You do this by summarizing your income and outgo for the last 12 months. Make copies of Worksheet No. 3 and use it to put this summary together—it's called a *cash flow* or *income and expense statement.*

This will require some time, so pull out your most recent tax return for your sources of income and taxes paid; your check stubs and monthly credit card statements will help you determine your cash expenses. The difference between your income and expenses is what's available for savings and investment. If you have a *surplus,* this should have been saved or invested, and your net worth should have increased by at least this much during this period.

But what if this bottom number is *negative?* *You have work to do* because you either borrowed or withdrew money from savings to cover this "loss." Moreover, even if this figure was *positive* but was *less than 10% of Line 1* (Salaries and Wages), you need to analyze closely your *variable* expenses to find ways to reduce them if you hope to implement an investment program.

Why? Your *fixed* expenses are difficult or impossible to cut out—you're obligated to pay them. This leaves you with discretion over only your variable expenses.

Now, draw up a *forecasted* cash flow statement for the next twelve months, using last year's statement as a point of departure. Add anticipated pay raises and additional investment income to last year's figures, then subtract your estimated taxes.

Your fixed expenses will likely remain unchanged, so you (and your family) need to examine closely your discretionary outlays to see where you can retrench or sacrifice. The more obvious areas are clothing, personal care, recreation and entertainment.

With enough adjusting, you should be able to produce a budget that will give you the "excess funds" you need to start your investment program. If not, then you'll need to reassess your objectives—perhaps they are too ambitious for your current situation.

SUGGESTION: Build savings and investments into your budget as a "fixed expense" rather than letting it be a residual or what happens to be left over after all your spending. Make it a *regular commitment* as if it were a rental or mortgage payment. It'll take discipline, but you can do it.

STAGE 4: CHOOSING INVESTMENTS THAT MEET YOUR OBJECTIVES

As we know now, those investments appropriate for you will depend on your objectives. And these objectives largely depend on what stage of your life cycle you're in. In other words,

which stage you're in will help decide what types of investments to consider because the objectives and tradeoffs differ in each period. So, a useful step is to consider where you are in the scheme of things.

A Life Cycle of Investing *

Three basic stages can be used to define your investing life cycle:
- Early-to-Mid Life
- Mid-to-Late Life
- Retirement
1. *Early-to-Mid Life (20-40 Years Old).* In your early 20's? At this age, most people are looking for new experiences, acquiring personal possessions, new friends and potential mates. If you're young and single, it's a time of few responsibilities AND a perfect time for socking away some money—even though the future seems remote and your income is low. This also applies to young couples with two careers and no children.

    SUGGESTION: Force yourself to set aside money for the future. Because you're not interested in current income, you might be interested in speculating for short-term profits—win or lose, you'll discover that the investing game isn't so easy, and you will learn to use more-informed strategies in the future.

    Twenty-five to 40 years old? Having children? Your income is higher but the financial strains of children, mortgage payments (or saving for a downpayment on a house) are burdensome. This is the time you need the most life insurance and the time to start building an education fund. Remember, the earlier you start, the easier it'll be to put those kids through school.

    SUGGESTION: Take part of that next pay raise and put it to work earning a return. Perhaps postpone that expenditure on a

* W. G. Shepherd, Jr. "Your Personal Assets," <u>Forbes</u>. September 14, 1984.

large-ticket, "have-to-have" purchase. Remember, rate of return is important BUT so is the *rate of investment* (how much you put aside)—you want the "power of compounding" working for you.

2. *Mid-to-Late Life (40-65 Years Old)*. Forty to 50 years old? If you're working and earning a good salary, you'll probably be interested in long-term growth and possibly short-term profit (if you can afford the risks)—but retirement is not that far away.

   The children are leaving the nest; the mortgage is mostly paid off. Your life insurance needs have dropped off sharply. Now's the time to really start squirreling away money into investments—as much as possible. Reducing taxes may become important. (If you're a widow/widower and not employed, *current income* should be your priority.)

   SUGGESTION: Since this is probably your first chance to build assets in a significant way, don't let this opportunity get away from you.

   Fifty to 60 years old? You're at your peak earnings. Save or invest everything you can, but minimize your taxes. Retirement is just around the corner. (But also take time to indulge yourself—you've earned it.)

   It's also a time to begin thinking about how to distribute assets to your family or grandchildren. You're not only building a retirement fund but also preparing your estate.

3. *Retirement*. If you're retired and no longer earning a salary, you'll doubtlessly have a need for *current income*. Depending on how you've played the investing game, income may or may not be the overriding need.

If you're well off (e.g., pensions and investment income cover 100% of your expenses), you may be looking for some growth possibilities—to build up your estate or to make a tax-deductible contribution to your favorite charity. Moreover, remember that your chief enemy now is *inflation*, which can be deadly by eroding the purchasing power of your fixed-income investments.

   SUGGESTION: Keep as much funds as possible earning income. Finish your estate planning and use gifts or trusts to reduce any possible estate taxes. If your estate is sizable (greater than $500,000 - $750,000), you might consider life insurance as a way to cover estate taxes. Otherwise, don't worry about it.

Investments for Different Objectives

Your choice of investments is dictated by your objectives, but you also need to answer the following questions:

- How much money do you need to accumulate?
- How many years do you have to accumulate this amount of money?
- How much can you save each year?

With answers to these questions, you're ready to turn to deciding (1) how to allocate your investable funds among different *types* of investments (the "portfolio decision"), and (2) how to select *individual* investments such as IBM stock or A.T.& T bonds (the "asset decision").

With regard to the first decision, Appendix B presents a number of *suggested "model portfolios,"* based on different investment objectives. These should provide guidelines for structuring your own portfolio. You may want to look them over quickly and then return to them after you finish reading this guide.

With regard to the second decision, Exhibit 1-1 presents the types of investments that might be suitable for your own objectives. In the remainder of this guide, we take up each one individually and discuss those factors to consider before investing in them.

TERMS TO KNOW

Balance sheet--personal
Capital growth
Capital gains yield
Cash flow (income and expense) statement
Current income
Current yield
Life cycle of investing
Net worth
Return
Safety of principal
Total return

Exhibit 1-1
Types of Investments to Meet Different Objectives

MAXIMUM SAFETY OF PRINCIPAL

Savings and money market deposit accounts
Money market funds
U.S. Savings bonds
Treasury securities
High-grade corporate and municipal bonds

CURRENT INCOME

Money market instruments (T-bills, CDs, commercial paper and bankers' acceptances)
Money market funds
Treasury securities
Corporate and municipal bonds
GNMA securities
Income-oriented mutual funds
Unit trusts
Annuities
Preferred stock

CAPITAL GROWTH

Common stocks
Real estate
Growth-oriented common stock mutual funds
Stock options

2 INVESTMENT ALTERNATIVES TO MEET YOUR OBJECTIVES

Chapter Objectives

1. Characteristics of Fixed-Income Investments
2. Characteristics of Variable-Income Investments

This chapter contains an overview of the important characteristics of the types of investments covered in this investment guide. These investments can be divided into two categories: *fixed-income* investments (e.g., money market instruments, bonds and preferred stock) and *variable-income* investments (e.g., common stocks, real estate and options). The following discussion moves from the least risky to the riskier investments.

CHARACTERISTICS OF FIXED-INCOME (DEBT) INVESTMENTS

Money Market Instruments (Chapter 8)

Money market instruments are short-term, high-quality debt obligations (less than one year maturity) that pay interest income. Individual investors typically do not hold these securities because (1) they trade in large denominations of $10,000 or more and (2) their yields are not much higher than interest rates on bank money market accounts. As a rule of thumb, you should have $25,000 or more before seriously considering investing directly in these securities. Otherwise, it's better to put your money in an interest-earning bank account or mutual fund.

1. *U.S. Treasury Bills (T-bills).* These are obligations of the federal government with maturities up to one year, although commonly issued with three- and six-month maturities. Issued on a discount basis (interest included in the par or face value received at maturity) in minimum denominations of $10,000. *Very liquid and the safest marketable security.* See Exhibit 2-1 for information on how to buy T-bills.

Exhibit 2-1
How to Buy U.S. Treasury Securities

U.S. Treasury Bills

Newly-issued bills can be purchased through a commercial bank or brokerage house. Commissions range from $10 to $35 per bill. Can also be purchased with a "noncompetitive bid" in the U.S. Treasury's weekly auction of T-bills. Orders may be easily placed by writing the main or branch office of your nearest Federal Reserve bank. Your letter should state the amount desired and include a check for the bills' face value. A refund for the discount on the bills will be sent to you. No fee or commission is charged for this service.

Write the Bureau of the Public Debt, Dept. F, Washington, D.C. 20239 to order application forms and a free booklet, "Information About Treasury Bills Sold at Original Price." Be sure to indicate whether you're interested in 13-week, 26-week or 52-week bills.

Note: Buying through a bank costs $15, *plus* you lose 3 days' interest and four days' discount on the discount interest. Buying through a Federal Reserve bank (check by mail), you lose a week's interest and, at maturity, get no interest for five more days.

Existing bills can be purchased on the open market through a brokerage house. Minimum purchase amount is $10,000 and in multiples of $5,000 over the initial amount.

U.S. Treasury Notes and Bonds

Newly-issued notes and bonds can be purchased directly from a Federal Reserve bank during the quarterly financing operation of the U.S. Treasury in a manner similar to T-bills described above.

Existing notes and bonds can be purchased from brokerage houses. Minimum purchase amount is $1,000, but $10,000 is considered to be a "round lot."

---

2. *Commercial Paper.* These are unsecured promissory notes issued by financially-strong corporations in denominations of $100,000. Also issued on a discount basis. Maturities range from a few days to 270 days. Most investors in commercial paper are *other* corporations. Slightly higher risk and less liquid than T-bills. Yields are

typically 0.5 percent to 1 percent more than T-bill yield.

3. *Negotiable Certificates of Deposit (CDs).* Money market CDs are negotiable time deposits issued by commercial banks in denominations of $100,000 to $1 million. Issued with one- to 180-day maturities. Quite liquid and slightly higher risk than T-bills. Yields usually 1 percent higher than T-bill yield.

4. *Bankers' Acceptances.* A "letter of credit" or draft that is originated in the financing of a foreign trade transaction, typically in denominations of $100,000. Issued as a discount instrument with maturities usually set at 180 days. Because payment on these drafts are guaranteed by a bank, the risk of default depends on the financial strength of the bank. However, there has never been a loss to investors. Because of the very low risk, the returns on bankers' acceptances are similar to those on T-bills.

5. *Eurodollar Deposits.* Dollar-denominated deposits (liabilities) of foreign banks or subsidiaries of domestic banks located outside the U.S. These fixed-rate *time* deposits range in size from $250,000 to $5 million, with maturities of one day to *several years.* Yields are comparable to U.S. money market rates.

6. *Repurchase Agreements (Repos).* Sales of securities (usually government securities) by institutions that guarantee the *repurchase* of these securities at a prespecified price and maturity (normally only a few days). Repos are relatively safe, and their yields are slightly higher than T-bills. "Retail repos" are now offered by many banks and S&Ls in denominations as low as $2,000 (these are not securities, however).

Exhibit 2-2 presents the yields for different money market instruments and maturities that existed in 1984 and early 1985. The Wall Street Journal or your broker is a good source for obtaining current yields on money market instruments—refer to Exhibit 2-3.

Exhibit 2-2
Interest Rates for Different Fixed-Income Securities

Financial Instrument	Maturity	January [*] 1985	One Year [**] Earlier
SHORT TERM			
Treasury-Bill [***]	90 days	8.00 %	9.16 %
Commercial Paper	30-59 days	7.98-8.13 %	9.15-9.30 %
	60-89 days	8.00-8.13 %	9.10-9.25 %
	90-179 days	8.00-8.15 %	9.10-9.25 %
	180-270 days	8.05-8.15 %	9.05-9.20 %
Certificates of Deposit	30-59 days	8.00-8.25 %	9.00-9.15 %
	60-89 days	8.00-8.35 %	9.13-9.50 %
	90-179 days	8.00-8.45 %	9.13-9.55 %
	180-269 days	8.35-8.80 %	9.25-9.60 %
	270-365 days	8.75-9.15 %	9.50-9.70 %
Bankers Acceptances	90 days	8.05 %	9.25 %
Eurodollar Deposits	90 days	8.49 %	9.68 %
Treasury Bill [***]	180 days	8.45 %	9.47 %
	1 year	9.02 %	9.75 %
INTERMEDIATE TERM			
Treasury Notes	3 years	10.43 %	10.77 %
	5 years	11.03 %	11.26 %
Federal Agencies	5 years	11.29 %	11.41 %
Municipals	5 years	7.50 %	7.25 %
LONG TERM			
Treasury Bonds	10 years	11.51 %	11.56 %
Federal Agencies	10 years	11.77 %	11.76 %
Municipal Bonds	20 years	9.51 %	9.60 %
Corporate Bonds	30 years	13.33 %	12.83 %

[*] Average rates for week ending January 18, 1985.
[**] Average rates for week ending January 20, 1984.
[***] Bond equivalent yield.

SOURCE: Continental Bank, Chicago, Illinois, 1985.

U.S. Treasury Notes and Bonds (Chapter 8)

These are intermediate and long-term obligations issued at a *stated* or *coupon* rate of interest by the federal government. Interest is paid semiannually. They are the safest and most liquid long-term marketable securities available. Because of their lower risk, government securities yield less than highly- rated corporate debt securities. While subject to federal income taxes, they are exempt from state and local taxes.

Treasury notes (T-notes) are issued with maturities of one to seven years, while *Treasury bonds* (T-bonds) are issued with typical maturities of 20 and 30 years. However, with so many issues outstanding, you can usually purchase any maturity you desire. Both securities are issued in $1,000 minimum denominations.

Federal Agency Bonds (Chapter 8)

These are debt obligations issued by federal and federally-sponsored agencies. Federal agencies, such as Farmers Home Administration (FHA) and Postal Service, are part of the federal government. Most agency debt, however, has been issued by federally-sponsored agencies such as Federal Intermediate Credit Banks and Federal Land Bank.

Agency securities' yields are usually 0.5% higher than comparable Treasury securities even though they are almost as safe as Treasuries. Part of the reason is that their marketability is much less because of low trading volume, relatively high commission costs and lack of investor interest.

Although available in minimum denominations of $10,000, the standard trading unit is $100,000 or more.

Interest on federal agency bonds is subject to federal income tax, and state and local taxes usually apply to most issues. Exceptions to such state and local taxing, such as Federal Home Loan Bank issues do exist—you'll need to check on the specific issue before you buy.

Municipal Bonds (Chapter 8)

Issued by state and local governments to finance schools, highways, sewers, utilities, etc., "munis" usually fall into two categories:

- *General obligations bonds*—backed by the full faith and credit of the state or local government that issued them.
- *Revenue bonds*—backed by a specific income source such as a toll bridge or highway.

Because general obligation bonds are backed by the overall financial resources and taxing power of the issuer, they generally have lower risk and returns than revenue bonds. The principal and interest payments on revenue bonds can be made only from the revenues generated by the project's assets that were financed by the bond proceeds—no other recourse is available if revenues fall short.

Municipal bond interest is exempt from federal income tax (hence the name "tax exempts") and from state and local taxes in the state of issue. Capital gains, however, are taxable. Tax reform has eliminated the federal tax-exempt status of "private purpose" munis that are used to finance projects such as sports stadiums or farm loans. You'll need to check on their tax status before purchasing them, e.g., in a prospectus. Chapter 8 goes into more detail on the distinction between taxable and tax-exempt municipals.

Mortgage-Backed Securities (Chapter 8)

These are certificates on a pool of home mortgages in which your pro rata share of the interest and principal payments are "passed-through" to you monthly.

Most popular mortgage-backed securities are issued by two federal agencies—Government National Mortgage Association (Ginnie Mae) and Federal National Mortgage Association (Fannie Mae). Both securities are relatively safe investments. Ginnie Maes are directly backed by the U.S. government, while Fannie Maes have the implicit backing of the U.S. government. Yields are typically 0.5 percent to 1.0 percent higher than comparable Treasury securities. Minimum denominations are $5,000.

Corporate Bonds (Chapter 8)

Promissory notes of corporations with 20- to 30-year maturities when issued. Most bonds pay interest semiannually and return the principal on a specific date of maturity. They are usually sold in $1,000 denominations.

They may be secured or unsecured. Secured bonds have a pledge of specific property such as land, building or equipment for repayment of the bond. *Unsecured bonds* or *debentures* only have the general credit of the issuer backing them.

Because of their higher risk, corporates yield more than government bonds. The yield for a specific bond will depend on its overall credit rating.

Exhibit 2-2 also contains the yields on intermediate- and long-term fixed-income securities in January 1984 and 1985.

Preferred Stocks (Chapter 9)

Preferred stocks are "hybrid" securities that pay a fixed income (dividend) like a bond yet are legally an equity security. The dividend is stated as either a *dollar amount* or as a fixed *percentage* of par value.

They have no maturity but may be callable if the market price is considerably above par value.

Their chief attraction is as a reasonably stable source of income. While riskier than a bond, they're less risky than common stock. In the event of liquidation of the issuing corporation, preferred stock has "preference" over common stock in the distribution of assets.

CHARACTERISTICS OF VARIABLE-INCOME INVESTMENTS

Real Estate (Chapter 15)

Real estate is a heterogeneous product that covers a wide range of long-term investment options: home ownership, raw land, developed or income-producing property, mortgages, real estate investment trusts (REITS), real estate syndications or limited partnerships.

Real estate's chief attractions used to be the preferential tax treatment of capital gains, substantial leverage (small downpayments and large, long-term mortgages) and extensive tax benefits. Tax reform has drastically changed this investment's appeal. A careful reading of Chapter 15's discussion on the impact of tax reform on different real estate investments is a must before you consider committing your money.

Negative aspects include relatively low liquidity, high transaction costs and poor marketability, plus some real estate investments may require considerable time and effort to manage.

Mutual Funds (Chapter 16)

Mutual funds pool the money of a number of investors and then invest these monies in a diversified portfolio of securities that are consistent with their stated investment objectives. You receive a certain number of *shares* that represent your invested money. The market value per share is referred to as its *net asset value* (NAV).

Income earned on a fund's assets in excess of expenses is distributed as *dividends*. If the fund's assets appreciate in value and capital gains are realized, these gains are also distributed to shareholders as *capital gains* or you can redeem your shares at the appreciated price.

The main advantages of mutual funds are full-time professional management, diversification, ease of acquisition and redemption, and the ability to invest *indirectly* in any type of security that meets your investment objective. Only a small investment is required to invest in most mutual funds.

Mutual funds are highly desirable for investors who either do not have the ability or time to manage their investments themselves.

Common Stocks (Chapters 10-13)

Shareholders of common stock are the legal owners of a corporation and thereby share in the ultimate risk and reward of the corporation. If a company fails to earn an adequate return on its assets, the stock price will fall below its book value. If the company goes bankrupt, you usually get nothing back on your investment. In contrast, if the corporation is successful, you likely will receive rising dividends and substantial capital gains.

Common stocks involve high risk due to the potential loss of invested capital—yet, profit potential is virtually unlimited. They are also one of the most complicated securities to evaluate.

Stock Options (Chapter 14)

Options are not securities, rather they are *rights to buy or sell* securities. A *call* option holder has the right to *buy*. A *put* option holder has the right to *sell*.

Exchange-listed options, e.g., on the Chicago Board Options Exchange, offer standardized maturities and exercise (strike) prices on the stocks underlying the options.

Options can be used as a speculative investment offering short-term profits (*buying* calls or puts), a *conservative* investment to realize *higher income* from securities you own (*writing* covered calls) and a hedge to protect the value of securities you own (*writing* covered calls, *buying* puts).

TERMS TO KNOW

Bankers' acceptances
Call option
Commercial paper
Common stock
Corporate bond
Debenture
Eurodollar deposits
Federal agency securities
Federal National Mortgage Association (Fannie Mae)
General obligation bond
Government National Mortgage Association (Ginnie Mae)
Money market instrument
Mortgage-backed security
Municipal bond
Mutual fund
Negotiable certificates of deposit (CDs)
Net asset value
Preferred stock
Put option
Real estate
Repurchase agreement (repo)
Retail repos
Revenue bond
Secured bond
Stock option
U.S. Treasury bill
U.S. Treasury bond
U.S. Treasury note

3

UNDERSTANDING RISKS AND RETURNS

Chapter Objectives

1. The Meaning of Return
2. How to Calculate Returns and Yield
3. The Meaning of Risk
4. How Risk is Measured
5. Major Sources of Risk
6. Understanding the Benefits of Diversification
7. Other Important Investment Considerations

The value of an automobile largely depends on the satisfaction you expect to receive from it. Because price and value are not necessarily the same, you would never pay a price in excess of the value you believe is offered. Similarly, when you make an investment, you never want to pay a price in excess of anticipated value.

The valuation process for investments, however, is more complicated. The important characteristics that determine value are *return* and *risk*.

Therefore, you need to understand return and risk as well as *how to measure them* if you are going to make sound investment decisions. Another important ingredient in making good investment choices is the concept of diversification.

In this chapter, we examine the various dimensions of return, risk and diversification and how they will affect your investments. Let's look first at the notion of return.

WHAT DO WE MEAN BY RETURN?

Although investment returns are not guaranteed, it's *expected* return that causes you to invest in a particular security. The return can be viewed, therefore, as the reward for investing, and the *size* of the return becomes a critical factor in selecting your investments.

Components of Return

Investment returns may be derived from more than one source. The *receipt of income* is the *most common source. Appreciation in value,*

being able to sell the investment for more than its original price, is the other source of return. We refer to these two sources as *current income* and *capital gains (or losses),* and their combination as the *total return.*

1. *Current Income.* Normally is received periodically in the form of interest, dividends, rent, etc. It is measured by the amount of *cash* you actually receive from owning an investment.
2. *Capital Gains (or Losses).* The other source of return comes from a change in the market value of your investment. You invest a certain amount and expect to receive not only current income but also to get back your originally invested funds.

With a bond, you get back your money at its maturity. With investments lacking a maturity, such as common stocks, or if you sell an investment *before* its maturity, what amount you get back is uncertain. If you sell your investment for *more than* its original price, you have a *capital gain.* If you sell your investment for less than its original price, a *capital loss* is realized.

Calculating Annual Income and Capital Gains (Losses)

Suppose you purchased the following investments on January 2, 1984:

1. 50 shares of IBM: purchase price = $100 per share; pays a $0.95 dividend per share

---

quarterly, or $0.95 x 50 shares = $47.50 per quarter.

2. 5 Florida Power 9s2000 debenture bonds: purchase price = $1,000 per bond; pays $22.50 in interest per bond each quarter or $22.50 x 5 bonds = $112.50 per quarter.

Now assume that one year later you sold the IBM stock and Florida Power bonds for $110 per share and $950 per bond, respectively. From this information, we can now calculate your current income and capital gains (losses) from these two investments.

Referring to Exhibit 3-1, we see that the total dollar returns are:

	50 Shares of IBM Stock	5 Florida Power Bonds
Current Income	$ 190	$ 450
Capital Gain (Loss)	500	(250)
Total Dollar Return	$ 690	$ 200

Because our original investment was the same in both, it's clear that IBM turned out to be your best investment *that year* because it provided a

total return of $690 versus only $200 from the bonds. Caution: While IBM was preferred to the Florida Power investment, you need to consider the differential risk inherent in each investment.

Measuring Returns as Yields

Rather than measuring returns in *dollars*, most investors measure returns on a *yield basis*, i.e., as a *percentage amount*. In doing so, two things are accomplished: (1) you find out how much you earned *per dollar invested*, and (2) you can *compare the yields* from different investments. To measure an investment's *holding period yield* (HPY), the following formula is used:

$$HPY = \frac{Current\ Income + Price\ Change}{Beginning\ Price}$$

To adapt this measure to specific investments, for example, the HPY becomes:

$$Bond\ HPY = \frac{I_1 + (P_1 - P_0)}{P_0} = \frac{I_1}{P_0} + \frac{(P_1 - P_0)}{P_0}$$

$$Stock\ HPY = \frac{D_1 + (P_1 - P_0)}{P_0} = \underbrace{\frac{D_1}{P_0}}_{\substack{Current \\ Yield}} + \underbrace{\frac{(P_1 - P_0)}{P_0}}_{\substack{Capital \\ Gains \\ Yield}}$$

Where

I_1 = interest income received over the holding period.

P_0 = price of security or value of investment *at beginning* of the period.

P_1 = price of security or value of investment *at the end* of the period.

D_1 = dividends received over the holding period.

Notice that we can break up the total yield into two components, just as we did with the dollar

---

Exhibit 3-1
Calculating the Current Income and Capital Gains (Losses) on Two Hypothetical Investments

	50 Shares of IBM Stock		5 Florida Power Bonds	
Source of Income	Per Share	Total Investment	Per Bond	Total Investment
1. Current Income:				
March 1984	$ 0.95	$ 47.50	$22.50	$112.50
June 1984	0.95	47.50	22.50	112.50
Sept. 1984	0.95	47.50	22.50	112.50
Dec. 1984	0.95	47.50	22.50	112.50
	$ 3.80	$190.00	$90.00	$450.00
2. Capital Gain (Loss):				
Ending Value	$ 110	$5,500	$ 950	$4,750
Less: Original Investment	100	5,000	1,000	5,000
Gain (Loss)	$ 10	$ 500	($ 50)	($ 250)
3. Total Dollar Return:				
[(1) + (2)] =	$13.80	$ 690	$ 40	$ 200

returns, i.e., into a *current yield* and a *capital gains yield*.

To illustrate how easy it is to use the HPY formula, let's look back at our IBM and Florida Power investments and figure out what their annual holding period yields were.

Referring to Exhibit 3-2, we see that you had a 4% and 13.8% *total* yield on your bond and stock investments, respectively. Further note that the bond's yield was composed of a 9% current yield and a 5% capital *loss* yield. Similarly, the stock had 3.8% current yield and a 10% capital *gain* yield. (To test your grasp of HPY's Worksheet No. 4 gives data on different types of investments for you to practice calculating HPY's.)

Exhibit 3-2
Calculating the Yields on the Two Hypothetical Investments Described in Exhibit 3-1

1. On a Per Bond or Share Basis:

Florida Power's HPY

$$= \frac{\$90 + (\$950 - \$1,000)}{\$1,000}$$

$$= \frac{\$90}{\$1,000} - \frac{\$50}{\$1,000}$$

$$= 0.09 - 0.05 = 4\%$$

IBM's HPY

$$= \frac{\$3.80 + (\$110 - \$100)}{\$100}$$

$$= \frac{\$3.80}{\$100} + \frac{\$10}{\$100}$$

$$= 0.038 + 0.10 = 13.8\%$$

2. On a Total Investment Basis:

Florida Power's HPY

$$= \frac{\$450 + (\$4,750 - \$5,000)}{\$5,000}$$

$$= \frac{\$450}{\$5,000} - \frac{\$250}{\$5,000}$$

$$= 0.09 - 0.05 = 4\%$$

IBM's HPY

$$= \frac{\$190 + (\$5,500 - \$5,000)}{\$5,000}$$

$$= \frac{\$190}{\$5,000} + \frac{\$500}{\$5,000}$$

$$= 0.038 + 0.10 = 13.8\%$$

NOTE: In calculating the HPY, it does not matter whether you do it on a per share or bond basis or on a total investment basis.

A Word About Analyzing Yields

A holding period yield can be determined for any specified period of time such as a week, a month, six months, a year, five years, etc. However, because interest rates and other returns are normally stated on an annual basis, HPYs for other than a one-year holding period need to be *annualized*. This is a relatively straightforward process and is done as follows:

$$\text{Annual HPY} = \text{HPY} \times \frac{\text{Number of Periods Per Year}}{\text{Length of Holding Period}}$$

For example, if you earned 3.5% on a stock over a three-month period and 2.0% on another stock over an eight-week period, your *annualized* yields would be

$$\text{Annual HPY} = 0.035 \times \frac{12 \text{ Months}}{3 \text{ Months}} = 14.0\% \text{ per annum}$$

$$\text{Annual HPY} = 0.02 \times \frac{52 \text{ Weeks}}{8 \text{ Weeks}} = 13.0\% \text{ per annum}$$

Worksheet No. 5 contains HPYs for different holding periods that you can practice converting to annualized yields.

A Few Observations

1. It is usually best to calculate returns on a holding period yield basis rather than a dollar return basis.

2. HPYs can be calculated on a per share, per bond or total investment basis.

3. To be comparable, HPYs on different investments need to be calculated over the same time interval, e.g., monthly, six months, one year, etc.

4. HPYs can be used to measure how well an investment did (its historical performance) or to estimate what you expect an investment to yield in the future. The first HPY is called the *actual* or *realized* return while the second HPY is referred to as an *expected* return.

5. Even if the capital gain yield was not realized during the holding period, it needs to be included in the return calculation.
6. It is possible that either the current income or capital gain components or both could be *negative*. For instance, a negative current income means you had to pay out cash in order to maintain the asset (refer to the real estate example in Worksheet No. 4).

WHAT DO WE MEAN BY RISK?

Let's now look at the opposite side of the investment picture—the *uncertainty* or *risk* associated with your investments' results. Risk is the chance that your actual return may differ from what you expected, either favorably or unfavorably. If, for example, you put your money into a six-month T-bill, you know *exactly* what return your investment will provide. Except for inflation, such an investment has no uncertainty—its risk is zero.

Most investments, however, involve a significant degree of risk because you can't determine with certainty what an investment will be worth at some future date. Of course, the degree of uncertainty varies considerably from one security to the next because each security involves a different amount of risk.

Normally, the more variable or the broader the range of possible returns is, the greater the risk is (and vice-versa). This just means that risky securities can produce returns that are well above or well below what is expected. For example, if you purchase a security that's expected to yield 10% but with a range of *minus 5%* to *plus 18%*, you face the risk that the actual return may differ considerably. In contrast, low-risk securities' actual returns will be very close to their expected returns.

Clearly, knowing the risk inherent in a security should take on a great deal of importance to you. The reason is because you should accept a higher degree of risk only if there is also the potential for greater profits.

For example, if two securities offer the same potential gain, you should choose the one expected to provide a return with greater certainty. Therefore, if you are going to make wise investment decisions, you need to be aware of both the expected return and the inherent risk of alternative investment opportunities.

Major Sources of Risk

An investment's total risk may arise from any number of sources of risk. The major sources of risk you must contend with are described in detail in Exhibit 3-3. They are:

- Business risk
- Inflation risk
- Financial risk
- Default risk
- Interest rate risk
- Market risk

A number of these risk sources are interrelated. For instance, default risk is largely due to business risk and financial risk. On the other hand, market risk is heavily influenced by interest rate and inflation risk.

Measuring Risk

1. *The Range.* Refers to a security's highest and lowest price or return for a particular time period, e.g., 52 weeks. The high-low prices of stocks, for example, are easily obtained each weekday in financial newspapers such as The Wall Street Journal. Many investors trade stocks or bonds based on their price range. For example, if a stock is near its yearly low, it may be a good time to buy. Similarly, if a stock is trading near its high, this may be a good time to sell. *One problem*—the range cannot usually be used for comparing securities' riskiness. For example, in 1984, Gearhart Industries' price range was $11 to $32, while Northwest Industries traded on a $41 to $62 range. Both had a range of $21, but an increase from $11 to $32 is about a 200% change, while $41 to $62 is only a 50% increase. Clearly, Gearhart's price was less stable than Northwest's, yet their ranges say that they were equally risky.

1. Business Risk—depends on the operating conditions faced by a firm and the variability in these conditions that affect the degree of uncertainty associated with a company's profitability and its ability to pay investors interest, dividends and any other returns. For instance, declines in profitability/dividends will negatively impact the price of a firm's securities. Sources of business risk are type of business, management competence, changing costs, introduction of new products, general economic conditions, overcapacity in the industry, competition, demographic shifts, consumer tastes, etc.

2. Financial Risk—depends on how a firm finances its operations with debt versus equity (degree of leverage). Because borrowed money or debt requires fixed interest payments, the amount of (residual) earnings available for dividends will be more variable than if no debt and its interest costs were present. In other words, the greater the variability in stockholders' returns, the greater the chance of the firm going bankrupt.

3. Interest Rate Risk—depends on fluctuations in the prevailing level of interest rates, which cause future market values and income to fluctuate. Fixed-income securities are most directly affected by this type of risk, although all investments are affected to some degree. For example, as interest rates increase, the value of fixed-income securities fall, and vice-versa.

4. Inflation Risk—depends on the impact inflation has on the purchasing power of income or values received in the future.

    Usually measured by the Consumer Price Index, an index that measures the cost of a "market basket" of goods and services for an average American family, e.g., food, shelter, medical expenses, clothing, etc. Inflation reduces the buying power of any income/capital appreciation received.

5. Default Risk—depends on the ability of a debt issuer to service its financial obligations (interest payments and principal repayments). Refers to the possibility that the return realized on an investment will be less than promised. Default can range from a postponement of interest payments to the legal liquidation of a bankrupt firm's assets to satisfy its debt obligations. Default risk is usually viewed as resulting from a combination of business and financial risk.

6. Market Risk—depends on changes in investor psychology toward investments. It is risk that tends to be caused by factors independent of a given security. For instance, although the profitability and financial condition of a firm remain unchanged, adverse political, social or economic news can cause its securities' prices to fall or fluctuate widely within a short period of time due to investors' general reactions. Interest-rate and inflation risk are an important part of the forces behind market risk.

2. *Variability.* A risk measure that considers not only the two extreme prices but *all* prices that were traded. This is done by analyzing the *dispersion* around the average or the expected price. If there's not much difference between most prices, then the dispersion and hence variability is small. If most prices were near the extremes, then the dispersion (variability) was large. The larger this dispersion, the greater is the risk.

Variability is most often measured using a statistic called the *standard deviation.* The larger the standard deviation, the greater is the risk because you are less certain of the ultimate outcome. Nevertheless, variability is a two-edged sword because the greater an investment's variability the greater the chance of loss and, correspondingly, the greater the chance of gain.

To illustrate, Exhibit 3-4 compares the relative returns and variability for various investments from 1947 to 1980. As this exhibit demonstrates, you must bear more risk, in general, to realize more return. This is known as the *risk-return tradeoff,* which will be studied in more detail below.

Exhibit 3-4
Historical Return and Risk (Variability) of Various Investments, 1947-80

Type of Investment	Average Return	Risk (Variability)
1. Treasury Bills	3.5%	2.1%
2. Treasury Bonds	2.6	6.2
3. Corporate Bonds	2.4	6.7
4. Preferred Stocks	3.3	9.2
5. Real Estate (Residential)	6.9	3.3
6. NYSE Stocks (a)	11.6	17.7
7. OTC Stocks (b)	14.8	21.8

(a) Common stocks listed on the New York Stock Exchange (NYSE)
(b) Common stocks traded in the Over-the-Counter market (OTC).

SOURCE: Adapted from N. Jacob and R. Pettit, Investments, Richard D. Irwin, Inc., 1984.

3. *Volatility.* * Also referred to as "beta," it is a measure that is usually applied to a stock. It measures how much a security can be expected to react or respond to changes in the general level of stock prices. Beta or volatility is calculated by comparing a security's past price movements relative to the movement of the stock market as a whole.

Beta is essentially an *index of riskiness.* For example, a beta of 1.00 means that an issue has historically moved in line with the market. If the market advanced 10%, the stock's return also rose 10%. If the market fell 10%, so did the stock's return.

On the other hand, a stock with a beta equal to 1.50 tends to rise or fall 50% faster than the market, while one with a beta of 0.80 has tended to rise or fall 20% slower than the market. Most beta values are relatively close to 1.0, while less than 10% of stocks' betas are greater than 2.0.

Volatility vs. Variability

Beta is a *relative risk* measure because it reflects only a security's stock market risk. In contrast, *variability* is an *absolute* or *total risk* measure: it includes price fluctuations that result from changes in an individual company's financial condition, growth prospects, and other factors unique to the company as well as market effects (beta).

Variability measures the extent to which a security's price fluctuates *regardless of how the market moves.* Beta, on the other hand, measures the extent to which a security tends to rise or fall with the market. Moreover, beta is only appropriate as a risk measure if you hold a *diversified* portfolio of securities. *Variability* or *total risk* should be used if you hold only a limited number of securities (less than 6-10).

It's important to recognize that, while stocks with high variability tend to have high betas, this relationship does not always hold. For instance, you can find many stocks with high variability and low betas, and vice-versa.

Just remember that a stock with a high variability and a low beta can be expected to rise *less* on a stock market advance than one with a low variability and a high beta. Also, over time, a stock's riskiness can increase or decrease, so you need to monitor it continually.

Where Can You Find a Measure of a Security's Risk? Your broker can usually find out what a security's variability or volatility risk is. Most major brokerage houses compute these risk measures for the stocks they follow.

In addition, a number of investment advisory services provide this information as part of their regular service, e.g., Value Line Investment Survey, Dailygraphs (William O'Neil & Co., Inc.), Standard & Poor's Corp., etc. Exhibit 3-5 provides a sample of widely-held common stocks' variability and beta risk measures.

Exhibit 3-5 The Variability and Volatility (Beta) of Common Stocks Widely Held by Individual Investors		
Stock	Variability	Beta
Low Risk		
1. American Electric Power	16%	0.31
2. Eastman Kodak	20	0.69
3. Exxon	19	0.85
4. Proctor & Gamble	19	0.60
5. Texaco	20	0.88
Average Risk		
1. Golden Nugget Inc. °	45%	1.09
2. Gulf Oil	30	1.02
3. Levi Strauss	30	0.99
4. Minnesota Mining & Mfg.	27	0.98
5. Polaroid	33	0.98
High Risk		
1. Donaldson. Lufkin Jenrette	45%	1.71
2. Mattel Inc.	55	2.14
3. National Semiconductor	49	1.83
4. Prime Computer Inc.	50	2.28
5. U. S. Home	47	2.19

° Notice that Golden Nugget, a gambling stock, is an example of a security with high variability but relatively low beta risk.

SOURCE: Dailygraphs Stock Option Guide, William O'Neil & Co., Inc., January 27. 1984.

---

* Value Line Convertibles Survey. Vol. 15. No. 46. December 10. 1984, pp. 19-20.

GOOD DIVERSIFICATION PAYS OFF

In setting your portfolio strategy, you should *first* determine how much risk you are willing to accept. Inevitably, of course, risk and profit potential tend to go hand in hand. That is, you cannot simply choose securities of the lowest risk without sacrificing return.

On the other hand, if you hold an *improperly diversified* portfolio, you may be exposing yourself to more risk than its potential returns warrant. Let's now turn to a discussion of these issues.

The Tradeoff Between Risk and Return

The risk of an investment is directly related to its expected return. If you expect higher returns, then you must take on increased risk. This can be demonstrated by examining the recent performance of different securities.

Referring to Exhibit 3-6, notice that as you go down the list of securities, the year-to-year fluctuation in the individual returns increases dramatically. Also note, though, that there is a close correspondence between return and risk, whether measured by the range of returns or volatility.

For example, the average returns on U.S. governments and higher-risk common stocks were 7.2% and 10.6%, respectively, while these two securities' volatility measures were 0.56 and 1.34.

In fact, because most investors are risk averse, there has been an historical tendency for a given increase in risk to be associated with a proportional increase in return. This general relationship is depicted graphically in Exhibit 3-7.

Three observations about this graphical relationship need to be made.

1. This is an approximate relationship over a long investment period. That is, don't expect this relationship to hold exactly every year. It is possible that lower-risk investments could outperform higher-risk ones. For example, in 1982 bonds performed better than stocks even though they generally have less risk (refer to Exhibit 3-6).

2. Within a specific type of investment, a broad range of risk-return characteristics exist, e.g., there are very risky as well as low-risk stocks.

3. Once you select an appropriate type of investment, you still need to decide which individual security or property to purchase.

Exhibit 3-6

Annual Holding Period Yields and Risk Measures of Long-Term Marketable Securities, 1971-1982

TYPE OF INVESTMENT	1971	1972	1973	1974	1975	1976	1977	1978	1979	1980	1981	1982	AVG	RANGE HIGH	RANGE LOW	VOLATILITY (RISK INDEX)
1. U.S. Government Bonds	16.2	5.3	-0.4	4.9	9.6	14.2	-0.9	-0.4	-1.1	-3.3	-0.8	42.7	7.2	42.7	-3.3	0.56
2. GNMA Mortgages	N.A.	6.1	2.5	3.9	10.4	16.3	1.5	2.2	0.2	0.4	1.5	40.1	7.7	40.1	0.2	0.52
3. Corporate Bonds (High Quality)	11.9	10.0	-0.4	-4.5	15.1	17.3	3.5	-1.9	-2.9	-5.4	0.2	39.4	6.9	39.4	-5.4	0.57
4. Preferred Stocks (High Quality)	9.5	6.7	0.3	-7.2	14.3	16.3	4.8	-2.1	-6.5	-2.0	5.2	31.1	5.9	31.1	-7.2	0.50
5. Common Stocks (Low Risk)	13.1	30.1	10.4	-14.1	19.2	16.7	-11.4	10.3	18.2	15.9	5.8	31.5	12.1	31.5	-14.1	0.64
6. Common Stocks (High Risk)	-7.1	4.3	-35.7	-40.6	60.4	49.7	-8.6	16.0	40.1	72.6	-20.0	-3.6	10.6	72.6	-40.6	1.34

SOURCE: R. M. Soldofsky. "Risk and Return for Long-Term Securities: 1971-1982," <u>Journal of Portfolio Management</u>, Fall 1984, pp. 57-64.

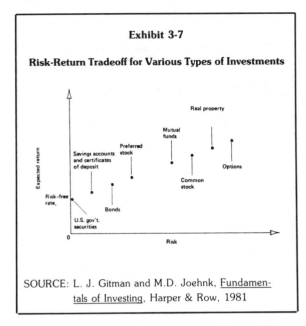

Exhibit 3-7

Risk-Return Tradeoff for Various Types of Investments

SOURCE: L. J. Gitman and M.D. Joehnk, <u>Fundamentals of Investing</u>, Harper & Row, 1981

Diversifiable vs. Nondiversifiable Risk

The *total risk* or *variability* of a security consists of two components: diversifiable and nondiversifiable risk. *Diversifiable* risk is that part of an investment's risk that can be reduced through diversification. It results from random or uncontrollable events *unique to an investment* such as a lawsuit or a labor strike.

Nondiversifiable risk is that part of total risk that results from forces that affect all investments (is not unique to a particular investment), such as inflation, war and international events. Therefore,

Total = Nondiversifiable + Diversifiable
Risk   Risk   Risk

Diversification Reduces Diversifiable Risk

The importance in recognizing the distinction between these two risk components is that you can greatly reduce diversifiable risk by holding a diversified portfolio of securities. Studies have shown that a careful selection of six to ten securities can almost eliminate diversifiable risk, e.g., $2,000 in each of ten stocks.

In contrast, nondiversifiable risk (like the market risk discussed earlier) *cannot be avoided*. Each security has its own unique amount of this risk, which is represented by its beta risk.

You can reduce diversifiable risk in two ways:

1. By holding securities of firms in different industries, e.g., utilities, airlines, steels, autos, etc., and/or

2. By holding *different types* of investments, e.g., bonds, stocks and real estate.

Exhibit 3-8 shows how quickly diversification across stocks can reduce risk as we move from a one-stock portfolio to a larger-sized stock portfolio. Notice that most of diversification's risk-reduction benefits occur after spreading your funds over 5-10 stocks.

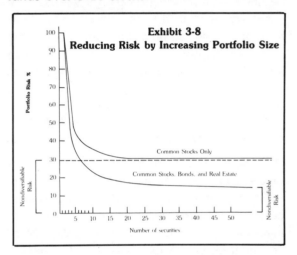

Exhibit 3-8
Reducing Risk by Increasing Portfolio Size

And note that no matter how many stocks you hold in a portfolio, you are still left with about 30% of an average stock's total variability. This is the market or nondiversifiable risk that cannot be eliminated. Finally, *if you also* diversify across types of investments—such as bonds, real estate, etc.—the nondiversifiable risk can be reduced even further.

The reason that diversification minimizes risk is because higher returns exert a *balancing effect* against lower returns. This results in most of your portfolio's return variability being "dampened out."

Diversification and Investor Confidence

A related aspect of diversification is its effect on your confidence that your portfolio's performance will achieve or be near the *average market return*. Clearly, this confidence depends on the dispersion of your portfolio's returns around the market's return.

In Exhibit 3-9, we summarize the average reduction in the range and variability of portfolio returns achieved by increasing the number of stocks in a portfolio. Panel A shows, for example, that in moving from a one-stock portfolio to an eight-stock portfolio, an average reduction in dispersion of 69% can be obtained. Note further that even more reduction in the range of returns can be achieved by moving to a 16-stock portfolio (80%).

Panel B indicates that comparable benefits can be obtained from diversification if we use total variability as our risk measure. Thus, both measures of dispersion clearly demonstrate that increasing the number of stocks in your portfolio increases your confidence of obtaining the market return.

OTHER IMPORTANT INVESTMENT CONSIDERATIONS

While the risk-return tradeoff and benefits of diversification are critical considerations in constructing your investment portfolio, you need to be aware of four other elements affecting your investment: (1) liquidity, (2) marketability, (3) investment effort and expertise, and (4) taxes.

Liquidity

Liquid assets are easily and quickly turned into cash, with *little or no risk of principal loss.* Examples are your checking and savings accounts or a money market mutual fund. On the other hand, long-term bonds and stocks tend to be illiquid because of the danger of receiving less than your purchase price if you should find it necessary to sell them to obtain quick cash.

Marketability

Marketability refers to the ease or difficulty of buying or selling a security or asset at its market value. This is related to but distinct from liquidity. For instance, market value is the price a buyer and seller would agree on if neither were under pressure to trade quickly. Large corporations' stock such as IBM are very marketable. In contrast, if you want to sell a rent house, you need

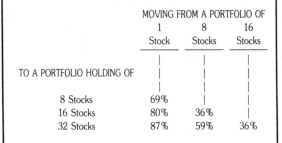

Exhibit 3-9
Percentage Reduction in Dispersion
of Portfolio Returns

A. Range of Returns' Dispersion

	MOVING FROM A PORTFOLIO OF		
	1 Stock	8 Stocks	16 Stocks
TO A PORTFOLIO HOLDING OF			
8 Stocks	69%		
16 Stocks	80%	36%	
32 Stocks	87%	59%	36%

B. Total Variability

	MOVING FROM A PORTFOLIO OF		
	1 Stock	8 Stocks	16 Stocks
TO A PORTFOLIO HOLDING OF			
8 Stocks	65%		
16 Stocks	75%	29%	
32 Stocks	83%	51%	32%

SOURCE: R. Upson, P. Jessup and K. Matsumoto. "Portfolio Diversification Strategies, "Financial Analysts Journal, May/June, 1975, pp. 86-88.

to be patient or be willing to sell at a distressed price.

Investment Effort and Expertise

Selecting and managing certain types of investments requires little or no time commitment or special knowledge. For example, stocks and bonds can be maintained with little effort whereas other investments, such as a rent house, may require constant management.

Similarly, it's easy to understand the relevant characteristics of a savings account or Treasury bill—their risk, expected return, liquidity, marketability and tax treatment. Other investments such as real estate or stock options require very special knowledge. Thus, you need to consider carefully the expertise, talent and time required to choose and manage your investments properly.

Taxes

You only keep the *after-tax* portion of your returns. Tax considerations are extremely important, especially for those in a high tax bracket. Understanding how investment income is taxed requires you to familiarize yourself with our tax system and what your marginal tax rate is. A detailed discussion of your investments' tax implications is postponed until Chapter 19.

SUMMARY

To summarize what we have learned in this chapter, Exhibit 3-10 gives you an overview of the investment considerations you need to keep in mind with respect to various types of investments.

Exhibit 3-10

A Checklist of Factors to Consider Before Investing in Various Types of Investments

	Risk	Return	Liquidity	Marketability	Expertise Required	Time Involved	Tax Advantages
SHORT-TERM DEBT							
Passbook Accounts	None	Low	Excellent	Excellent	None	None	None
U.S. Savings Bonds	None	Low	Good	Excellent	None	None	Minimal
Money Market Securities	Little	Varies	Good	Excellent	None	Little	Minimal
Money Market Mutual Funds	Minimal	Varies	Excellent	Excellent	Little	Little	None
LONG-TERM DEBT							
Treasury Bonds	None	Varies	Good	Good	Little	Modest	Minimal
Corporate Bonds	Varies	Varies	Good	Good	Little	Modest	Substantial
State/Local Bonds	Varies	Varies	Poor	Poor	Varies	Varies	Minimal
EQUITIES							
Common Stocks	Substantial	Varies	Average	Usually Excellent	Substantial	Substantial	Varies
Preferred Stocks	Varies	Varies	Average	Usually Excellent	Varies	Varies	Small
Listed Options	Substantial	Varies	Poor	Excellent	Substantial	Substantial	Minimal
MUTUAL FUNDS	Varies	Varies	Average	Excellent	Little	Little	Varies
REAL ESTATE	Substantial	Varies	Poor	Poor	Substantial	Varies	Substantial

Adapted from Ben Branch, Investments: A Practical Approach, pp. 50. Published by Longman Financial Sources Publishing, Inc., a Longman Group USA company. ©1985 by Longman Group USA Inc. Adapted with permission.

TERMS TO KNOW

Beta risk
Business risk
Capital gains yield
Current yield
Default risk
Diversifiable risk
Diversification
Expected return
Financial risk
Holding period yield

Inflation risk
Interest rate risk
Liquidity
Market risk
Marketability
Nondiversifiable risk
Range of returns
Realized returns
Standard deviation
Variability
Volatility

4 WHAT IT TAKES TO BE A SUCCESSFUL INVESTOR

Chapter Objectives

1. The Importance of Assessing Your Attitudes and Temperament in Becoming a Successful Investor
2. Eight Guidelines for the Successful Investor

So you want to be a successful investor. Why?

Because you want to enhance your financial future. You want to strengthen your financial security—for yourself if you're single, for your family as the children grow up and go to college, for you and your wife to enjoy a better standard of living, to be able to travel, to stay ahead of inflation, to be comfortably independent when you reach retirement.

These are some of many good reasons for investing. Every investor has his/her reasons. Whatever these reasons, they mean one thing: you're looking ahead; you're planning; you want to "succeed" as an investor. We all do! And it can be done:

- IF you clearly define your objectives
- IF you adhere strictly to time-tested investment rules
- IF you allocate adequate time to investigate and follow up on investment ideas
- IF you apply plain common sense, with minimal emotional involvement
- IF you maintain patience and understand that luck is part of investment success

Do these requirements sound like an impossible list? Not if you're serious about becoming a successful investor. It can be done. It has been done—millions of times, but only by those with the determination and self-discipline to do it.

Many apparently sound investments end up falling short of expectations, and leave the investor frustrated—or worse, a financial loser. This usually occurs because the investor fails to recognize his/her own financial attitude and temperament.

In this chapter, we examine this important aspect of a successful investment program. We point out specific, realistic guidelines for you to follow if you truly want to increase your chances of becoming a successful investor.

YOUR FINANCIAL ATTITUDE AND TEMPERAMENT

How you manage your investment portfolio depends on the type of individual you are. Investors don't fall into a single mold. If they did we wouldn't have "bulls" and "bears."

Different motivations, different attitudes toward risk, breadth of knowledge, types of experience and differing abilities to evaluate alternative investments make each investor unique.

This requires you to "know thyself". Take a personal inventory of your stengths and weaknesses. (Be brutally frank with yourself on this inventory.) Only then can your investment objectives and the best types of investments *for you* be properly determined.

How much time and effort can you devote to your investments? The changes in the securities markets over the past ten years are overwhelming. Never in U.S. financial history have so many investment choices been available to investors. Investment returns and safety in the 1980's and 1990's will be affected by the highly uncertain outlook for inflation, interest rates, employment and record federal and trade deficits. Never before have we seen such volatility in interest rates and market prices.

In such an environment, the *less time and effort* you devote to your investments, the more *conservative* your selections should be. So ask yourself these important questions:

1. Are you unwilling or unable to keep up with business news and financial reports?
2. Do you prefer not to manage your own investments (or do you feel you don't have enough time)?
3. Do you want little risk exposure and yet are unhappy with simply investing in a passbook savings account?

If you answer these questions "yes," then, initially the best strategy is to put *most* of your money into money market accounts or mutual funds. Money market funds invest only in safe, short-term securities such as Treasury bills, commercial paper and certificates of deposit (CD's) issued by banks. They can be converted to cash quickly in case you have a sudden, unexpected need for cash.

Can you only spend 30 minutes a week on research and review? If so, stick with *high-quality* investments. While not very exciting, they are not likely to disappoint you.

Do you want to actively manage your own investment program and are you willing to assume high risks in the quest for high gains? This high-risk approach to investing is obviously not suitable for most investors. To follow this approach requires an unusual set of personal characteristics:

- highly motivated
- knowledgable about securities with years of investing experience
- confident in the ability to judge security values
- ability to absorb substantial capital losses
- adequate time to keep close tabs on developments in the securities markets

Most of us fall somewhere between the two extreme investment approaches: low-risk, low-yield and high-risk, high-yield. But knowing where *you fall in this spectrum is essential.*

Are you interested enough and will you take time enough to read books and magazines, subscribe to investment advisory services and study financial data and statistics? Then many of the suggestions in this investment guide are for you, and, as a result, you will make more money. *Success requires effort.* Remember:

Successful investors don't do a percent or two better than the norm—they do 100 percent better!

What is your emotional temperament? Are you a cautious, get-the-facts, no-nonsense person? Or are you a guess-the-future, buy-on-rumors, make-a-fast-buck style person? More investment mistakes are made because of impulse buying or inadequate assessment and monitoring of investments' potential gains and losses than for any other reason.

Perhaps more important than style is *peace of mind.* If an investment will cause you to worry—don't make it. Or, if you have already done so, sell it—you are "over-invested." Money itself is never more important than peace of mind. It is better to sleep well than to eat well.

The successful investor is one who looks before he/she leaps. He/she does not allow emotions to dictate behavior. A risky investment that suffers heavy losses is the surest way to damage the long-run potential for building your assets. A cautiously developed investment program will provide more favorable long-run results than an impulsive, risky one.

GUIDELINES FOR SUCCESSFUL INVESTING

Wall Street is well known for its many generalizations and other "conventional wisdom" concerning sound investing. Below, we describe the more useful "Do's" and "Don'ts" for successful investing, which are based on the accumulated experience and trial-and-error results of successful investors.

DO Stick with a Specific Investment Plan or Rules

We cannot emphasize too strongly that, to be successful, you must have an investment plan that recognizes and accepts the fact that some losses are bound to occur. No investor (however successful) has been right on *every* investment. Investigate before you invest, and avoid buying or selling on impulse or a hunch. *Don't be in a hurry!*

Make all investments according to your plan.

Don't deviate from it—especially for emotional reasons. Following your investment rules will be more rewarding than breaking them. They were designed to be followed; otherwise, they will mean nothing.

DO Act Promptly

We don't mean impulsively. But, after fully assessing the situation, if your judgment dictates a buy or sell decision, don't be reluctant. Act! It's well and good to make every dollar possible, but don't quibble over the "last quarter point"—you may regret it if the market moves away from you.

DO Diversify
(But Don't Over-Diversify)

Diversifying *across* different investment categories (e.g., stocks, bonds, etc.) as well as *within* certain categories, e.g., five to ten stocks from different industries—such as utilities, transportation, banking—can reduce risk without giving up much in the way of return.

But don't go overboard and try to cover the waterfront. When you and your investments are spread too thin you lose control—you only have so much time to analyze and monitor your investments.

At the other extreme, many investors have only one or two securities. This prevents them from receiving the benefit of proper diversification—reduction of risk.

How many securities you want to study or hold depends on your individual "time" situation, but rule of thumb says 8 to 10 for most "average" investors; perhaps 15 for the more experienced who have more time.

DO Stay Out When in Doubt

This is one area where the average investor goes wrong. He/she sees the market moving and itches to get in and be a part of it. But to increase your odds for success, you should wait until, *after thorough study,* you find a situation which you are convinced should prove profitable. Patience to wait for certainty of mind is a profitable virtue. There are plenty of oppor-

tunities out there. It's not the winners you don't buy, it's the losers you don't buy that will make the difference!

A major fault of many investors is that they try too hard to make too much money too fast. Take your time. Rarely does a security's price take off quickly. Rather, appreciation is slow and often erratic. Few investments achieve substantial appreciation in less than two years. Once you do have a position in the market, if even the slightest doubt arises as to the soundness of that position, either get out entirely or reduce your holding to the point where you don't worry and can sleep. *You don't have to be in the market all the time.* There is no such thing as a permanent investment.

DO Limit Losses, Let Profits Run

This is one of the most important rules to follow—all successful investors use it. At first glance, this might seem easy to follow. But human nature ends up making the average investor do the opposite! The trouble is that one does not intentionally start out to let losses run or to limit profits.

If certain trading rules are not followed, you will find that you have unconsciously done just that. Why? Because it is easy to take a profit, but it is difficult to take a loss. (Who wants to admit he/she is wrong or has made a mistake?) Take comfort in knowing that even the most astute investor is wrong on occasion.

Avoid feeling that when the market moves against you, the market is wrong and will eventually correct itself to reflect your opinion of the situation. You may want to wait until a stock comes back to break-even. In many cases, you may wait a long, long time. In other cases, the stock may never come back. Result: you held on against the current trend and let your losses run. Before this happens, admit you erred and get out. Your losses can be recouped quicker in another investment.

Another related guideline is to "never throw good money after bad." This warns against "averaging down"—buying more shares of a stock when its price declines. You'll only compound your mistake.

DON'T Buy on "Hot Tips" or Rumors

To be successful, you must take time to learn enough about a security and the current economic forces which affect it in order to make intelligent investment decisions. Besides, by the time you receive a tip or hear a rumor, it's too late—hundreds of investors have already heard it and have acted on it *if* it has any merit. Don't "buy in haste and repent in leisure."

DON'T be Overly Optimistic or Pessimistic

Learn to recognize the two prime motivating forces in investing—greed and fear (or hope). Discipline yourself to avoid these extremes in emotions about the market and/or securities you own. Avoid fads or securities in vogue. When a stock becomes popular, watch out—it's probably overvalued.

And don't rely on the "greater fool theory"—that prices will keep rising and you will be able to sell to someone else foolish enough to pay more than its worth. You may end up being the fool. Remember: "Bulls and bears make money, but hogs get slaughtered."

Realistically, even an exceptional investment cannot perform above-average forever. Investors' moods and economic conditions fluctuate over time, and these will affect even the most seemingly infallible investment. Pre-establish your price objective (e.g., a doubling in price), sell when it is realized, and don't look back.

DON'T Go Against the Trend

You need to be aware of the overall trends in the economy, interest rates, the stock market and securities in which you are interested. Never buck a trend in progress. The average (unsuccessful) investor concentrates on believing that he/she is right and the market is wrong. Remember: one has to be right at the right time. And the right time is when the market itself is acting in accordance with your opinion. This means you need to recognize the trend of the market and stay with it until the trend changes in order to realize maximum profit.

5 HOW SECURITIES MARKETS WORK

Chapter Objectives

1. To Describe the Role of Different Segments of Security Markets
2. To Explain How to Buy Securities--Selecting a Broker, Brokerage Firm, Type of Account to Open and Types of Orders
3. To Discuss the Mechanics of How Securities Markets Work and the Role of Regulation

You as well as many investors may find the buying and selling of securities somewhat mysterious. This is partly due to the lingo used with regard to investing and partly due to the stories about how much money is earned (and lost) on trading securities.

This chapter removes some of the mystery by examining the various segments of the security markets--the role and mechanics of security exchanges, how to buy securities, types of orders and accounts, the costs of investing and so on.

TYPES OF SECURITY MARKETS

The Primary or "New Issue" Market

Billions of dollars worth of newly-issued securities are brought to market each year. These securities are called *new* or *primary* issues. New sales of Texaco stock or Treasury bills, for instance, take place in the primary market. Basically, though, the new issue market is a *bond* market. For example, 3/4s of all new *corporate* issues are bonds. Including *government* issues makes this percentage even higher. The remaining percentage is usually younger ("start up") companies that use this market to issue their shares of common stock for the first time.

An *investment banker* or *underwriter*, such as Merrill Lynch or Salomon Bros., acts as the middleman in the primary markets. (This is not to be confused with a commercial bank.) If a company is well known, its new issue is bought by the investment banker at an agreed-upon price and then quickly resold to investors at a higher price. The difference is the underwriter's profit.

Underwriting a new issue guarantees a successful issuance. But to spread around the purchase cost, selling risk and geographical allocation of the issue among investors, a group of investment bankers--called an *underwriter syndicate*--is formed. In many ways, they act like a stockbroker. (Exhibit 5-1 contains an advertisement for a new stock offering called a "tombstone," that lists the underwriter syndicate members and the offering price.)

How is a new issue price set? The price for a new issue may be *negotiated, privately agreed-upon,* or *auctioned competitively* (such as state and local bond issues). Usually, *prevailing prices for comparable issues already being traded* as well as *current market conditions* are used to establish an issue's price.

The Secondary or "Used Issue" Market

Once a new security (bond, common or preferred stock) is sold in the primary market, the *secondary market* provides the means for trading this *existing* or *"used"* security among investors. This trading may occur on a *listed* or *organized exchange,* such as the New York Stock Exchange (NYSE), or in a more informal but still highly organized market known as the *over-the-counter* (OTC) *market.*

Organized vs. OTC Market. In both cases, professionals "make a market" in a security by holding an inventory of it. This provides marketability and allows its easy transfer from sellers to buyers. Market makers are called *specialists* on organized exchanges and *dealers* in the OTC.

Organized exchanges provide a *fixed location* where trading in various securities occurs. This contrasts with the OTC market which is not physically located in any one place. It actually is a *communications network* over which securities are traded.

Pricing Securities in an Auction vs. Negotiated Market. Secondary markets are either an auction or negotiated market. In an *auction market,* such as the organized exchanges, *prices are determined by the bidding of market participants called brokers.* These brokers are intermediaries that represent you in an attempt to obtain the best possible price. For this effort, they collect commissions. And they don't care about whether you are buying or selling or even about what is being bought or sold.

A *negotiated market* involves a *dealer network* that makes a market by standing ready at all times to buy/sell securities at their specified prices. In contrast to brokers, dealers do have a vested interest because they buy (sell) securities from (to) you. Their *profit* in these trades comes from the difference in their *bid-ask spread*--the price at which they will buy (bid) and sell (ask). The OTC markets for stocks and government securities are examples of a negotiated market.

1. *New York Stock Exchange (NYSE).* The largest and most   prominent secondary market for stocks. Over 2,000 issues are traded here, which represent over 75% of the dollar volume traded in the U.S.-- hence its name, the "Big Board." Companies must apply to have their securities traded here. It has the strictest listing requirements of any organized exchange in the world.

   About 1,400 members, who have purchased "seats," conduct their business here. Typically, they are partners or directors of brokerage firms.

   Most members act as brokers for their customers' buy/sell orders (*"commission brokers"*). Twenty-five percent of all members are *"specialists"* who are assigned specific stocks and one of the 89 trading posts on the exchange's trading floor. A small number of members trade only for their own account (*"floor traders"*).

2. *American Stock Exchange (AMEX or ASE).* The smaller AMEX (the "Curb" exchange) is the only other nationally organized exchange. Its organization and trading procedures are similar to the NYSE.

   It has, however, fewer seats (650) and stocks listed (1000). Its listing requirements are also less strict. Smaller (especially energy and natural resource) companies dominate the types of firms traded here.

Exhibit 5-2 presents a comparison of the listing requirements for the NYSE and AMEX.

Exhibit 5-2
A Comparison of Listing Requirements on the NYSE and AMEX*

Requirement	NYSE	AMEX
OWNERSHIP		
1. Number of Publicly-Traded Shares	1,000,000	400,000
2. Number of Shareholders Holding 100 Shares or More	2,000	1,200
FINANCIAL		
3. Last Year's Pre-Tax Income	$2.5 Million	$0.75 Million
4. Last Two Years' Pre-Tax Income	$2.0 Million	N.A.
5. Last Year's Net Income	N.A.	$0.40 Million
6. Tangible Assets	$16 Million	$4 Million
7. Market Value of Common Stock	$16 Million	$3 Million

* Subsequent to listing, violation of any of these requirements by a company may lead to its stock being "delisted."

---

3. *Regional Exchanges.* A number of regional exchanges also exist, including:
   Boston Stock Exchange
   Cincinnati Stock Exchange
   Midwest Stock Exchange
   Pacific Coast Stock Exchange
   Philadelphia Stock Exchange.
   While patterned after the NYSE, these exchanges' listing requirements are more lenient. They tend to specialize in smaller companies with limited geographical interest. Most, however, carry securities traded on the NYSE or AMEX (called *dual listing*). Their chief attraction is lower commissions.

4. *Over-the-Counter (OTC) Market.* Larger, well-known companies' *stocks are usually listed on an exchange. In contrast, numerous smaller firms tend to be found in the OTC market (over 10,000 stocks).*
   Trades take place by telephone or other telecommunication devices. The National

Association of Securities Dealers (NASD), a self-policing organization of dealers, requires at least two market makers (dealers) for each security. Typically, five to ten dealers are involved.

OTC markets exist for stocks, bonds, federal securities, municipal bonds, commercial paper, negotiable CDs, mutual funds as well as other various securities. Taken together, these securities make the OTC the largest market in the world.

There are actually three levels to the OTC stock market:

- The "national market" is for larger, more actively-traded securities such as Apple Computer and MCI Communications. They have enough of a diversified shareholder base that they are considered national in scope.
- The "regular market" has less actively-traded securities that don't qualify for "national listing."
- The "additional OTC" market contains thinly-traded securities that tend to have only local or regional interest.

NASDAQ. The NASD *Automated Quotation* system is a nationally-computerized system that provides up-to-the-minute quotations on over 3,500 OTC stocks. This is how your broker finds out what current bid-ask prices are. Before this system was installed in 1971, your broker had to telephone around to get quotes--an obviously time-consuming, inefficient process. The NASDAQ system has made it possible to find the best price for you quickly at the touch of a button.

If a stock is not on the NASDAQ system, it is reported in the "pink sheets" available at your brokerage firm. The pink sheets contain recent price quotes and a list of dealers who make a market in the security.

5. *Listed Options. Listed call-put options* are traded on the Chicago Board Options Exchange (CBOE), AMEX, NYSE, Philadelphia and Pacific Coast Exchange. They offer trading in standardized call and put option contracts that have 3-, 6- and 9-month expiration periods on a rotating monthly series. For example, one calendar series is January-April-July-October.

PARTICIPATING IN THE MARKET

Selecting a Broker and a Brokerage Firm

The first step in purchasing securities is to select a broker and brokerage firm that suits your needs. Chapter 17 covers this topic in detail, so we won't repeat it here.

Opening an Account

Before placing an order, you must open an account with a brokerage firm. It's a simple process--much like opening a charge account with a store. You will be asked for personal information such as your social security number, type of account and general financial information on your liquid assets and net worth.

It's also important to discuss your personal financial situation with your broker so that your investment objectives are clear. Instructions on the transfer and custody of securities must also be given to the broker (see below).

Types of Accounts You Can Open

1. *Cash Account.* A cash account allows you to make only cash transactions. That is, you pay the entire cost of the securities. It is the most common type used and is often referred to as a "Type 1" account.

2. *Margin Account.* A margin account allows you to buy securities with a *combination of cash and borrowed funds* and is referred to as a "Type 2" account.

   That is, you purchase a security partially with your money and partially with credit supplied by the brokerage firm. It is like making an initial downpayment on a house and borrowing the remaining funds for the purchase.

   By using your securities as collateral, you are permitted to borrow a certain percentage (currently 50%) of the purchase price, called *margin*. You pay interest on the borrowed amount. The interest rate is based on the *broker's loan* or *call money rate*--a rate that can fluctuate daily or weekly.

NOTE: If the dollar amount of collateral in your account falls below a specified level (25%-30% of your total holdings), you are required by law to put up more collateral (cash or additional securities). This is called a *margin call*.

If you don't do this, the broker will sell off some of your securities to raise the necessary cash to satisfy the loan requirements.

A WORD OF CAUTION: Investors use margin to increase their potential investment returns. If security prices are expected to rise, using borrowed funds can magnify the returns over what they would be if only cash were used. Exhibit 5-3 illustrates how this works.

HOWEVER, the *opposite result can occur if you are wrong and prices fall!* Exhibit 5-3 also illustrates *how margin works against you by magnifying your losses.*

LESSON: Because margin magnifies both gains and losses, using a margin account is a much riskier type of investing.

3. *Asset Management Account.* Brokerage firms now offer a special account called an asset management account. This account consolidates your checking, credit card, money market and margin accounts into one account. Your funds are "swept" back and forth to minimize your interest expenses on borrowed funds or to maximize your short-term yields.

For instance, say you *write a check;* your checking account is tapped first for the funds. Next, if necessary, your money fund is tapped. Finally, if funds to cover the check are still not enough, a margin loan is made. Your credit card purchases are handled similarly.

Exhibit 5-3
How Buying Securities on Margin Can Magnify Your Gains and Losses

ASSUME: 1. You buy 200 Exxon shares at $50 per share
2. Margin requirement = 50% (the percentage of the purchase price that can be borrowed)
3. Broker loan rate = 8%

A. Return on a Cash vs. Margin Purchase: Sell Exxon at $60 Per Share One Year Later

	Cash Purchase (No Margin)	Margin Purchase (Borrow 50%)
Purchase (200 shares x $50)	− $10,000	− $10,000 Cash = $5,000 Loan = $5,000
Sale (200 shares x $60)	$12,000	$12,000
Gross Profit	$ 2,000	$ 2,000
Less: Interest expense (8% x $5,000)	-0-	− 400
Net Profit	$ 2,000	$ 1,600
Rate of Return (Gain ÷ Equity)	$ 2,000 / $10,000	$ 1,600 / $ 5,000
	20%	32%

B. Loss on a Cash vs. Margin Purchase: Sell Exxon at $45 Per Share One Year Later

	Cash Purchase (No Margin)	Margin Purchase (Borrow 50%)
Purchase (200 shares x $50)	-$10,000	-$10,000 Cash = $ 5,000 Loan = $ 5,000
Sale (200 shares x $45)	$ 9,000	$ 9,000
Loss	-$ 1,000	-$ 1,000
Less: Interest expense (8% x $5,000)	-0-	− 400
Total Loss	− $ 1,000	− $ 1,400
Rate of Return (Loss ÷ Equity)	− $ 1,000 / $10,000	− $ 1,400 / $ 5,000
	−10%	−28%

On the other hand, say you *make a cash deposit.* This amount is applied first toward reducing any loan amount. Otherwise, it is placed in a money fund to earn interest. In many ways, this account simplifies your cash management problems--plus you can get one monthly statement summarizing all your financial transactions.

4. *"Street-Name" Account.* Once you have purchased a security, you have two choices on how the security is delivered:
   - Leave the security with the broker
   - Take delivery of the security

   If your securities are left with the broker, they are registered in a "street-name" (name of the brokerage firm) although you are the actual owner. *If you decide to take delivery,* the securities are registered in your name and a certificate of ownership is issued to you, e.g., a stock certificate.

   Pros and Cons of Using a "Street-Name." Street-name registration offers safe storage and makes trading easier by eliminating the handling of certificates. On the other hand, you may encounter some problems with a street-name account:
   - Dividends/interest may be credited to the wrong account (you have to catch the errors if it's to be corrected).
   - Delays in receiving dividends/interest --sometimes up to a month after they are paid.
   - Securities may be tied up during a bankrupt brokerage firm's reorganization.

   Pros and Cons of Taking Delivery. You are the registered owner, so no confusion over ownership can arise. In addition, all the "negatives" of using a street-name mentioned above are eliminated.

   However, you are responsible for the safekeeping of the securities, and you have to pay for this. Moreover, if the securities are lost, destroyed or stolen, it's your problem, i.e., your expense to have them replaced or your loss if they are stolen.

The Monthly Statement

If you have a "street-name" account, you receive a *monthly statement* of the securities that are being held by the brokerage house. This statement also includes any transactions that have taken place during the month: receipts of dividends/interest, margin interest paid, securities bought and sold, cash balances etc.

Exhibit 5-4 contains an example of a monthly statement and a description of the information it contains.

Types of Trade Positions

1. *Long Position.* A long position involves initially purchasing a security and is the most common type of transaction. A long position is taken in the hope that a security's price will increase and can be sold later at a profit.

   The objective in "being long" is to buy low and sell high. Being long entitles you to any dividends or interest paid plus the capital gains (losses if the security price falls). It is done when you are "bullish" about a security's future prospects.

2. *Short Position.* A more speculative trade is to initiate a short sale position. *A short sale involves initially selling a security* in the hope that the *security will decline in price.*

   While your objective is still "buy low and sell high," you *reverse* the order of your transactions from the case of a long purchase. That is, you sell first ("sell high") and *then when the price falls you buy the security back* ("buy low").

   You would do this when you were "bearish" on a security's future prospects.

   To initiate such a trade, your broker *borrows* the security or shares from the account of another customer (or another brokerage firm). He/she then sells the security to you. The sale proceeds are held in "escrow" until you liquidate your position by buying back the (replacing the borrowed) security.

   If the *security is purchased at a lower price* in the future, then you realize a *capital gain.* On the other hand, if the *security is bought at a higher price,* a *capital loss* is realized.

Exhibit 5-4

Example of an Investor's Monthly Statement for a "Street-Name" Account

FIDELITY

BROKERAGE SERVICES INCORPORATED

BRANCH MANAGER NAME IS

FOR STATEMENT QUESTIONS CALL
LOCAL
IN TEXAS   800-252-9433

YOUR ACCOUNT NUMBER IS

STATEMENT PERIOD	PAGE 1 OF 1
JUL 30 1983 THRU AUG 26 1983	SS/ID 453-70-7871

F I N A N C I A L   S U M M A R Y

			THIS PERIOD	YEAR TO DATE
OPENING NET MONEY BALANCE	7,247.30DR			
CLOSING NET MONEY BALANCE	2,061.57DR			
TOTAL MARKET VALUE-AUG 26	8,350.00	DIVIDEND	5.00	15.00
EQUITY-AUG 26	6,288.43	CREDIT INT EARNED	0.00	15.02
		MARGIN INT CHARGED	59.47	124.09

DATE	TRANSACTION	QUANTITY	DESCRIPTION	AMOUNT

REGULAR ACCOUNT ACTIVITY

DATE	TRANSACTION	QUANTITY	DESCRIPTION			AMOUNT
07-30			++OPENING BALANCE++			7,247.30DR
08-02	DIVIDEND RECEIVED		FOOD LION INC			5.00CR
08-09	MARGIN INTEREST ə 12.250%		AVG BAL	7,245DR	07/21-08/09	49.31
			END BAL	7,242DR	20 DAYS	
08-11	YOU SOLD	-200	FOOD LION INC ə 26 1/2			5,240.20CR
08-21	MARGIN INTEREST ə 12.500%		AVG BAL	2,438DR	08/10-08/21	10.16
			END BAL	2,002DR	12 DAYS	
08-26			++CLOSING BALANCE++			2,061.57DR

ACCOUNT TYPE	QUANTITY	SECURITY DESCRIPTION	SYMBOL	MARKET VALUE ON AUG 26 PER SHARE	TOTAL

POSITIONS IN YOUR ACCOUNT

ACCOUNT TYPE	QUANTITY	SECURITY DESCRIPTION	SYMBOL	PER SHARE	TOTAL
MARGIN	200	AMER INCOME LIFE INS CO	AINC	13 7/8	2,775.00
MARGIN	100	LIFEMARK CORP	LMK	26 1/4	2,625.00
MARGIN	200	RHODES INC	RHDS	14 3/4	2,950.00

This statement has three parts:

1. The top third of the statement summarizes the opening and closing balances for margin (the "DR" amounts), the total market value and equity in the account as well as the dividends paid ($5), interest earned ($0) and margin interest charged ($59.47).
2. The middle third contains all the transactions activity.
3. The lower third lists the stocks held by the brokerage firm and their market value.

SOURCE: Fidelity Brokerage Services Incorporated, 1983.

While you may borrow a security indefinitely, it must eventually be replaced by a close-out transaction. Moreover, as a short-seller, you must reimburse the original owner for any dividends paid during the short sale period.

Types of Orders

1. *Market Order.* An order to buy or sell a security as soon as possible at the best price available. It is the quickest way to fill your order because it is executed as soon as it reaches the exchange floor or market maker.

2. *Limit Order.* A limit order restricts the execution of the order to a specified price-- to buy (sell) at a specified price or lower (higher).

When you place such an order, it is transmitted to the exchange specialist dealing in the security. The order is noted in his/her book, indicating the price and number of shares desired. As soon as the specified market price (or better) trades, your order is executed as quickly as possible.

A limit order remains in effect (1) until a certain date, e.g., for the "day only," or (2) until canceled by you (good till canceled or "GTC") if it's never executed.

A Limit Order Example: Say that you place a limit order to buy 100 shares of Exxon currently selling at $52 at a limit price of 48½. If Exxon falls to 48½ *or less,* the specialist clears all 48½ orders received before yours and then executes your order *if the price is still at 48½ or below.*

3. *Stop-Loss (Stop) Order.* An order to buy (sell) a security when its market price trades at or above (below) a specified level. It is used primarily to protect your paper profits or to limit your losses in a security.

A Stop-Loss Order Example: Suppose you bought 100 shares of General Motors at $60 per share and that the price has now risen to $75. To protect your profits, you might enter an order at "72 Stop." If GM's price dipped to $72 or below, your stop order would be "triggered" and would *become a market order.* That is, you would be sold out *immediately* at the prevailing price, regardless what it was.

4. *Round- and Odd-Lot Orders.* Stock trading normally occurs in 100-share multiples known as *round-lots.* If your order involves less than 100 shares, it is treated as an *odd-lot.*

If your order calls for an *odd multiple* of 100, then it is *both* a round-lot an odd-lot. For example, if you want to buy 250 shares of Chrysler, then you have a round-lot of 200 shares and a 50-share odd-lot.

The processing of odd-lot orders will differ across brokerage firms. Such orders can be executed (1) on the exchange floor (through a computerized buy-sell system) or (2) "in house."

In the latter case, a brokerage firm such as E. F. Hutton handles the order by taking the opposite side of your trade. For instance, if you want to *buy* a security, they will *sell* you the security from their own portfolio at the prevailing (quoted) market price.

Regardless which process is used, you "pay" an extra ⅛ or 12½ cents per share for stock and a certain dollar amount for bonds.

MECHANICS OF THE MARKET

Executing Your Order

Perhaps the best way to describe how your order is executed is to walk through the different order-processing steps.

Let's say you are thinking of buying 100 shares of U.S. Steel. Using her computerized quotation system, your Paine-Webber broker tells you that U.S.S.'s current asked price is 25¾.

Deciding this is an attractive price, you instruct your broker to buy 100 shares "at market." Your broker will write an order and have it wired to her New York office. It is then phoned or wired to a clerk on the New York Stock Exchange floor.

Next, the clerk informs a Paine-Webber member partner of the order. This member partner then goes to the "post" where U.S. Steel is traded.

This member partner will then ask the specialist for U.S. Steel's current price. Assume it's "25½ bid, 25¾ ask," which says you could have the stock for $25.75 per share.

However, since Paine-Webber tries to do better for you, the member partner replies, "100 at 25⅝ to buy." The specialist (or another exchange member trying to sell for his customer) may respond, "Sold 100 at 25⅝."

Your transaction has now been completed-- both sides record each other's firm name and give the trade information to their phone clerks. In turn, your broker (and you) are notified of the trade.

Meanwhile, another clerk at the post records the following: the stock symbol, the price and number of shares. This information is then fed into a Market Data System Computer that stores it and communicates the details to over 12,000 tickers and quotation devices in the U.S. and other parts of the world.

Stock Symbols and the Ticker Tape. Actual transactions for listed securities appear on a "ticker tape" (electronic viewing screen) found in most brokerage firms. Each stock has a *ticker symbol.* For example, "X" stands for U.S. Steel, "XON" for Exxon and "MO" for Phillip Morris. All *listed* stocks have *3 or less letters* while OTC stocks have *4 or more.* A particular stock's symbol can be found in the S&P <u>Stock Guide</u> or from your broker.

How to Read the Tape. Each transaction's volume and price follow (below) the firm's ticker symbol on the tape. To illustrate,

X	PG
25⅝	6s52½

indicates your trade of 100 shares of U.S. Steel ("X") at 25⅝ while "PG 6s52½" stands for 600 shares ("s" = 00) of Proctor & Gamble at 52½.

Trades for 1000 or more shares are printed in full. For instance, "AAPL 3500s23⅞" means 3500 shares of Apple Computer at 23⅞.

Confirmation Statement

Each purchase or sell transaction as well as all open (limit) orders is acknowledged by a *confirmation statement.* Referring to the example found in Exhibit 5-5, this statement gives

- Number of shares bought (sold)--200 shares bought
- Company name--Rival Mfg.
- Unit price--14⅜ per share
- Total amount due--$2,940.01
- Trade date--May 25, 1983
- Settlement date--June 2, 1983

Two observations. First, notice that there is no explicit indication of the commission costs. The reason is because this stock was purchased "in house." That is, Rotan Mosle "makes a market" in this stock, so the stock was sold out of their own inventory at the best asking price. Then there was a "mark up" charged instead of an explicit commission. The *implicit* commission in this case was $2,940.01 minus $2,875.00 (200 shares x 14⅜) or $65.01.

Second, the *settlement date* refers to the date by which payment must be made. You have *five business days after the "trade date" to do this.* Similarly, *if you had sold* a security, the proceeds must "hit you account" by the fifth business day.

Exhibit 5-5

Confirmation Statement for the Purchase of 200 Shares of Rival Manufacturing

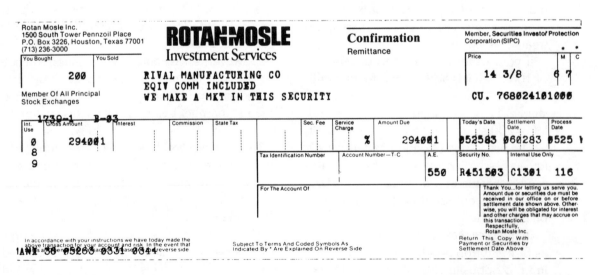

SOURCE: Rotan-Mosle Inc., 1983

The Costs of Investing: Commission Rates

Investing isn't free. Certain costs, such as commissions, transfer fees and taxes, can be significant in size for smaller investors--ranging from 2% to 5% of the dollar amount. You pay a commission on both the purchase and sale of securities, which is based on round-lot transactions.

While, technically, commission rates are "negotiable," only large or institutional investors can truly quibble about their rates. Here's one area where shopping around can save you money.

Discount vs. Full-Service Brokers. There are individual variations among different brokerage firms as to how commissions are calculated. Most *full-service brokers* base their commission fees on *both price and volume.* For example, for *common stock* transactions,

	Price per Share			
	$10	$20	$30	$40
Shares				
100	$ 36.30	$ 55.10	$ 71.00	$ 84.00
200	$ 72.40	$101.30	$130.70	$157.50
500	$143.25	$210.25	$277.25	$342.25

If you are an active trader, a full-service broker can "discount" the fixed-fee schedule amount by 20%-25%--*ask to see if they will.*

On the other hand, most discount brokers base their commissions on *either dollar amount or volume.* For example,

Dollar Amount	Commission Rate
Under $5,000	$28 + 0.8%
$5,001-$15,000	$28 + 0.6%
$15,000-$25,000	$28 + 0.5%

There also may be a *minimum* as well as a *maximum charge* per trade, regardless of the dollar amount involved.

Currently, each customer's account is insured up to $100,000 of securities held by the brokerage firm and up to $40,000 in cash balances. Some brokerage firms also insure their accounts for more than these limits through private insurance--you'll need to ask what these limits are.

NOTE: Don't confuse this as being insurance to guarantee the *dollar value* of your securities. Rather, it only assures you that the securities *themselves* will be recovered.

REGULATION OF SECURITIES MARKETS: THE SEC

The Securities and Exchange Commission (SEC) was created by Congress in 1933. Its purpose is to *regulate the organized securities markets.* The role it plays is to protect (unwary) investors from fraud and manipulation as well as to force corporations to provide "fair and adequate" information for investment purposes.

In addition to the SEC, there are two other layers of regulation--state laws and self-regulation by the industry. *State laws* (and the agencies they created) were designed to prevent an individual from buying a "piece of the blue sky"--hence the name "blue sky laws." In many ways, individual states have tougher rules and regulations on the sale of securities than does the SEC.

Industry self-regulation includes the National Association of Security Dealers (NASD) and the exchanges themselves. These organizations essentially control trading practices among their members.

TERMS TO KNOW

American Stock Exchange (Amex or ASE)
Asset management account
Auction market
The "Big Board" exchange
"Blue Sky" laws
Broker loan (call money) interest rate
Chicago Board Option Exchange
Commission broker
Confirmation statement
The "Curb" exchange
Dealer
Discount broker
Dual listing
Floor trader
Full-service broker
"Good till canceled" limit order
Investment banker
Limit order
Margin account
Margin call
Margin debt
Market maker
Market order
National Association of Securities Dealers
  (NASD)
NASDAQ--NASD Automated Quotation
  System
National OTC market
Negotiated market
New York Stock Exchange (NYSE)
Odd-lot order
Organized (listed) exchange
"Pink sheet" stocks
Primary (new issue) market
Regular OTC market
Round-lot order
Secondary (used issue) market
Securities & Exchange Commission (SEC)
Short sale
Specialist
"Stop-loss" order
"Street-name" account
Ticker symbol
Tombstone
Underwriter
Underwriter syndicate

MANAGING LOW RISK
INVESTMENTS

6 CASH RESERVES: SAVINGS ACCOUNTS, CDs AND SAVINGS BONDS

Chapter Objectives

1. The Difference Between Savings and Investments
2. Understanding the Power of Compound Interest
3. A Description of the Various Types of Deposit Accounts
4. Things to Look for in Selecting a Savings Vehicle for Your Cash Reserves
5. Money Market Funds and Series EE Bonds as a Store for Your Cash Reserves

Before seriously considering an investment in securities, you need adequate *cash reserves* for living expenses, emergencies, special purchases, etc. Wise investors see savings as the stable foundation of their investment portfolios, and they would no more neglect their savings than forget their broker's phone number.

Saving isn't just pitching pennies into a piggybank. While most people keep their cash reserves in a bank or S&L account, deregulation of the banking industry and increasing competition from mutual funds and brokerage firms have created a *wide range of savings options*. To such extent in fact that your savings must be *managed* as carefully as any investment.

All the various options stress safety, convenience and variety. The most troublesome aspect of all this is the *variety* of accounts from which you may choose. So it's worthwhile to examine what each has to offer you as well as things to look for before deciding on the one (or ones) best suited for you.

SAVINGS VS. INVESTMENTS

Let's take a moment to emphasize the differences between savings and investments. The *key features of savings* are *liquidity* and *safety*. *Liquidity* means you can withdraw your funds on short notice without the risk of giving up your principal (original deposits) and interest. *Safety* means that your principal is insured or is backed by the full faith and power of the U.S. government. Savings are also relatively *short-term* in nature.

Investments, in contrast, have a lower degree of liquidity and require a longer commitment of

funds that usually involves the risk of capital loss. There is the *potential* for greater rates of return compared to a cash reserve account, but you have no guarantee that this will occur. Therefore, investments should be made with funds that you don't need to have readily available.

A Note on Liquidity Vs. Marketability. Often the words "liquidity" and "marketability" are used interchangeably, but they don't mean the same thing. For example, *liquid* bank accounts allow quick withdrawals without risking loss of principal and interest. *Marketable* securities such as listed stocks offer an uncertain return, but you can quickly buy or sell them at their prevailing market price. Investments such as real estate are both *illiquid* and *nonmarketable*—there's no assurance of a profit or return of your invested capital. Nor is there certainty you can quickly locate a buyer.

THE POWER OF COMPOUNDING INTEREST

Interest is simply a charge for the use of another's money. If you borrow money to buy a car, you *pay* interest. Your bank *pays you* interest on your savings deposit.

A saver builds up cash reserves by depositing part of his/her current income into a savings account that earns interest. "Interest" is usually stated as a *percentage rate per annum* even if the money is deposited for only a few months.

To complicate matters, though, there are *different methods for calculating* interest. This means that the *stated* rate will not be the *effec-*

tive rate. The reason is because of the concept called *compound interest.* *Simple* interest refers to the payment (receipt) of interest *once a year.* *Compound* interest, on the other hand, means interest is paid (received) *more often* than once a year. In effect, you earn "interest on interest" during the year. That is, interest earned after a given period, say 3 months, is added to the principal amount and *included* in the next period's interest calculation. This compounding of interest is what causes the effective interest rate to be higher than the stated interest rate. And the more frequently compounding occurs, the higher the effective interest rate.

To illustrate the difference between different methods of calculating interest, assume you deposit $5,000 in an account that pays 10% per annum. Let's now contrast what your savings will be worth when interest is earned annually, quarterly and daily:

Time in Years	Interest Earned Annually (10.00%)	Interest Earned Quarterly (10.38%)	Interest Earned Daily (10.52%)
1	$ 5,500	$ 5,519	$ 5,526
5	$ 8,052	$ 8,193	$ 8,244
10	$12,968	$13,425	$13,591
15	$20,886	$22,000	$22,408
20	$33,637	$36,048	$36,945

First, notice that earning 10% on $5,000 can amount to a tidy sum if the money is left in the account (in fact, your money will double in seven years). Second, there can be quite a difference in your savings, depending on the compounding method used. For instance, after 20 years, you will have received an *extra $3,308* ($36,945 minus $33,637) in interest with daily versus annual compounding. The reason is that the *effective* interest rate is *10.52%* with daily compounding rather than 10.00%. Obviously, you should prefer the highest frequency of compounding possible. Most financial institutions now compound interest daily.

TIP: Be sure to ask what the effective, not stated or nominal interest rate is. Often times, one bank may offer what appears to be a higher

(but nominal) interest rate than the competition, but turns out to be a lower effective annual rate. It simply compounds interest less frequently.

SUGGESTION: If you're curious about how compound interest works, a pamphlet entitled "The Arithmetic of Interest Rates" is available at no charge from the Federal Reserve Bank of New York, Public Information Dept., 33 Liberty Street, New York, NY 10045. Write, or call (212) 791-6134.

WHICH SAVINGS ACCOUNT IS BEST FOR YOU?

Banks, S&Ls and credit unions offer many types of accounts. Despite promotional claims that each institution and each account is unique, they are actually quite similar. Most accounts are insured up to $100,000. You'll also find that yields on comparable accounts are quite competitive.

To be a wise saver, though, you need to shop around for the highest possible interest rate on the type of account that offers the features you want. Once you've done this, stay with it. Changing economic conditions may make another account appear more attractive later on. Yet the small fractional difference in yields will not affect your overall return much, and moving your funds from one institution to another is not worth the trouble. In addition, holding a number of different accounts spread over different institutions just creates a paperwork headache.

Types of Deposit Accounts

The more widely acceptable accounts are described below, although different institutions may have different names for them.

1. *Passbook Account.* About 13 percent of all bank deposits are traditional passbook accounts that pay a modest interest rate (5—5½%). The *effective* yield will differ, though, depending on the compound-

ing method and the date on which a deposit starts to earn and pays interest, e.g., interest paid from day of deposit to day of withdrawal. Only a small minimum balance is required, but no check-writing privileges available.

2. *NOW Checking Account.* Negotiable Orders of Withdrawal accounts have check-writing privileges and require a modest minimum balance ($250 to $1,500) and pay $5\frac{1}{4}\%$ interest. A monthly service fee may be charged as well as a fee when your balance falls below the minimum.

3. *SuperNow Checking Accounts.* The yield "floats" with short-term interest rates but requires a higher minimum balance of $2,500. Earns low passbook yield if balance falls below minimum. Various fees assessed for monthly services, each check written, deposits, automated teller, etc.

4. *Money Market Accounts.* The yield also floats with short-term market rates and usually requires at least a $1,000 minimum balance. Some allow a limited number of withdrawals per month (only three of which may be by check). These accounts are comparable to money market mutual funds (see below), but their yields are typically lower. However, they are federally insured, whereas money market funds are not.

These accounts will have varying maturities and yields. The more common ones are:

- 7-90 day account: interest rate based on the 13-week T-bill.
- 91-day CD: interest rate also based on the 13-week T-bill.
- 180-day CD: interest rate is usually $\frac{1}{4}\%$ higher than the average T-bill rate over the latest four-week period.

NOTE: These accounts offer no compounding, and there is a penalty for early withdrawal, e.g., three months' interest if held less than one year (penalty could be greater than the interest in some cases, so watch out!) or six months' interest if held for more than one year.

In addition, CDs of up to eight-year maturities can be found with different compounding methods. These should only be used to "lock in" a known interest rate and when your money is not needed until a certain future date.

5. *Real Estate Earnings-Based CDs.* A recent innovation offered by some financial institutions is CDs that provide a minimum, guaranteed rate of interest (usually 10%) plus the opportunity to receive additional interest from participation in real estate income and appreciation (up to a 17% total return). Minimum balance is higher ($5,000) and maturities are usually 9-10 years. While the principal and guaranteed return (paid quarterly) are federally insured, there's no assurance that you will receive more than the minimum interest rate. Moreover, you cannot withdraw your money until after five years—and then only at substantial penalty.

6. *Asset Management Accounts.* Most brokerage firms now offer accounts that allow you to combine investments and savings into a single account. The chief attraction is any income from your securities are automatically invested in a money market fund that earns interest. In addition, you can borrow money by using your securities and mutual fund as collateral.

Exhibit 6-1 is a quick reference chart for these accounts.

Things to Look for Before You Decide

1. *Interest Rate.* Usually the higher the quoted interest rate, the greater the interest received. To earn higher interest rates, you will have to deposit larger amounts of money for longer periods of time. S&Ls tend to pay a slightly higher interest rate than commercial banks for comparable accounts. Exhibit 6-2 gives representative interest rates for different accounts in late 1985 and 1986.

Exhibit 6-1
Types of Savings Accounts

Account	Interest Rate*	Minimum Balance	Maturity	Special Features
Regular Savings	Low	Very Minimal	None	No fees; no checkwriting
NOW Checking	Modest	Modest	None	No fees if minimum balance maintained
SuperNOW Checking	Varies with money-market rates	$2,500	None	Check-writing but extensive fees
Money Market or CD	Varies with money-market rates	$1,000	7 days to 8 years	Limited withdrawal rights (penalty assessed)
Real Estate Based	Minimum 9-10%	$5,000	8-10 yrs.	Additional interest possible from loan participation; minimum 5 years before withdrawal
Asset Management	Varies daily based on money-market rates	$1,000	None	Not government insured; extensive combination of financial accounts and services offered

*Refer to Exhibit 6-2 for recent representative interest rates on these accounts.

Exhibit 6-2
Recent Representative Interest Rates on Bank Savings Accounts

Type of Deposit and Maturity	December 31 1986	December 31 1985
SuperNOW Checking	5.16%	5.97%
Money Market Deposits	5.31	6.63
6-Month Account	5.81	7.39
1-Year Certificate	6.05	7.69
2-1/2 Year Certificate	6.45	8.22
5-Year Certificate	6.98	8.84

SOURCE: Rates offered by the 100 largest-asset banks and thrifts in the 10 largest metro areas, according to Bank Rate Monitor, North Palm Beach, FL, January 5, 1987.

2. *Compound Interval.* The more often interest is added to your account, the greater will be the amount upon which interest is computed. Different institutions will compound the interest on your account from once a year (certain money market accounts) to quarterly (credit unions) to daily. Generally, the more frequent the compounding, the more desirable it is. Again, just be sure to ask what the *effective* (rather than stated) interest rate is.

3. *Safety.* Most deposits are insured up to $100,000 by a federal government agency. Nevertheless, a few accounts are *not* insured or, if it's a state-chartered institution, there may be insurance provided by a private source. Just be sure to ask about insurance. Make certain you are protected—there's no cost to you.

   In addition, the law allows you to have separate insured accounts for each family member, joint-tenancy and trust accounts—each with $100,000 insurance coverage.

4. *Interest-Earning/Withdrawal Procedure.* Interest income can be affected by when interest begins to be earned and when it ends. Typical interest-earning periods are:
   - deposit by the tenth of the month, earn from the first
   - earn from the date of deposit
   - deposit after the first of the month, earn from the first of the *following* month

The first method is clearly preferred (if available) because you earn a full month's interest, even if you wait until the tenth day to make a deposit. Most institutions use the second method.

Perhaps more important but the least publicized (and most confusing) is the *withdrawal* procedure, i.e., what happens if you withdraw funds *before* a specified payment date? Which funds are assumed to be withdrawn? Newly deposited money or money on deposit since the last interest payment?

The *most* desirable withdrawal procedure is LIFO ("last-in, first-out) wherein it is assumed that any withdrawal is the money *most recently* deposited. This means interest is paid on the longer-term deposits, and hence more interest is earned. The *least desirable* method (and to be avoided!) is FIFO ("first-in, first-out) in which it is assumed that any withdrawal is money that has been on deposit the *longest*. Interest is then paid on the shorter-term deposits. *Be sure to inquire about which withdrawal procedure is used*—few people ever ask (or know)!

5. *Minimum Balance.* What happens if your account balance falls below the minimum? Normally, you'll earn a lower rate of interest (required by federal law). *How is the minimum calculated?* On any one day? On the average minimum balance? The average method is preferred and avoids extra costs if, for example there's just a one-day dip below the minimum.

6. *Check-Writing Privilege.* Money market accounts limit checkwriting to three monthly (that's federal law). Other accounts such as NOW accounts have no limits. Is there *a minimum amount per check?* There are no federal limitations here, but some institutions require a $100 or $250 minimum—some even a $500 minimum to discourage withdrawals.

7. *Service Charge.* This area has become a bit bewildering, making comparison shop-ping difficult. With deregulation, banks have "unbundled" their services and now require separate charges for each service. *Inquire about them:* Are there any costs for extra checks beyond three? for falling below minimum balance? for deposits? for automated teller? for credit cards? for over-drafts? for different average monthly balances? An example of the latter is the "tiered-fee" structure advertised by one bank:

"Earn an 8% annual yield with free banking for any balance over $10,000; only a $10 monthly charge plus $.25 per check when below $5,000."

To show you what can happen in this situation, assume your average balance is $4,000, and you write 12 checks per month. Your checks will cost $156 per year, and you'll earn $320 in interest, so your net yield is only 4.10%—or less than a passbook savings rate!

USING A MONEY MARKET FUND TO STORE YOUR CASH

A money market fund is a mutual fund that invests in an array of very short-term, relatively safe money-market instruments such as Treasury bills, commercial paper and bank CDs. It issues you shares against a portfolio of these securities that it buys in large denominations by pooling the funds of many investors.

Although they are not federally insured, only one money market fund has failed in their 12-year history, and those losses were very minimal. In return for a nominally higher risk, most money funds require an initial minimum deposit of only $500-$1,000, AND there is no minimum balance that has to be kept. The net return (after operating expenses and management fees of 0.25% to 1.00% of net asset value) is passed through to you. Wire transfers and checkwriting privileges (usually $500 minimum) allow you easy access to your funds.

Should You Use a Bank's Money Market Deposit Account or a Money Market Fund?

Bank money market accounts and money market funds are very similar. Nonetheless, while the interest rates on both float with short-term yields, the services each offers do differ.

1. You receive immediate credit for a new deposit with a bank. With a fund, it may take up to two weeks for your deposit to clear.
2. Bank accounts are government insured, whereas money market funds are not usually insured (some do have private insurance). The high-quality, short-term nature of its securities normally makes a money market fund relatively safe, however.
3. Money market funds are more impersonal than dealing with a bank. There is no local office for depositing/withdrawing funds. All business is done through the mail or a toll-free telephone call.
4. Money market funds generally require a smaller minimum balance, and there is no penalty for your balance falling below the minimum; i.e., you earn the same interest rate.
5. Some money market funds offer a "family of funds" that is a convenient way for you to move your savings into other types of mutual funds. These other funds have different objectives, including high growth (stock) and high income (bond) funds as well as taxable and tax-exempt securities.

Selecting a Money Market Fund

Once you decide to invest in a money market fund, which one of the nearly 200 money funds should you select? (Exhibit 6-3 contains a list of the money market funds available.)

Things to consider are:
1. *Safety*. Your principal is most secure in a money fund that invests only in government securities.
2. *Yield*. Higher yields (one percentage point

or more) can be earned in a fund that invests in non-government securities. Check out the fund's prospectus to find out what kind of issues it holds. If you're after yield, make sure only top-quality issues are held, e.g., General Electric or Chase Manhatten-type issues.
3. *Average Maturity*. Stay with funds whose securities have an average maturity of less than 40 days. This will keep your money earning current interest rates. For example, if a fund invests in longer-term issues and interest rates increase sharply, its yield will be lower relative to that of other funds with shorter maturities. WHY WORRY? Other investors could redeem their shares and could force the fund to sell some of its securities at a loss, jeopardizing your principal.

Financial newspapers and magazines carry advertisements for many money market funds. Your public library will also have the names, addresses and phone numbers of these funds. Simply telephone (most have a toll-free number) for a free copy of their current prospectus. Read it thoroughly to see if it fits your needs. Items to pay special attention to are the management fees, investment policies, performance, and services offered— especially check-writing and deposit/withdrawal procedures. Exhibit 6-4 describes how to invest in a money market fund.

Exhibit 6-4
How to Invest in a Money Market Fund

BY MAIL: Mail your check deposit with your application to the address given in the prospectus. Mail delay and check processing means it may take up to two weeks before your funds begin to earn interest. *(SUGGESTION:* Rather than use the fund's prepaid mail envelope, use your own stamped envelope. *WHY?* Prepaid mail permits require the postal service to count the envelopes before delivery—this could delay crediting of money to your account.)

BY WIRE TRANSFER: If your savings is *more than* $5,000, a wire transfer of funds may be better to ensure that your money is earning interest sooner.

Contact the money fund for instructions on how to wire money to the fund; obtain an account number; call you bank and have the money wired; and mail your application to the fund. Funds invested this way begin to earn interest the same day.

Exhibit 6-3
List of Money Market Funds

MONEY MARKET FUNDS

The following quotations, collected by the National Association of Securities Dealers Inc., represent the average of annualized yields and dollar-weighted portfolio maturities ending Friday, March 15, 1985. Yields are based on actual dividends to shareholders.

Fund	Avg. Mat.	7Day YLD.	30Day YLD.	NAV
AARP US Gvt f	44	7.99	8.05	3046.1
ActvAsst GovSc	57	8.05	8.06	161.2
AlexBCash Gvt	31	7.98	7.86	151.7
AlexBCash Prm	31	7.97	7.86	647.3
Alliance Capital	47	7.95	7.87	916.9
AllianceGvt Res	39	7.86	7.65	191.1
Alliance TaxEx	67	5.10	5.15	284.2
AmCap Resrv a	42	7.92	7.67	317.5
Am Genl MM a	45	8.11	8.11	40.6
Amer Natl MM	19	8.05	7.95	13.4
AutomCash Mgt	27	8.15	8.07	852.7
AutomGvt MTr	50	8.28	8.24	1154.4
Babson Prime	36	7.93	7.82	61.0
BenhamCal TF	39	4.35	4.42	76.4
BenhamNatl TF	24	4.93	5.09	15.6
BirrWilson MFd	27	7.25	7.23	56.9
BLC Cash Mgt	19	7.68	7.47	25.7
Boston Co Cash	45	8.00	7.95	234.9
Bull&Bear DRs	27	7.69	7.52	84.7
CalvrtSocInv af	22	7.96	7.87	41.1
Calvrt TF MM	113	5.52	5.61	273.7
CAM Fund	23	7.69	7.51	31.6
CapCash MgtTr	17	8.15	7.75	121.0
Cap Preservtn	44	7.50	7.46	1832.6
Cap Preservtn 2	2	7.85	7.79	558.6
CardGovt SecTr	28	8.25	8.23	410.3
CarngieGov Sec	18	8.10	7.98	162.3
CarnegieTax Fr	25	4.46	4.52	137.8
Cash Equiv MM	28	7.89	7.83	4743.7
CashEq GovSec	26	7.67	7.68	462.5
CshMgt TrAm a	18	8.24	8.19	630.0
Cash Rsv Mgt a	57	8.83	8.80	5.1
CentennlMM Tr	31	7.63	7.40	156.9
CignaMM Fd b	(z)	(z)	8.18	242.9
CimcoMM Trst	42	8.41	8.30	14.2
CMA GovtSec a	47	8.26	8.78	1732.1
CMA MnyFd a	58	8.05	9.28	15885.1
CMA Tax Ex	57	4.75	5.63	3349.2
Col Daily Inc af	27	7.57	7.51	487.7
Colonial MnyM	26	7.71	7.62	12.8
CommMnyF a	30	8.05	7.93	1106.0
Comp Cash M a	27	7.65	7.51	160.0
Current Interest	49	8.03	7.79	863.0
CurrentInt USG	52	7.95	7.90	92.1
Daily cash Fdl	31	7.80	7.63	1835.4
DailyCash Govt	7	7.71	7.67	56.1
DlyCashTxEx c	28	4.54	4.52	130.6
DailyDollar Rs	54	7.97	7.78	177.2
Daily Incm Fd	47	8.10	7.97	500.7
DailyTaxFree c	41	5.19	5.28	834.4
DBL GvtSc Prtf	54	8.32	8.29	190.5
DBL MM Portf	58	8.58	8.54	1348.6
DBL Tax Free	55	4.82	4.86	290.6
DWS Liqd Asset	59	8.22	8.26	6784.6
DWS USGvtMM	58	7.98	7.99	426.1
DelaCashRsrv f	49	8.15	7.99	1500.1
DelaTaxFr MF	76	4.63	4.69	50.0
DelaTreas Rsrv	46	7.78	7.69	54.4
DrevfsInst Govt	87	8.73	8.66	992.0
DrevfsInst MM	88	8.28	8.37	815.0
DrevfsLiq Asst	67	8.42	8.35	8.5
DrvfusGvt Sers	96	8.78	8.74	964.5
DrvfMnyMk Ser	72	8.29	8.23	818.5
DryTaxEx MM	85	5.10	5.12	2187.1
EatonVan Cash	26	7.93	7.79	210.9
EGT MMTrust f	37	7.59	7.50	77.2
Equit MMkt Ac	46	7.89	7.92	264.6
Fahnestock Dly	42	7.89	7.80	149.5
FBL MnMkFd b	25	7.10	7.05	31.9
FedMaster Trst	28	8.08	8.03	2704.4
FedrlTaxFree c	46	4.92	5.01	3604.6
FidelCash Resv	37	8.01	7.94	4243.1
FidelDlyIncm b	36	8.23	8.18	2673.1
FidUS Govt Res	32	7.97	7.92	365.8
FidMM USTrea	1	8.29	8.16	237.1
FidMM Domstc	34	8.38	8.26	1466.7
FidMM Govmnt	36	8.42	8.36	777.3
FidMass TaxFr	47	4.49	4.55	223.1
FidTaxExmpt c	68	5.16	5.27	2347.5
FnclDlyInc Shr	19	8.13	7.98	229.3
FnclPlanFed Sc	57	5.76	5.77	5.2
FirstInstTax Ex	40	4.52	4.63	33.6
FstInvCshMgt f	26	7.94	7.65	380.6
FstTrMM GenP	48	7.90	7.75	34.9
FstTrMMFd Gv	58	7.63	7.77	18.1
FstTrust TaxFr	66	4.59	4.81	15.0
First Variable	29	7.93	7.80	643.7
FlaMutlGvt Sec	(z)	(z)	6.36	3.4
Founders MMk	20	7.90	7.74	25.4
Franklin FedM	2	7.59	7.51	150.2
FrnklnMnyFd a	33	7.66	7.58	1032.9
Frnkln TaxEx c	15	4.32	4.53	76.1
FundGov Invst	47	7.88	8.08	1037.8
GenlGovt Secur	100	8.21	8.22	96.5
GenlMoney Mkt	83	8.24	8.22	403.0
GIT Cash Trust	10	7.42	7.36	5.0
GovtInvstTrst a	21	7.61	7.49	310.3
GovtSecur Cash	30	8.08	7.98	78.6
Gradison Cash	45	8.13	8.01	481.3
GradisonUS Gv	38	7.75	7.82	23.0
Guardian Cash	22	7.78	7.67	17.9
Hilliard Gov't	20	7.56	7.58	123.9
Hutton AMA Fd	55	8.68	8.62	1877.0
Hutton Govt Fd	39	8.24	8.20	1071.5
IDS Cash Mngt	34	8.08	7.99	983.3
IDS Stratgy Fd	35	6.34	6.17	10.5
IDS TxFrMny c	72	4.88	4.88	69.7
IntegrlMM Sec	36	7.72	7.65	50.5
JohnHanc Cash	35	7.84	7.76	401.5
JonesDly Pssp f	38	7.71	7.59	656.8
Kemper Gvt MM	27	7.63	7.52	90.3
Kemper MnyM	29	8.09	8.05	4934.3
Keystone LiqTr	33	7.59	7.48	275.0
KidderP GovtM	36	7.81	7.74	145.7
KidderP PrmAc	39	7.96	7.91	479.5
KidderP TaxEx	73	4.95	4.97	421.7
Lndmrk Cash	(z)	(z)	7.86	157.3
Lndmrk TxFr	(z)	(z)	5.07	83.4
LeggMasn Csh f	41	7.74	7.65	232.1
Lehman CashM	27	8.17	8.03	892.5
Lehman GvtFd	10	8.27	8.22	414.9
Lehman TxFree	60	5.04	5.09	331.4
LexGvtScMM a	78	7.41	7.41	17.9
LexMoneyMkt a	82	8.10	7.96	224.2
LexTaxFrDly c	48	5.15	5.40	71.0
LFRoth EarnLq	37	8.09	8.20	364.5
LF Roth Exmpt	22	4.39	4.57	92.0
LibrtyCash Mgt	27	7.29	7.20	31.5
LiquidCapitl Tr	29	8.15	7.98	1274.5
LiquidCAshTR f	2	8.64	8.68	1001.2
LiquidGrn TxFr	88	4.87	4.96	16.1
LiquidGreen Tr	39	7.76	7.72	202.3
LordAbbet Cash	30	7.75	7.59	201.2
LuthBrMon Mkt	35	7.77	7.70	507.7
ManCshActTr a	25	7.70	7.56	43.4
MAP GovtFund	50	7.43	7.69	12.9
MassCashMgt a	28	7.80	7.80	719.6
McDonald MM	45	7.63	7.54	170.0
MerrLGovtFd a	48	8.07	7.91	1484.1
MerrLInstFd af	41	8.16	8.10	1095.1
MerrLRdyAst a	50	8.01	9.27	12468.6
MerrLRetRsv a	48	7.62	8.68	1553.9
Midwst Incm Tr	39	7.63	7.57	153.3
Midwst IT Cash	37	7.61	7.50	58.5
MnyMgtP Govt	30	7.54	7.18	6.1
MnyMgtP Pr	23	7.91	7.75	28.6
MoneyMkt Instr	30	7.51	7.44	99.1
MoneyMktMgt f	35	7.73	7.66	273.9
Money Mkt Trst	32	8.13	8.04	2040.9
MoneyMart Ast	32	8.17	8.13	3432.1
MorganKeegn f	37	7.64	7.52	77.3
MuniCashRsv c	72	5.38	5.37	1.5
MuniFundInv c	36	4.88	4.97	1572.7
MtlOmCash Res	51	7.72	7.73	56.0
MtlOmMny Mkt	44	7.99	8.04	287.8
Natl Cash Resv	39	7.42	7.32	38.2
NEL Cash Mngt	38	8.12	8.03	821.0
NEL US Govt	46	8.01	8.27	42.0
NatlGovt Fund	38	7.39	7.47	43.4
NatlMMkt Fund	27	8.07	7.94	1687.2
NatlTax Exmpt	72	4.65	4.69	121.4
Nationwide MM	42	8.18	8.03	461.2
Newton Money	36	7.62	7.54	15.1
NLR Cash Port	37	7.92	7.82	1461.8
NLR Govt Prt	30	8.06	7.94	60.0
NuveenTaxEx c	53	5.01	5.06	1943.9
Nuveen TaxFr	44	4.84	4.93	120.1
Oppn Mny Mrkt	26	7.95	7.85	1294.6
Oxford CshMgt	181	8.06	7.99	201.0
PacHrzGov MM	93	8.13	7.99	459.0
PacHrzMM Prt	25	8.21	8.12	304.7
PaineWb Cash f	40	8.25	8.17	4284.3
Parkway Cash	37	8.05	7.94	418.5
Phoenix MMkt	(z)	(z)	8.12	49.7
Plimoney Fund	42	7.59	7.47	41.2
PrimeCash Fd	16	8.13	8.02	94.5
PrudB GvtSec	29	7.82	7.69	261.1
PrudB TaxFr c	(z)	(z)	5.07	311.6
PutnmDlyDiv a	44	7.99	7.88	295.7
Renaisnc GvFd	1	8.52	8.50	44.1
Renaissnc MM	21	8.35	8.27	125.8
Reserv CPA GV	6	7.81	7.71	18.8
Reserv GOV'T	2	7.91	7.92	260.7
Reserv PRIMR	35	8.09	8.12	1638.9
Reserv INTRST	64	5.16	5.38	186.0
Reserv NY	60	4.69	4.88	63.0
RMA MonyMkt	40	8.14	8.01	1161.0
RMA Tax-Free	62	4.52	4.66	468.3
RMA USGov	44	7.85	7.77	179.8
RowePrPrRes f	41	8.05	8.10	3100.0
RowePTxEx cf	65	5.09	5.16	951.0
RowePUSTrea f	38	8.04	7.99	158.0
Safeco MnyMk f	26	7.94	7.85	39.7
St Paul Money	20	8.00	7.79	90.6
ScuddCashInv f	37	8.06	7.95	1063.1
ScuddrGvt Mny	44	7.50	7.44	142.6
ScuddrTaxFr cf	34	4.52	4.53	285.5
Secur Cash Fd	15	7.94	7.77	54.9
Select Mny Mkt	32	7.39	7.32	23.2
SelgmnCM Prm	27	7.61	7.54	418.0
Sentinel Cash b	35	7.67	7.59	38.8
SentryCash Mgt	27	7.85	7.65	29.5
ShrsnDailyDiv f	45	8.05	8.02	3750.3
ShrsnDaily TxF	58	4.69	4.77	439.9
ShrsnFMA Cash	44	8.10	8.08	1137.0
ShrsnFMA Govt	47	8.10	8.16	272.0
ShrsnFMA Mun	51	4.78	4.83	446.2
ShrsnGovt Agen	43	8.33	8.40	1379.4
ShrtTmIncm Fd	42	7.86	7.79	152.5
ShortTerm Govt	46	7.83	7.77	296.7
ShortTermYld a	18	7.52	7.43	16.3
Sigma MnyMkt	10	7.58	7.52	7.6
SthFrmBur Csh	19	7.45	7.36	27.5
Standby Reserv	38	8.05	7.99	262.2
SteinRoeCsh Rs	39	7.92	7.84	909.1
SteinRoe Govt	26	7.31	7.20	27.9
SteinRoe Tax	55	4.66	4.75	156.9
Summit Cash	46	7.98	8.81	497.4
Sutro MM Fd f	37	7.59	7.46	111.4
TaxExmpMM c	48	4.71	4.72	569.6
TaxFrInst Tr	66	4.92	5.02	1052.8
TaxFree Mny c	35	4.64	3.48	469.2
TempInvest Fd	41	8.51	8.47	5493.8
Trnsam CashRs	32	8.48	8.38	297.5
Trinity LiqdAst	20	8.31	8.13	235.0
Trust CashRes f	34	7.60	7.52	149.1
TrFdTreas Prtf	50	8.20	8.21	1661.2
TrFdUS Agency	36	8.45	8.41	377.6
TrFd Commercl	37	8.14	8.17	109.1
TrFd Obligation	37	8.17	8.11	1538.4
TrShtTr FedFd	39	8.34	8.39	1698.6
TrShtTFed TFd	40	8.32	8.35	1323.4
TrShTer US Gvt	46	8.43	8.46	6751.5
TrstUSTrea Obl	47	8.37	8.33	3163.5
TuckerA CashM	45	7.82	7.70	423.5
TuckerA GvtSc	33	8.00	7.94	105.4
TuckerA TxEx	78	4.86	4.94	80.1
UMB Federal	31	8.26	8.19	110.0
UMB Prime	36	8.24	8.18	67.0
UnitedCshMgt a	49	7.99	7.85	343.6
USAA FedSMM	77	7.64	7.58	32.3
USAA MutlMM	27	8.30	8.09	296.9
US Treas SecFd	58	7.89	7.93	106.8
ValueLineCsh a	43	8.06	8.00	483.6
ValLineMM Prt	22	4.80	4.81	21.7
VangdMMFed f	42	8.17	8.12	495.2
VangrdMM Pr f	41	8.39	8.24	1703.1
Vangrd Insure f	24	7.75	7.58	50.2
VangMunMM cf	75	5.12	5.18	577.3
VantageCsh Prt	39	7.93	7.81	283.9
VantageGvt Prt	34	8.01	7.90	52.6
WayneHum MM	23	7.64	7.48	68.5
WebstrCash Rs	38	7.96	7.91	1374.1
Working Assets	42	7.76	7.68	51.5

Footnotes: (Eligible funds not included declined to provide information.)

a-Yield may include capital gains and losses. b-Account size varies yield due to fixed charges. c-Primarily federally tax exempt securities. f-As of previous day. z-Unavailable.

SOURCE: The Wall Street Journal, March 18, 1985.

A monthly publication, Donoghue's Moneyletter, P.O Box 401, Holliston, MA 01746, is an excellent advisory service on money funds. The Donoghue Money Fund Directory, Wiesenberger's Investment Companies and Forbes' Annual Survey of Mutual Funds (August or September issue) provide complete listings of money funds—check with your local library for these services.

NOTE: If you are in a high tax bracket, one of the tax-free money funds may provide a higher after-tax yield. They are similar to other money funds except they invest in short-term tax-exempt securities of state and municipal governments.

SERIES EE BONDS*

U.S. savings bonds are no longer the poor savings vehicle once thought. In 1982, this bond's maximum fixed interest rate of 8.5% could not compete with the 15% rate on bank deposits. People avoided them like the plague. To rekindle sales, significant changes were made. The Series EE bond now pays a *variable* interest rate—adjusted semiannually—equal to 85% of the average yield on five-year Treasury securities.

In early 1985, the Series EE bond rate was 10.94%--a yield considerably higher than those on banks' CDs and money market funds. By November 1986, this rate has fallen to its minimum, *guaranteed* rate of 7.5%--still much higher than other savings rates. As a result (because of "the decline in market interest rates during the past year"), the Treasury changed the rules by slashing the 7.5% guaranteed rate to 6%, beginning November 1, 1986. (NOTE: Savings bonds issued previously weren't affected in any way.) In effect, this ruined one of the best bargains around. Nevertheless, Series EE bonds are still competitive at today's rates. But remember, the adjustment in future savings bond rates will *lag* behind if interest rates begin to rise once again.

Attractive Savings Features

Besides offering the highest safety available anywhere, the EE bond has other attractive features:

1. *No Principal Loss.* EE bonds are purchased for one-half their face value (at a discount) in amounts as little as $25. The difference between the face value and purchase price reflects the interest you will receive as a lump sum at maturity. Therefore, the savings bond's value can never be less than your original investment. *NOTE:* You may receive more or less than the face amount, depending on prevailing interest rates and how long you hold the bond.

2. *Variable Interest Rate.* A new savings bond rate is calculated each May and November. It is based on the average Treasury yields for the preceding six months. For example, say you bought a Series EE bond in November 1986 and

*K. Slater. "Once Lowly Regarded U.S. Savings Bonds Now Offer Improved Investment Features." The Wall Street Journal, November 12, 1984, p. 39.

sell it in November 1998. When you sell it, the Treasury yields for the 24 six-month periods for 1986-98 period would be averaged, then 85% of this average rate would be applied to your initial sum, compounded semiannually. You're guaranteed *at least* 6% even if Treasury yields were below that, and there's no limit on how high the rate can go. *A WORD OF CAUTION:* This is true only if you hold your bond for at least five years. If sold earlier, the bond's yield reverts to a fixed rate that ranges from about 4% after one year to less than 6% after 4½ years. You should view this as a "penalty for early withdrawal."

3. *Tax Advantages.* Two tax advantages can increase your after-tax return. First, like other U.S. government securities, interest income from savings bonds is exempt from state and local tax. Second, the federal tax on this income can be *deferred until the bond is redeemed,* rather than paying tax as the interest accrues annually.

If you are nearing retirement, this deferral feature can make savings bonds especially attractive. Here's how it works: Invest now, when you're in a high tax bracket, and defer paying taxes on the interest until after retirement, when your tax bracket may be lower. *SPECIAL NOTE:* If you are a civil service employee, savings bonds are even more attractive. The reason is that you will be in a very low bracket the first few years after retirement because you don't pay any taxes on your government pension until your contributions have been recovered. Carefully selecting your bonds' maturities to fall in the first few retirement years can be smart investing.

Finally, another tax option for retirees is to *exchange* EE bonds for HH bonds. By making this exchange, you postpone *again* paying federal income tax on the interest built up on the EE bonds. You'll pay that tax when you redeem your HHs or the HHs reach maturity after 10 years. Meanwhile, you get a semiannual check for interest on the HH bonds. However, the rate is fixed at only 7.5% and is taxable.

Exhibit 6-5 contains a summary of the Series EE bond's general characteristics.

TERMS TO KNOW

Asset management account
Check-writing privilege
Compound interest
Effective interest rate
Family of funds
Interest-earning procedure
Interest-Withdrawal procedure
Minimum balance
Money market deposit account
Money market fund
NOW account
Passbook account
Real estate earnings-based account
Simple interest
Stated (or nominal) interest rate
SuperNOW account

Exhibit 6-5
Characteristics of Series EE Savings Bond

1. *Interest Rate:* Minimum rate is 6%. Rate is adjusted periodically (every May and November) to keep it equal to 85% of the preceding six months' average yield on the five-year Treasury notes.
2. *Purchase Price:* $25 to $5,000. Each bond purchased at deep discount to its maturity (face) value. Purchase price is one-half of face value.
3. *Maturity:* 12 years.
4. *How to Buy Bonds:* Easiest way is through a payroll deduction plan (60% of the $ billion purchased in 1984 were acquired this way). Banks and other financial institutions sell them, or by mail from the Bureau of the Public Debt, Washington, D.C. 20226.
5. *Fees or Commissions:* None.
6. *Maximum Annual Purchase:* Each individual is allowed $30,000 for himself/herself and $30,000 owned jointly with a spouse or child.
7. *Redemption:* Cannot be redeemed in the first six months after purchase (unless there's an emergency). After that, any bank can redeem it for you. (*NOTE:* Interest is paid only twice a year so the best time to redeem is right after a six-month anniversary. Otherwise, redeeming even a few days before can cost you *several months'* interest.)

7
REDUCING RISK WITH LIFE INSURANCE

Chapter Objectives
1. Who Needs Life Insurance?
2. Deciding How Much Insurance You Need
3. Choosing the Best Policy for You
4. The Difference Between Nonparticipating and Participating Insurance
5. Tips on Buying Life Insurance
6. Selecting the Right Insurance Agent

Life insurance is not the solid investment it is often represented as being. However, for some individuals, this may be their best (only) investment alternative.

Despite this, adequate life insurance at minimum cost can contribute to long-term financial security. Just remember, though, to keep two things separate:

- Insurance for *pure risk protection* against loss of income
- Insurance as an *investment*

In this chapter, those points you'll want to consider before deciding on a life insurance program are presented.

WHO NEEDS LIFE INSURANCE?

If you have a family or other dependents you'll probably want to protect them from the financial hardship of losing your income due to untimely death.

Life insurance provides a lump sum of money (usually tax-free) that your dependents can use immediately and/or invest to replace income loss.

If you have (1) no family or dependents or (2) a sufficiently large estate, you probably don't need insurance. In the first case, no protection is needed. In the second, protection is already provided.

Since you may not fall into either category, you'll need an understanding of the essentials of life insurance. Only then can you make the best decision on your life insurance program-- especially when you consider the vast array of insurance policies.

HOW MUCH INSURANCE DO YOU NEED?

The basic considerations in deciding how much life insurance is needed revolve around the money or personal assets that will be required to provide the following:

- *An executor or "last expense" fund*--to administer your estate, to pay expenses such as funeral, medical costs and outstanding debts. These expenses obviously can vary greatly, depending on individual family circumstances, so this need should be reviewed periodically as those circumstances change.
- *A family income*--to cover the time period from death until the youngest child/dependent reaches the age of 18 (or finishes college).
- *A lifetime income for the surviving spouse*-- to ensure a living income for the spouse after the family income period.

Regarding the last consideration, if the spouse has a profession or career, he/she might be able to provide self-sufficiency. If so, this aspect of life insurance may be downplayed.

It should be clear that estimating the need for life insurance translates into determining the desired family income at different stages in life.

The most common approach is the "six-times-salary" formula (see Exhibit 7-1). Experience indicates that life insurance (and other death benefits) should equal at least 6 times your annual salary.

Interest income on such an amount (plus Social Security) should allow the surviving family to maintain its current standard of living without tapping the principal. The principal could then be used for emergencies, education and long-term needs.

One drawback. This simplistic method has a serious drawback--it's a general formula that ignores what phase of your life cycle you are in.

As we learned in Chapter 1, planning for financial security depends on your age, family status, financial condition, etc. For example, a 39-year-old man with a family of non-employed wife and two young children has entirely different insurance needs from one who has an employed wife and one college-aged child.

Typically, your insurance requirements will decline as your assets increase and life expectancy decreases. To account for life-cycle considerations, Worksheet No. 6 provides a more detailed formula to follow. Included is a discussion of each step and an example of how to apply it.

We suggest that you work through both formulas in order to get a range of what your insurance needs might be.

WHICH POLICY IS BEST FOR YOU?

The life insurance industry has become very imaginative in packaging its products in a great variety of ways.

The result is that it's difficult to compare different policies and rates (cost per $ 1,000 of insurance)--even for sophisticated buyers. Moreover, it is difficult to make generalizations about the "best" policy for you.

The best policy is the one that you decide fits your needs. And this will depend upon your current (and anticipated) estate, income tax bracket, ability to pay and family situation.

Understanding a particular policy requires a basic knowledge of the two traditional forms of insurance:

- Term life insurance
- Whole or ordinary life insurance

All other policies, such as the newer variable life and universal life, are just variations of these two policies.

Term Life Insurance

Term insurance provides low-cost, "pure death" protection only. No other provision for further benefits are included. (Group plans are usually term insurance.)

Annual premiums are the lowest when you're young and increase as you become older, i.e., as you become more of a risk to the insurer--see Exhibit 7-2.

There are three basic types of term life insurance:
- Straight term
- Renewable and convertible term
- Decreasing term

Let's look at each of the three.

1. *Straight term* provides the *least expensive* protection for a specified time (most often 1 year). *Disadvantage:* Its main limitation is its temporary nature. For example, suppose you survive the policy period but a need still exists. If you lose insurability because of poor health, changes in financial condition or occupation, you may not be able to purchase insurance.

2. *Renewable and convertible term* is purchased with yearly, 5-year or 10-year *(guaranteed) renewable provisions.* The premium is constant *(or level)* over each policy period but increases every time you renew--see Exhibit 7-3.

Exhibit 7-3

Illustration of Annual Premiums for a 5-Year Renewable, $100,000 Policy:

At Age	Premium
20	$ 111
30	$ 116
40	$ 194
50	$ 501
60	$1,153

The convertible provision permits you to convert to a whole (ordinary) life policy at any time while the policy is in force. No evidence of insurability (no medical reexamination) is required at conversion.

Advantage: This term insurance eliminates straight term's disadvantage of being temporary. For instance, your insurance needs may change or you may become uninsurable (a remote possibility). Convertible term lets you switch to whole life with no question asked--term insurance does not.

3. *Decreasing term* insurance also offers a level premium but has two distinguishing

features:
- It covers a 20- or 30-year period.
- The amount of coverage declines slowly year by year.

Advantages: This plan is ideal for those situations where you need the highest protection during the early years but your need declines over time.

Examples would be to provide protection for the repayment of a home mortgage or for your dependents when they are most vulnerable. Then, as your retirement funds, savings, investments, etc. grow, your insurance needs are reduced.

Exhibit 7-4 illustrates that, with a level premium, you underpay for coverage in the early years and overpay in the latter years. (This is the reverse of how whole life works.)

Exhibit 7-4

Illustration of a 20-Year, Decreasing Term's Cost and Coverage (Age 40)

Year	Annual Premium	Amount of Coverage
1	$320	$100,000
5	$320	$ 91,000
10	$320	$ 74,500
15	$320	$ 35,500

Whole (Ordinary or Permanent) Life Insurance

Whole life insurance also has *level* premiums but, as the name implies, provides coverage over your entire life.

It combines term insurance with a tax-deferred saving feature. The difference between the total premium you pay and the amount that covers mortality and administrative costs goes toward the *cash value* of the policy. This cash value then earns a *predetermined, guaranteed interest rate* (albeit a very low 3-4% rate).

Advantages. Whole life offers two advantages:
- Cash values (savings) build up which can be borrowed for emergency needs. The borrowing rate is usually 6-8%.
- At retirement, the premiums remain the

same rather than increasing sharply because of advancing age. (*NOTE:* If coverage is *not* desired, the cash value can be taken out under different annuity options that can be easily blended into your overall retirement program.)

Disadvantages. This is the most expensive form of insurance. More death protection per dollar spent can be obtained with term insurance. Moreover, in the earlier years, very little cash value accumulates because your premium goes mostly toward paying agents' sales commissions and mortality and administrative costs. Finally, your savings usually earn less than the market rate of interest.

Despite these drawbacks, whole life is the only way to get guaranteed protection at a fixed premium for life.

Recent Improvements in the Traditional Whole Life Policy

Record high interest rates and inflation during the late 1970s and early 1980s forced insurance companies to design new products and to give you an opportunity to earn more on policy cash values.

Two major products have emerged: *variable life* and *universal life* policies.

1. *Variable life insurance*, while very similar to whole life, has one major difference--your *cash value is not guaranteed*. Rather it changes, depending on the return your funds earn. So your cash values don't increase at a fixed rate but fluctuate daily with the value of your account's securities. This can, of course, shrink as well as grow.

   Some variable life insurers offer more investments choices than others. For example, you can choose between different portfolios (mutual funds) for your cash value, e.g., a stock fund, bond fund or money market fund. In effect, you become your own portfolio manager, switching between funds when you like. Several companies, on the other hand, give you the option of letting their strategists do the switching.

Note: Managing your own portfolio means that the risk of failure or success is solely yours, not the insurer's as in years past. If the market or your own investment decisions go against you, variable life will prove to be a *very expensive* way to buy insurance. On the other hand, if you think stocks, bonds or money funds will keep pace with or exceed inflation, variable life overcomes a major criticism of whole life-- the loss of purchasing power on a fixed cash value and death benefit.

2. *Universal life insurance* also emphasizes investment performance but allows you to vary both the amount of premium and the level of death protection (within certain limits).

   When your finances are tight, you can cut back on the premiums. When you have extra cash, you can beef up your policy's cash value by increasing your contributions. The insurer lets you do this by simply adjusting your death benefits and cash values to be consistent with your actual payment.

   Your cash value grows at a rate of interest guaranteed for *that* year *but* the insurer can *raise* or *lower the rate each year.*

The "Latest Twists" in Variable Life Policies

"Universal variable" policies, sometimes called "Universal II", are now available. These policies combine the flexible premiums and death benefits of universal life with the investment choices of variable life. That is, you can shift your cash values from fund to fund.

In short, the cash value can grow faster than in universal policies but you must act as your own portfolio manager--deciding when to move out of stock, for instance, and into bonds or money market instruments.

"Flexible premium variable life" policies also are emerging. This new policy builds cash value in a manner identical to variable and universal life. The twist is that you can choose to have the insurance premiums paid directly from the accrued cash value.

Single-Premium Whole Life Policies: An Old Idea That's New

With tax-oriented investments leveled by the Tax Reform Act of 1986, the life insurance industry is giving new life to an old idea--*single premium whole life insurance* (SPWL). This "new" type of policy is actually 200 years old; it's just that tax reform has stimulated the creative juices of life insurers to update it and redesign it to fit today's tax laws.

As with conventional life insurance, SPWLs pay a death benefit to the survivors. But it's not just life insurance--it's being marketed as a tax-favored savings and investment vehicle, with death coverage as an extra kicker.

As the name implies, you buy an SPWL policy with a single, up-front premium of $5,000 or more. So, in contrast to policies with annual, level premiums, this plan accumulates immediate, substantial cash value because virtually all of that premium is invested to earn interest on a tax-deferred basis. But, obviously, you need much more money initially to take advantage of it. The death benefit is paid from the earnings on the cash value.

Typically, you are guaranteed a fixed interest rate on the cash value for the first year, or first few years. After that, the rate can fluctuate, either according to a specified formula or at the insurance company's discretion. SPWLs are currently yielding about 6%-8% a year (that's the net yield, after the cost of insurance and other expenses have been deducted). Because of its tax-deferred feature, this implies a doubling of cash value in about 10 years. There are also SPWLs that offer a variable return through a variety of investment alternatives such as investing in a stock, bond or money market fund. But, these are subject to market risk.

Another very appealing insurance feature is that you can turn the earnings into cash by borrowing them (and no one will make you pay it back). Because this money can be borrowed at no out-of-pocket cost (or at a 1%-2% interest rate at most) and because it doesn't count as income, you get it *tax-free*. This is an important advantage over competing investments such as

IRAs or annuities (see below)--such investments face a 10% penalty for early withdrawal (before age 59½).

Thus, SPWLs give you easy access to cash values through tax-free policy loans at little or no cost, provide a competitive return on the "inside buildup" of earnings without any tax consequences, provide financial security through guaranteed life insurance benefits, and pass proceeds to beneficiaries free of income tax.

Deferred Annuities: A Tax-Favored Investment with No Death Benefits

Another "hot" insurance product that escaped the hand of tax reform and is expected to receive greater attention is the deferred annuity. ("Annuity" means payment of a *level* stream of cash.) Basically, a *deferred annuity* is just a single-premium whole life policy stripped of its death coverage. Or, as others would have it, an SPWL is a more complex form of an annuity--one with more bells and whistles.

With an annuity, you make either a single lump-sum or several investments in a contract. The earnings then accumulate on a *tax-deferred* basis. At a future date you select, periodic payments begin to be made. This makes them a useful financial planning tool for meeting a child's college expenses or adding to your retirement income. While there are no death benefits, an annuity does guarantee the beneficiary at least the amount invested if the annuity holder should die during the accumulation period. And, as with an IRA, money withdrawn in a lump sum or in annuity payments after retirement age is subject to ordinary income tax on the amount attributable to earnings. However, withdrawals before age 59½ are generally subject to both ordinary income tax plus a 10% penalty. That is, there are no borrowing privileges as with whole life policies.

There are two types of deferred annuities--fixed and variable. *Fixed annuities* allow you to lock in a guaranteed rate of return for up to 5 years and insure the return of your principal at any time. But, unlike federally-insured savings accounts, this safety feature is only as good as the reputation and financial strength of the insurance company backing it. As with any life insurance policy, it's a good idea to buy only from a company that earns a top rating (A+) from the industry watchdog, A. M. Best Co. Your insurance agent can tell you what the Best rating is before you buy.

Variable annuities, as the name implies, offer a "variable" rate of return because the buyer can select and periodically change how the money is allocated among a family of stock, bond and money market funds. So, you receive the tax benefits of an annuity *and* flexibility in your investment choices. Just remember, your tax-deferred return will vary with the market performance of the annuity investments you choose.

When you do begin receiving income from your annuity, a portion of each payment is treated as a "return of principal" and, therefore, is not subject to taxes (an annuity, just like insurance, is purchased with after-tax dollars). Finally, many people no longer qualify for a tax-deductible IRA. This leaves them with only the choice of a *non-deductible IRA,* but this has a $2,000 a year limitation. (See Chapter 18 for more details.) Not so with annuities, there are no restrictions on the maximum annual contribution.

A Summary of Whole Life's Tax Advantages

All versions of whole life have two important tax advantages:

- Earnings on cash values are tax-exempt while the policy is in force.
- If you surrender your policy and withdraw the money, you are taxed only on the amount that exceeds what you paid in (this includes the part of the premium that didn't go into the cash value).

NOTE: All insurance shares a common tax feature--the death benefit is added to the insured's taxable estate. That is, it's not taxed as ordinary income or as capital gains. This means if you die in 1987 and your estate is less than $600,000, there will be no federal estate taxes.

A Few Words of Caution on Whole Life Policies

Whole life policies and its many "hybrids" involve enormous fees that lower investment returns. There are *sales commissions*—either at the "front-end" or, more subtly, in the form of higher annual fees. In fact, first-year charges alone are so large that if you bought a policy and dropped it in the first 5 years, you would have little to show, even with strong investment performance. In addition, you can expect the higher fees to cut into your overall return by 2 to 3 percentage points, even over a longer time period.

Finally, there are *surrender charges* of as much as 8%-10% at the outset, declining by stages to zero after 7-10 years. But this may not pose a real problem since you can get the money out of the account by borrowing.

Also, don't become too enamored by the advertising claims about whole life policies' investment features. First, they do reduce your investment flexibility. Even with variable policies, you're offered only a handful of "mutual fund" choices, and their returns are tied to the particular investments made by the company--for better or for worse. Moreover, the performance figures on these funds aren't readily available. And, if the policy has "switching privileges," you may be limited to the number of switches among funds you can make per annum, e.g., four per year.

Again, watch out for the word *guaranteed.* "Guaranteed return" means only for a short period of time. After that, your return is uncertain. "Guaranteed safety of principal" doesn't mean federally-guaranteed as with a bank CD. It means guaranteed by the issuing company, so make sure it's financially sound.

NONPARTICIPATING VS. PARTICIPATING INSURANCE

Both term and whole life insurance are sold on a *nonparticipating* and *participating* basis. You need to consider carefully the distinction between the two.

Nonparticipating insurance presets the premium you actually pay. The *stockholders* of a nonparticipating company receive the policies' profits.

Participating insurance (offered by mutual life insurance companies) is, in contrast, owned by the policyholders. This means they share in the company's income.

This "sharing" occurs as follows. Participating premiums are set at a rather high level. Then, depending on the profitability of the company, a "dividend" is declared that serves to reduce your premium. The *net cost* of your policy usually ends up being slightly less than that of a nonparticipating policy.

WARNING: There is the risk of a higher participating insurance premium in some years should the company have poor investment and claims experience.

TIPS ON BUYING LIFE INSURANCE

Which Type of Policy?

For protection? Which type of policy depends upon your family situation: ages, financial position and ability to save or invest. In general, young families with tight budgets need large amounts of death protection, so *term* insurance makes the most sense. More mature families usually need much less insurance; *whole life* seems appropriate in this case.

As an investment? If you feel comfortable with your ability to save and invest excess funds, stick with term insurance. Others might turn to whole life because it includes a "forced savings" plan.

Cost? From a pure wealth-maximization viewpoint, *term* insurance is preferred because the death benefits are obtained at at the lowest cost. On the other hand, the modified whole-life policies are attractive within an overall financial plan. They are very flexible and can be used in a variety of ways, depending on your financial plan during each phase of your life cycle. If unusually high coverage is needed temporarily, a whole-life policy can be augmented with term insurance during this time.

Fixed premium desired? If you don't want to face an increasing premium, stay with whole or universal life where the premium is based on the guaranteed (not the current) rate.

How to Find the Lowest Cost Coverage

Comparing insurance rates can be a nightmare because dividends/current interest rates change *every* year.

Write the National Insurance Consumer Organization (NICO) for its annual pamphlet, "How to Save Money on Life Insurance," for useful ideas. (NICO, 344 Commerce St., Alexandria, VA 22314).

The best universal life policies have smaller sales charges and better rates for insurance than do variable life policies.

By Mail. One way to keep policy costs low is to buy by mail. USAA Life Insurance Co. in San Antonio, Texas is currently recommended by NICO.

Through Agents. NICO says the best universal policy is offered by Connecticut Mutual Life.

BEWARE: Some insurers offer policies with "no sales charge," but they require huge term-coverage and surrender charges.

Coverage for Your Dependents?

The prime objective of insurance is to prevent your financial plan from failing due to untimely death. Coverage of dependents may or may not serve to attain this objective.

If your *spouse's income* is vital to the financial plan, this chapter's principles would apply equally well to him or her. As for children, insurance agents often suggest an *endowment policy* to provide funds for college or burial expenses. (An endowment policy, much like whole life, requires level payments for 10-20 years and pays the policy's face value at maturity or before if the insured dies prematurely.)

As a savings vehicle, an endowment policy is *very inefficient.* This is because premiums are much higher than those for a whole life policy issued at the same age. The reason is that reserves equal to the policy's face value must be accumulated in a shorter period of time than with whole life. Also, in the highly remote chance that a dependent child dies prematurely, the burial expenses can normally be paid out of current income or the liquid portion of your assets.

Multiple Policies?

If you have a number of policies, it may be smart to combine them into a single policy. The reason is that there is usually a $10-$20 *annual policy fee.* Check with your agent. You may be able to eliminate these costs.

SELECTING THE RIGHT INSURANCE AGENT

A good insurance agent is a specialist who can be valuable in designing your life insurance program. (If nothing else, he or she can explain clearly the myriad of available options!)

Two Things to Look For

- Certification as a *Chartered Life Underwriter* (CLU). A CLU has been certified as having a substantial body of knowledge about life insurance as well as accounting, economics, law and taxes.
- Dedication to a career of life insurance, e.g., the agent has been selling life insurance for more than 5 years.
  NOTE: If you feel confident about your ability to select the right insurance, a year's worth of premiums can be saved by avoiding an agent's sales commission. For example, you can purchase insurance through a group plan of your employer, professional organization, or alumni association. Some companies also sell policies by mail or phone.

LATE BULLETIN

In 1986, the Florida supreme court overturned a state statute that prevented life insurance agents from offering *discounts* on insurance premiums. If this recent ruling works its way through the other 49 states where such "give ups" against agents' sales commissions are forbidden, expect lower insurance premiums. This is especially important because agents' commissions usually consume over half of your policy's first-year premium. Watch for more competitive (lower) premiums ahead. All this translates into more of your money going to work for you sooner.

TERMS TO KNOW

Chartered Life Underwriter (CLU)
Decreasing term insurance
Deferred annuity
Fixed annuity
Flexible premium variable life insurance
Mutual life insurance company
Nonparticipating insurance
Participating insurance
Pure risk protection
Renewable and convertible term insurance
Single-premium whole life policy
Straight term insurance
Term life insurance
Universal life insurance
Universal variable insurance
Variable annuity
Variable life insurance
Whole (ordinary or permanent) life insurance

FIXED INCOME SECURITIES

8 DEBT SECURITIES FOR HIGH YIELD AND SAFETY

Chapter Objectives

1. Why Invest in Debt Securities?
2. Basics of Bond Investing
3. Determinants of Bond Prices and Yields
4. Things to Consider About Bonds

Debt securities have traditionally been conservative investments, held by large institutions because they offered good current income and safety of principal. Recent inflation and volatile interest rates changed all that. To cope with these new forces, the debt markets now contain a diversity of fixed-income securities with differing returns, risks, liquidities and tax implications.

While money market instruments are a big part of the debt market, they're mostly a low-risk pure income investment vehicle. Therefore, our primary focus in this chapter will be on the longer-term segment of the debt market, where income is also important but the prospect of capital appreciation (depreciation) must also be considered.

In this regard, we'll cover the basics of bond investing, what determines bond prices and their volatility as well as things to consider before investing your money. Remember, debt securities can still be a conservative investment if you stick to high-quality issues and adopt a long-term ("buy-and-hold") perspective.

GENERAL INVESTMENT CHARACTERISTICS

The investment characteristics of debt securities were outlined in Chapter 2. We suggest you read over this material again before continuing to read.

The main characteristic to keep in mind is that a debt security is a loan to whatever entity issued it. In return, the issuer promises to repay the loan at a specified future date and, in the meantime,

to pay the buyer a fixed rate of interest. So, a bond, for example, is just an "IOU" and, whenever you buy a bond, you become a creditor of the government or corporation that issued it.

BONDS VS. COMMON STOCKS

How then is a bond different from a stock? When you buy a stock, you don't become a creditor—you become an owner. The corporation whose stock you purchased promises nothing. Hopefully, though, it will do well, increasing its earnings year to year. You will participate in this if the price of its stock goes up, and through higher dividends. On the other hand, a bondholder doesn't benefit from rising profits.

But, there's no guarantee that this will happen. In fact, the opposite could occur. If it does, the stock's price will fall and your investment may be worth only a fraction of its original value.

Like a stock, a bond's price will fluctuate. If you have to sell it before it matures, you may receive more or less money than you paid for it. But, if you hold the bond until it matures, you will get back the face or par value of the bond (its principal). Of course, a bond issue occasionally goes into default (the issuer is unable to pay interest or principal).

WHY INVEST IN DEBT SECURITIES?

Like most other investments, debt provides two sources of income:

- *current income* in the form of periodic (fixed) interest payments, especially for those who need income for living expenses.

- *potential capital gains* if interest rates fall. On the latter, it's important to keep in mind that interest rates and prices of fixed-income securities *move in opposite directions*. That is, if rates increase, bond prices fall and vice-versa.

This means that if you sell an issue *before* it matures, you may receive more or less than what you originally invested. If you hold to maturity, however, you *know* what you'll receive—its principal or par value.

Moreover, bonds are "senior securities" whose claims on income and assets come before other corporate securities such as common and preferred stock.

Debt's most attractive feature--high current income--used to be a disadvantage because it was fully taxed. By lowering individual tax rates and by eliminating the preferential capital gains tax, tax reform has actually *increased* the relative attractiveness of high fixed-income securities compared to securities such as stocks that emphasized capital gains over current income.

Nevertheless, because debt's income is fixed, a disadvantage is that this return can be *eroded by inflation*. To illustrate, Exhibit 8-1 presents the 30-year performance of debt securities after adjusting for inflation. Several comments can be made:

- After inflation, returns on *long-term bonds* have been *both negative and quite variable*. Contrast this with *shorter-term debt*, where returns were *higher* and *more stable*.
- In the short term, average returns tended to increase with maturity but peaked at 12-18 months, while risk continued to increase steadily with time to maturity.

CONCLUSION: Long-term bonds' returns did not compensate for the extra risk. So, it paid to keep money invested short-term rather than long-term. Of course, there's no assurance this will be repeated in the future. Also remember, bonds pay a *fixed income* but this *doesn't mean* they have a *fixed yield* or *return*.

Perhaps the biggest *disadvantage* is the large denominations of debt issues. Because of this,

---

Exhibit 8-1

Risk-Returns on Debt Securities After Adjusting for Inflation, 1953-1982

Maturity	Annual Average Return (Continuous Compounding)	Variability (Standard Deviation)
0-6 Months	1.04%	2.37%
6-12 Months	1.11	3.00
12-18 Months	1.12	3.57
18-24 Months	1.05	4.08
24-30 Months	0.92	4.44
30-36 Months	1.01	5.01
3-4 Years	0.75	5.51
4-5 Years	0.33	6.21
5-10 Years	0.47	6.98
20-year Governments	−0.93	9.47
20-year Corporates	−0.42	10.18
Common Stocks (S & P 500 Index)	5.19	18.40
Consumer Price Index (Inflation)	4.32	3.60

SOURCE: M. C. Scott. "Bond Bets: Keep Them Short." AAII Journal. February 1984.

---

many experts think a minimum of $50,000-$100,000 is needed to obtain a well-diversified bond portfolio. This is why most individual investors end up investing in *unit trusts* or *mutual funds*, where the minimum investment is much lower (see discussion below).

BASICS OF BOND INVESTING

Bearer vs. Registered Bonds

Bearer bonds are issued and traded with no records of ownership. Like cash, the holder ("bearer") is the owner. If the bond is lost, it's your loss—so, *such bonds need to be kept in safekeeping*. Interest is received by "clipping the coupons" and presenting them to your bank for collection. This means you have to keep up with the payment dates.

With *registered bonds*, the issuer keeps a record of who owns them. This enables interest payments to be mailed to you automatically.

Types of Bond Yields

Bonds are purchased mainly for their yields. However, there are four different yields that you need to be familiar with.

1. *Coupon or Nominal Yield* — is the annual interest earned as a *percentage* of a bond's *par value.* For example, a $1,000 par bond paying $120 a year has a 12% coupon yield ($120 ÷ $1,000).
2. *Current Yield* — is the annual interest paid as a *percentage* of a bond's *current market price.* (This is to a bond what dividend yield is to common stock.) Continuing our example, if the bond's price is $960, it's current yield is 8% ($120 ÷ $960).
3. *Yield-to-Maturity (YTM)* — is, as its name implies, the *total percentage yield* you receive if you buy the bond and hold it to maturity. In contrast to the current yield, the YTM or promised yield includes both the bond's interest income and its price appreciation (depreciation), which is the difference between the bond's current price and its par value. When investors refer to the *market rate of interest* being 10%, they are saying that the YTM is 10%.
4. *Discount Yield* — is the annualized percentage from par or value at which a discount instrument sells. It applies to short-term obligations such as Treasury bills or commercial paper.

How to Read Market Quotes

1. *Treasury Bills* — are quoted on a discount yield basis by maturity rather than in prices.

Maturity Date	Discount		Yield
	Bid	Asked	
10-24	7.14	7.10	7.33
10-31	7.18	7.14	7.39
11-7	7.19	7.15	7.41

As an example, the T-bill maturing on October 24 can be *sold* at a (bid) price yielding 7.14%, while it could be *purchased* for a 7.10% return. The "7.33% yield" in the last column is the T-

bill's return on a *coupon-equivalent* basis. Exhibit 8-2 explains how a T-bill's price and yield are calculated.

Exhibit 8-2
How Discount Interest Works on Treasury Bills

T-bill prices are expressed as a percentage of $100. To calculate the price, the following formula is used:

$$\text{Price} = 100 - \frac{\text{Days to Maturity}}{360 \text{ Days}} \times \text{Discount Yield}$$

EXAMPLE: Take a 90-day $10,000 T-bill, which has a 9.6% discount yield. Its price would be

$$\text{Price} = 100 - \left(\frac{90 \text{ days}}{360 \text{ days}} \times 9.6\right) = \$97.60 \text{ per } \$100$$

So, this T-bill would cost you $9,760 ($10,000 × $\frac{\$97.60}{\$100}$).

NOTE: T-bill yields are quoted on an *annualized* basis, that's why we had to take 90/360 or ¼ of 9.6% — your interest is earned for only 90 days, not a whole year.

REMEMBER: T-bill yields cannot be compared to other, coupon-bearing instruments. The reasons:

1. T-bills are sold at a discount instead of at par or face value, and
2. T-bill yields are quoted on a 360-day calendar year instead of 365 days. This means your *effective* (or *coupon equivalent*) *yield* is *higher* than the discount yield and is the correct yield to use for comparison purposes. Your banker or broker should be able to calculate the effective yield for you.

---

2. *Longer Term Governments,* such as Treasury notes and bonds as well as agency bonds, are quoted as a *percentage of par value in 32nds.* For example, the "10½s1989" T-note is quoted as

Rate	Mat	Date	Bid	Asked	Bid Chg.	Yld.
10½s	1989	Jun n ...	97.16	97.24	+ .2	10.74

This note's coupon yield is 10½%, and it matures in June 1989 (the "n" tells you it's a note rather than a bond). Its 97.24 asked price says you would *pay* 97 24/32% of par value. For a $10,000 note, this translates into a 97.75% x $10,000 = $9,775 price. The change from the prior day's closing bid price was +2/32nds, and the yield-to-maturity is 10.74%.

Exhibit 8-3

TREASURY BONDS, NOTES & BILLS

Tuesday, March 19, 1985

Representative mid-afternoon Over-the-Counter quotations supplied by the Federal Reserve Bank of New York City,' based on transactions of $1 million or more.

Decimals in bid-and-asked and bid changes represent 32nds; 101.1 means 101 1/32. a-Plus 1/64. b-Yield to call date. d-Minus 1/64. k-Non U.S. citizens exempt from withholding taxes. n-Treasury notes. p-Treasury note; non U.S. citizens exempt from withholding taxes.

U.S. TREASURY BONDS AND NOTES

Rate	Mat. Date		Bid	Asked	Bid Chg.	Yld.
9⅝s,	1985	Mar	100	100.4	.....	4.85
13⅜s,	1985	Mar n	100.2	100.6	– .1	6.15
9½s,	1985	Apr n	100.1	100.5	.....	7.79
3¼s,	1985	May	99	100	– .1	3.21
4¼s,	1975-85	May	99.3	100.3	.....	3.58
9⅞s,	1985	May n	100.4	100.8	+ .1	8.32
10⅜s,	1985	May n	100.5	100.9	.....	8.20
14⅛s,	1985	May n	100.23	100.27	– .1	8.10
14⅜s,	1985	May n	100.24	100.28	– .1	8.14
14s,	1985	Jun n	101.8	101.12	.....	8.68
10s,	1985	Jun n	100.5	100.9	.....	8.77
10⅝s,	1985	Jul n	100.12	100.16	.....	9.08
8¼s,	1985	Aug n	99.17	99.21	.....	9.06
9⅝s,	1985	Aug n	100	100.4	.....	9.22
10⅝s,	1985	Aug n	100.10	100.14	.....	9.54
13⅛s,	1985	Aug n	101.11	101.15	– .1	9.26
10⅞s,	1985	Sep n	100.19	100.23	.....	9.45
15⅞s,	1985	Sep n	103.2	103.6	– .2	9.54
10½s,	1985	Oct n	100.12	100.16	.....	9.64
9¾s,	1985	Nov n	99.27	99.31	– .1	9.80
10½s,	1985	Nov n	100.8	100.12	.....	9.93
11¾s,	1985	Nov n	101.3	101.7	.....	9.78
10⅞s,	1985	Dec n	100.19	100.23	+ .1	9.90
14⅛s,	1985	Dec n	102.30	103.2	.....	9.96
10⅝s,	1986	Jan n	100.13	100.17	.....	9.97
10⅞s,	1986	Feb n	100.20	100.24	.....	10.02
13½s,	1986	Feb n	102.26	102.30	.....	10.03
9⅞s,	1986	Feb n	99.25	99.29	+ .1	9.99
14s,	1986	Mar n	103.16	103.20	.....	10.20
11½s,	1986	Mar n	101.5	101.9	– .1	10.16
11¾s,	1986	Apr n	101.13	101.17	+ .1	10.26
7⅞s,	1986	May n	97.19	97.23	+ .1	10.02
9⅜s,	1986	May n	98.31	99.3	+ .3	10.23
12⅝s,	1986	May n	102.11	102.15	+ .1	10.38
13¾s,	1986	May n	103.17	103.21	+ .1	10.31
13s,	1986	Jun n	102.31	103.3	+ .1	10.36
14⅞s,	1986	Jun n	105.10	105.14	.....	10.24
12⅝s,	1986	Jul p	102.18	102.22	+ .1	10.46
8s,	1986	Aug n	97.3	97.7	.....	10.17
11⅜s,	1986	Aug n	101.4	101.8	.....	10.40
12⅜s,	1986	Aug p	102.7	102.11	+ .1	10.58
11⅞s,	1986	Sep p	101.20	101.24	.....	10.60

Rate	Mat. Date		Bid	Asked	Bid Chg.	Yld.
7½s,	1988-93	Aug	77.20	78.4	+ .8	11.65
8⅝s,	1993	Aug	82.26	83.2	+ .3	11.86
11⅞s,	1993	Aug n	99.2	99.6	+ .4	12.03
8⅝s,	1993	Nov	82.20	82.28	+ .4	11.84
11¾s,	1993	Nov	98.10	98.14	+ .5	12.05
9s,	1994	Feb	83.31	84.7	+ .5	11.92
4⅛s,	1989-94	May	91.30	92.30	+ .18	5.10
13⅛s,	1994	May	105.8	105.12	+ .4	12.14
8¾s,	1994	Aug	82	82.8	+ .4	11.94
12⅝s,	1994	Aug p	102.22	102.26	+ .4	12.12
10⅛s,	1994	Nov	89.26	90.2	+ .2	11.88
11⅝s,	1994	Nov	97.21	97.25	+ .4	12.02
3s,	1995	Feb	92.2	93.2	+ .16	3.85
10½s,	1995	Feb	91.27	92.3	+ .5	11.88
11¼s,	1995	Feb p	95.25	95.27	+ .4	11.98
10⅜s,	1995	May	90.29	91.5	+ .8	11.90
12⅝s,	1995	May	103.22	103.30	+ .1	11.95
11½s,	1995	Nov	97.22	97.30	+ .4	11.85
7s,	1993-98	May	68.14	68.30	+ .6	11.68
3½s,	1998	Nov	92.1	93.1	+ .23	4.17
8½s,	1994-99	May	76.14	76.30	+ .1	11.91
7⅞s,	1995-00	Feb	71.12	71.28	+ .2	11.96
8⅜s,	1995-00	Aug	74.12	74.28	+ .2	11.99
11¾s,	2001	Feb	97.10	97.18	+ .4	12.10
13⅛s,	2001	May	106.22	106.30	+ .8	12.14
8s,	1996-01	Aug	71.14	71.30	+ .8	11.94
13⅜s,	2001	Aug	108.12	108.20	+ .3	12.15
15¾s,	2001	Nov	126.23	126.31	+ .2	11.98
14¼s,	2002	Feb	115.16	115.24	+ .13	12.05
11⅝s,	2002	Nov	96	96.8	+ .6	12.15
10¾s,	2003	Feb	89.18	89.26	+ .4	12.16
106s,	2003	May	89.18	89.26	+ .4	12.15
11⅛s,	2003	Aug	92.12	92.20	+ .5	12.14
11⅞s,	2003	Nov	97.31	98.7	+ .6	12.12
12⅜s,	2004	May	101.19	101.27	+ .5	12.13
13¾s,	2004	Aug	112.3	112.11	+ .3	12.09
11⅝s,	2004	Nov k	95.27	95.31	+ .6	12.17
8¼s,	2000-05	May	72.6	72.22	+ .6	11.84
7⅝s,	2002-07	Feb	66.14	66.30	+ .6	11.90
7⅞s,	2002-07	Nov	68.5	68.21	+ .10	11.90
8⅜s,	2003-08	Aug	71.9	71.25	+ .7	12.00
8¾s,	2003-08	Nov	73.27	74.3	+ .6	12.09
9⅛s,	2004-09	May	76.20	76.28	+ .7	12.10
10⅜s,	2004-09	Nov	86.5	86.13	+ .5	12.12
11¾s,	2005-10	Feb	97.4	97.12	+ .3	12.09
10s,	2005-10	May	83.15	83.23	+ .4	12.07
12¾s,	2005-10	Nov	104.4	104.12	+ .6	12.17
13⅞s,	2006-11	May	112.24	113	+ .2	12.15
14s,	2006-11	Nov	113.30	114.6	+ .6	12.13
10⅜s,	2007-12	Nov	86.4	86.12	+ .6	12.09
12s,	2008-13	Aug	98.22	98.26	+ .6	12.15
13¼s,	2009-14	May	110.4	110.12	+ .8	11.93
12½s,	2009-14	Aug k	102.27	102.31	+ .5	12.12

SOURCE: The Wall Street Journal, October 1, 1985

Exhibit 8-3 provides a sample of Treasury note and bond quotes.

3. *Corporate-issued debt,* in contrast to government securities, are quoted as a percentage of par value in ⅛'s. For instance,

Bonds	Cur Yld.	High	Low	Close	Net Chg.
Xerox 8⅝s99	11.	81⅞	81⅛	81¼	+1½

This Xerox bond has an 8⅝% coupon and matures in 1999. Its current yield is 11%, and its closing price was 81¼% of par or 81.25% x $1,000 = $812.50 — a net change of + 1½% or $15.00 per bond from the prior trading day's close.

ABOUT BOND PRICES

Level of Bond Prices

A bond's value is determined by four factors:

- coupon interest
- par value
- term (years) to maturity
- yield-to-maturity

Because the first three are always known, it's a bond's yield- to-maturity that largely affects its price. More importantly, it's *changes in this yield* that cause bond prices to vary.

Changes in Bond Prices

Three very important relationships need to be kept in mind about the volatility of bond prices. As interest rates change,

- bond prices move in the opposite direction
- long-term bond prices fluctuate more than short-term bond prices, and
- lower coupon bonds' prices fluctuate more than higher coupon bond prices.

WHAT DETERMINES YIELDS?

The level of bond yields generally depends on three factors:

- General economic conditions
- Outlook on inflation
- Default risk

Economic Conditions

When you invest in debt securities, you are essentially loaning money to the government or a corporation. In a strong economy, the high demand for money will push yields up. On the other hand, during a recession, the demand for loans is weaker, so yields fall. In a sense, then, interest rates are the "price" (cost) of money, responding to demand and supply just like any other commodity's price does.

Inflation

Inflation erodes the purchasing power of future income. To offset this potential loss, investors demand an "extra premium" in yields.

For example, say that, in a *zero* inflation environment, a 1-year T-bill yields 6%. Now, let's say that the inflation rate is expected to jump to 4% over the next year. This means the same T-bill would now have to sell to yield 10% or else no one would buy it. Moreover, because inflation varies over time, securities with different maturities will have different inflation premiums added into their yields.

Default Risk

You always face the possibility an issuer may default on its interest and principal payments. Fortunately, a bond's risk of default can be determined by referring to its *bond rating.*

These ratings are provided by credit rating agencies such as Moody and Standard & Poor's. These agencies give you an independent judgment of an issuer's financial strength and overall creditworthiness. By relying on their ratings, you have a useful way to screen out issues lacking the quality you desire. Your broker can help you here.

From Exhibit 8-4, you can see that these ratings range from Triple-A (highest quality) to D (in default). Moreover, the rule is: The higher quality an issue has, the lower its yield will be.

Exhibit 8-4 How Agency Ratings for Bonds Work			
Investment Quality	Moody's	S & P	Description
High Grade	Aaa	AAA	Highest rating possible that indicates extremely strong capacity to pay interest and principal
	Aa	AA	High quality with strong capacity to pay interest and principal
Medium Grade	A	A	Good quality but may be susceptible to adverse economic conditions
	Baa	BBB	Adequate capacity to pay interest and principal but this could be weakened under adverse economic conditions
Speculative	Ba	BB	Only moderate protection of interest and principal during both good and bad times
	B	B	Lack characteristics of other desirable investments. Payments over long term not safe
Default	Caa	CCC	Poor quality—in danger of default
	Ca	CC	Highly speculative that may be in default
	C	C	Lowest rated bonds
		D	In default on interest and/or principal payments

SOURCE: Moody's Bond Record and Standard & Poor's Bond Guide.

A WORD ON TAX-EXEMPT ISSUES

Municipal bonds, Treasury issues and many federal agency obligations share a common trait: their interest is *partially* or *fully tax-exempt*. For instance, Treasuries and agency obligations are federally taxed but are exempt from state and local taxes. Many munis, on the other hand, escape taxation at *all* levels.

Your After-Tax Yield

An important consideration before you invest in a tax-exempt is to determine what your yield will be when compared to the *after-tax* yields on similar quality, taxable bonds. To do this is fairly straight forward if you know your marginal tax bracket.

For tax-exempts, your after-tax yield is simply the stated yield since no taxes are paid. For a *taxable issue*, its after-tax yield is given by

Taxable Yield × (1—Marginal Tax Rate)

For example, assume you're in the 33% tax bracket, and you have a choice of investing in (1) a muni that yields 8% or (2) a corporate bond that yields 11%. In this case, the muni's after-tax yield is 8%, and the corporate's after-tax yield is

$$11\% \times (1 - 0.33) = 7.37\%$$

So, you're better off investing in the municipal bond because you receive a higher *after-tax* return. This is why municipal yields are often 20%-30% below those on taxable issues, and they become more appealing the higher your tax bracket is. That is, notice what happens if you're in the 15% tax bracket instead. In this case, the corporate's after-tax yield is

$$11\% \times (1 - 0.15) = 9.35\%$$

and the corporate becomes a more attractive investment.

Ratings

Ratings on the investment quality of most muni bonds are readily available. However, because most municipal bond issues are small, munis tend to have *poor liquidity* and *marketability*. This means there's a limited market for them, so you may be forced to take a price discount if you sell before maturity.

Tax Reform

Municipals are still good investments, but tax reform has made things more complicated. *Reason:* The new tax bill has created new municipal bond categories—each having different tax implications. Basically, the less essential a given type of bond is, the more unfavorably they are treated for federal income tax purposes. In a nutshell, this is how things work:*

1. *"Public-Purpose" Bonds*—these are securities issued to meet essential governmental functions such as school and highway financing. These continue to be tax-exempt.

2. *"Non-Governmental Purpose" Bonds*— these bonds are held to be for "non-governmental purposes" under the new law, e.g., bonds issued to finance student loans or housing. The upshot is that such bonds issued after August 7, 1986 must have their interest treated as a "preference item." What this means is that the interest income must be added to your taxable income if you have to calculate the *alternative minimum tax*. (The 21% alternative minimum tax applies when it results in a larger tax bill than under the normal tax calculations.) For most people, this is of little concern. For example, a family of four with an adjusted gross income of $100,000 can have over $60,000 in preference items (including municipal interest) before facing the alternative tax.

3. *"Taxable Municipals"*--these are issued for "non-essential" governmental purposes, e.g., financing pollution control facilities, sports stadiums and farm loans. While not exempt from Federal taxes, they may be exempt from state and local taxes in the states in which they're issued. *NOTE:* There's a limited market for these, and their newness is still untested.

---

* A. Peers, "Municipals May Still Be Good Bets, If You Can Decipher the Tax Bill," The Wall Street Jounal, September 10, 1986, p. 29.

TIP: There are so many exceptions and special situations with regard to these three categories that you'll be venturing into a potential quagmire. For instance, munis issued to finance hospital and airport construction may or may not be tax-exempt, depending on the circumstances. It's best to read carefully the legal opinion given in the bond prospectus to determine what category the issue falls into. *Better yet, stay with bonds issued before August 7, 1986*--they're generally not taxable.

In sum, over the long run, munis may end up being the best tax-advantaged investment because other tax-favored investments were harder hit by tax reform.

THINGS TO CONSIDER

Be Conservative

Buy and hold high-quality issues to maximize current income. *Trading* bonds is speculative and requires considerable expertise, not only in bond fundamentals but also also in forecasting future interest rate changes.

Consider Bond Funds or Unit Trusts

Buying bonds requires considerable capital, so building a diversified portfolio is expensive. An alternative is to buy shares in a *bond mutual fund* (see Chapter 16) or a unit trust, where the minimum investment is as low as $1,000.

These two are similar in that they're not a debt security. Rather, they are *shares* representing ownership in a diversified portfolio of bonds that pays dividends from interest income that is earned. In addition, both of their values change in response to movements in interest rates.

There are big differences, though. A unit trust's portfolio of bonds never changes (a simple buy-and-hold strategy), while a mutual fund has a managed portfolio. This means the risk of losing principal because of rising rates is lower because unit trusts have fixed portfolios. Investors can simply hold their shares until maturity, when the bonds are paid off at face value. Because mutual fund portfolios are constantly changing, they don't have a fixed maturity and it's more difficult to avoid interest rate risk.

If you are most concerned about current income and if you believe interest rates are headed south, you might want to buy a trust and not a mutual fund, since the fund will have to add lowering yielding securities while the trust offers a fixed return. Conversely, funds offer some protection against rising interest rates because they can invest new money at prevailing rates.

Also, a unit trust is illiquid because there's no secondary market for it, whereas a fund's shares can always be sold back to the mutual fund.

Returns on unit trusts are generally about one-quarter to one percentage point higher than those offered by bond funds. Unit trusts, however, do have annual fees like mutual funds and upfront sales charges as high as 5% that make returns slightly lower than those on individual bonds. Management fees for mutual funds run around 0.65% of fund assets, whereas unit trusts only charge about 0.18%.

While the costs (management fees) of mutual funds are generally higher than a unit trust, funds offer better diversification. A unit trust usually holds 10-35 different issues; a mutual fund may have as many as 100 different securities. Finally, unit trusts "self-destruct" (usually after 10 years) when the bonds mature and the proceeds are distributed—while funds are on-going, buying and selling bonds continually.

A major consideration in choosing a trust or fund is the *quality* of the bonds in their portfolio. Examine their prospectus and stick with a trust or fund that is made up of securities with "investment grade" ratings—"A" or higher. Also, about half of the unit trusts available carry some form of insurance protecting bondholders against default. Such insurance usually gives a trust a triple-A credit rating, but it can reduce your returns by 30 to 40 basis points (*one basis point is one-hundredth of a percentage point*).

Deep Discount Bonds

If you need money for a specific future need, e.g., house downpayment, children's college fund or retirement, one way to save tax-advantaged money is to buy quality discount bonds that mature when you'll need the money. (A "discount bond" is a bond selling for less than par value.) At maturity, your gain (par value minus purchase price) will be taxed at the lower long-term capital gains rate.

Check Out the Indenture Provisions

Look for a *sinking fund provision*, it'll increase the bond's safety. Also watch out for *call privileges*, especially if it's a "premium bond" (one that sells for more than par value). With today's relatively low interest rates, an issuer may call an issue for redemption—most likely at a price less than you paid.

Is there any *security?* Certain bonds, called *secured bonds*, have specific property backing them as collateral to guarantee interest and principal payments. *Unsecured bonds* or *debentures* are backed only by the general creditworthiness of the issuer.

Bond Swaps

This involves liquidating one bond position and (simultaneously) buying a different issue to replace it. Swaps are usually done to increase yields ("yield pick-up swap") or to generate year-end capital losses to reduce taxable income ("tax swaps").

High-Coupon Bonds

Now that interest rates have dropped from their nosebleed heights of the early 1980's, one possible way to improve your returns is to *buy high-coupon bonds that won't be callable for a few more years.* If rates stay down, there's a good chance the issuer will refund this high-cost debt to take it off the books. To get you to tender, they'll offer a premium over the market price.

Flower Bonds

If you're an affluent senior citizen, you might use "flower bonds" to reduce estate taxes. These are low-coupon government securities selling at a deep discount. Their main appeal is that they will be accepted at face value to pay estate taxes when the owner dies.

New vs. "Seasoned" Issues

Yields on new issues usually tend to be higher than on existing issues of the same quality or issuer.

Space Your Maturities

Structure your portfolio with staggered maturities from 1 to 15 years. This will allow you to *reinvest* your annual proceeds at *higher* interest rates if market rates should increase. If they fall, you'll have to reinvest at lower rates but your longer-term maturities will have appreciated in value.

NEW PRODUCTS

Every year, new financial products hit the market, designed to meet every conceivable investor need. We focused on the basics of bond investing and, therefore, couldn't cover every aspect of the debt markets. However, following is a short description of the newer, more popular debt instruments you might want to consider.

Zero Coupon Bonds

Perhaps the hottest item, "zeroes" pay no interest (the coupons have been "stripped off"). You buy the "corpus" which is issued at a *deep discount* from face value—up to 60%-90% depending on the term to maturity. At maturity, you get your money back plus all compounded interest, based on the yield at the time you bought the bond.

MAIN ADVANTAGE: Having to reinvest interest payments at a future, unknown interest rate is not a problem, plus you'll know exactly how much your money earned.

MAIN DISADVANTAGE: Taxes have to be paid on the *imputed* interest as if you had received it in cash. This makes zeroes more attractive as a tax-sheltered investment for IRAs or custodial trusts for children.

Mortgage-Backed Bond Funds

High-yielding Ginnie Maes can now be purchased for as little as $1,000 by purchasing shares in mutual funds or unit trusts. This approach solves the problem of having to reinvest monthly interest and principal payments—they do it for you.

Floating-Rate Notes

Coupon rates on these "floaters" are adjusted periodically as interest rates change.

MAIN ADVANTAGE: You're protected against inflation and loss of principal during periods of rising interest rates.

MAIN DISADVANTAGE: Adjustments *lag* actual changes in market rates and there's a floor and ceiling to how much coupons can change.

Put Bonds

These have a built-in protection against price erosion because of rising interest rates. They give you the right to redeem at par at different points in time, e.g., annually.

MAIN ADVANTAGE: Regardless of how high interest rates go (and prices down), you can "put" or sell the bond back to the issuer for the full principal amount. Because of this, their prices are less volatile.

MAIN DISADVANTAGE: You get a lower yield for the lower risk. And, the more often you have the right to sell your bond back, the lower the yield.

Single-State Municipal Funds

Offered as either mutual funds or unit trusts, these investments are restricted to home-state municipal bonds. By doing so, a resident can avoid state and local taxes as well as federal taxes. The higher your tax bracket, the more attractive these funds' returns can be to you.

WORD OF CAUTION: The additional tax break of these "state trusts" isn't necessarily worthwhile. You may find that a "national trust" earns more than a single-state trust even after you pay state taxes on it, especially in states where the top state rate is less than 10%.

Junk Bonds

Most of us have heard of "junk bonds," lower-quality corporate bonds with ultrahigh yields that have been popular lately. While attractive because of their generous yields when compared to other bonds, there's a good reason for them

being called "junk"--they're extremely risky (quality ratings are B or lower). And now, with more of them floating around, this "house of cards" investment will come tumbling down if a few junk bond issuers begin defaulting. *My advice:* Look elsewhere with your money.

A FINAL WORD ON DEBT SECURITIES

Conservative investors who prefer steady income to the thrills and chills of uncertain capital gains--REJOICE! Tax reform is your friend. With no tax breaks for capital gains, income investors are on equal footing with growth investors for the first time since 1921. With lower tax rates, too, you keep more of each dollar of income earned.

TERMS TO KNOW

Alternative minimum tax
Basis point
Bearer bond
Bond swap
Callable bond
Coupon (nominal) yield
Debenture (unsecured) bond
Discount bond
Discount yield
Floating-rate note
Junk bond
Mortgage-backed bond
Municipal bond
National unit trust
Non-governmental purpose municipal bond
Par value
Premium bond
Public-purpose municipal bond
Principal
Registered bond
Seasoned bond
Sinking fund provision
Taxable municipal bond
Term (years) to maturity
Treasury bill
Treasury bond
Treasury note
Unit investment trust
Yield pick-up swap
Yield-to-maturity

9

WHAT YOU SHOULD KNOW ABOUT PREFERRED STOCK

Chapter Objectives
1. What is a Preferred Stock?
2. Investment Characteristics of Preferred Stock
3. How to Evaluate Risk and Return
4. When to Consider Preferred Stock as an Investment

Preferred stock (or just preferred) seems to be a rather obscure investment to many people. One reason for this may be that it's a "hybrid" security that's similar to both a bond and a common stock. Like a bond, it pays a fixed income (dividend) but has less safety because it has fewer rights. Like a common stock, it's legally an equity security. However, it lacks the same potential for higher dividends or price appreciation.

The name "preferred" comes from its "preference" (prior claim) with regard to the payment of dividends, and to a firm's assets in the event of liquidation.

Exhibit 9-1 contains a list of the other investment characteristics of preferreds.

Most preferreds have been issued by utilities or by companies when they acquired another firm. While over 1,000 issues are publicly traded, preferred stock is usually *not an attractive investment* for the average investor because its yield is *lower* and its risk *higher* than other comparable investments.

EVALUATING PREFERRED STOCK

Returns

The desirability of preferred stocks depends on the returns on comparable investments. As a fixed-income security, preferreds have the principal attraction of emphasizing *current income* or yield because they provide a stable stream of income just like a bond. This means preferreds compete with other fixed-income investments on a yield basis. *Result:* They don't *act* like a common stock.

Exhibit 9-1
General Investment Characteristics of Preferred Stock

1. *PAR VALUE*--establishes the amount that preferred stockholders are entitled to in the event of liquidation, usually $25, $50 or $100 per share.
2. *DIVIDENDS*--are an annual fixed amount which may be stated in dollars, e.g., Ohio Edison $3.50 Pfd., or as a percentage of par value, e.g., Ohio Edison 7.36% Pfd. Most preferreds usually offer a *cumulative dividend* feature. If a firm is unable to pay a dividend because of insufficient earnings, the dividend accrues to the next year as an *arrearage* or *dividends in arrears*. This obligation must be paid before any common stock dividends can be declared. A few preferreds are noncumulative. For obvious reasons, you should avoid this type of preferred. While unusual, some preferreds enjoy a *participating provision* that allows preferred stockholders to receive an extra dividend if the common stock dividend exceeds a certain level. For example, once the common stock dividend exceeds a certain level, additional dividends may be shared on a 50-50 basis between the preferred and common stockholders. A participating preferred is more desirable than a nonparticipating because common dividends tend to increase over time.
3. *VOTING RIGHTS*--are not normally carried by preferreds as they are by common stock. If a firm has financial problems and preferred dividends are omitted, preferred stockholders can elect a certain number of people to the board of directors. This allows them to protect their interests.
4. *CLAIMS ON ASSETS*--refers to the fact that a preferred has a prior claim on a firm's assets in bankruptcy (before common stockholders), but this is largely symbolic. By the time creditors that have claims prior to the preferred stockholders are satisfied (if they are satisfied), not much, if anything, is likely to be left over.
5. *NO MATURITY*--means a preferred does not have an explicit maturity date; is issued in perpetuity just as common stock is. May have, however, an implicit "maturity date" if there is a call or sinking fund provision (see below).
6. *SINKING FUND PROVISION*--requires the issuer to buy back a certain percentage of the issue directly from the stockholders if at any time the shares trade at or below par value (the firm annually sets aside and accumulates funds to do this whenever the market price is above par value).

This further means that a preferred's market price is determined by the prevailing level of interest rates. If, for example, interest rates fall, a preferred's price moves up along with bond prices, and when rates rise, its price falls.

To illustrate, the current dividend yield is defined as:

$$\text{Current Yield} = \frac{\text{Annual Dividend Per Share}}{\text{Market Price Per Share}}$$

If it pays a $4 dividend and its market price is $40 per share, its current dividend yield is:

$$10\% = \frac{\$4}{\$40} \qquad \frac{4.10}{46} = 8.91\%$$

Now, if prevailing yields on comparable investments fall to 8%, this preferred's yield would also fall to 8%. But, notice that this implies that its market price will have to increase 25% from $40 to $50, i.e.,

$$8\% = \frac{\$4}{?}$$

$$8\% = \frac{\$4}{\$50}$$

We can conclude, because its dividend is fixed, its price must increase (decrease) whenever market conditions cause its current yield to decrease (increase). This further illustrates why a preferred stock is like a bond--its price moves in the opposite direction to interest rate changes.

As shown in Exhibit 9-2, high-grade preferred stock yields historically have tended to be about one-half to one percentage point less than high-grade bonds. So, check on the prevailing yields on comparable quality bonds before considering any preferred stock.

TIP: Unless a preferred's yield is at least one percentage point higher than a comparable quality bond, it makes little sense to buy it for income--the bond is a better buy. One exception though--it's easier to buy preferreds because their face value is $25-$100 whereas bonds' face values are usually $1,000.

Why have preferred stock yields tended to be less than high-grade bonds? The reason is that corporations enjoy a special tax advantage with

Exhibit 9-2
Yields on High-Grade Preferred Stocks and Corporate Bonds

Year	(1) High-Grade Preferred Stocks	(2) AA-Rated Bonds	(1)—(2) Yield Spread
1970	7.29	8.32	-1.03
1971	6.75	7.39	-0.64
1972	6.85	7.49	-0.64
1973	7.23	7.94	-0.71
1974	8.23	9.10	-0.87
1975	8.01	8.77	-0.76
1976	7.97	8.75	-0.78
1977	7.60	8.24	-0.64
1978	8.25	8.92	-0.67
1979	9.50	10.46	-0.96
1980	12.35	12.85	-0.50

Source: Federal Reserve Bulletin and Standard & Poor's Stock Guide

regard to dividend income. They have to pay taxes on only 20% of any dividend received. In contrast, you pay taxes on the full amount. (If you are incorporated, e.g., a medical practice or other incorporated practice, you can profitably take advantage of this tax break by buying preferreds through your corporation.)

Because of this tax advantage, corporations buy preferreds aggressively, driving prices up and yields down to the point where it makes little sense for most individual investors to buy them. In fact, corporations own most of the preferred stocks.

Risk

As you know, an investment also needs to be evaluated in terms of its risk or the potential loss of capital value. Preferred has two potential risks:

1. Issuer's Risk. One risk with preferred stock concerns the financial strength of the issuer. A preferred stock's price can drop if a company's earnings fall because dividend payments may be suspended. While this is a rare event, you need to be aware it can happen.

   As we saw in Exhibit 9-1, preferred stockholders are low on the totem pole when it comes to the distribution of assets.

In the event of liquidation, you're likely to receive very little, if anything, for your investment. (This is another reason, besides yield, why bonds are "preferred" to preferred--they have many more legal protections.)

But how do you assess financial strength? One way is to examine the historical dividend payment record. Your broker can tell you how reliable the company's past payment record has been and whether there's much chance of future dividends being suspended.

Another way to assess an issuer's risk of "passing" on its dividend is to refer to the quality rating its preferred has, such as its rating by Standard & Poor's (S&P) or Moody's. Such agencies basically do your homework for you by measuring a firm's capacity and willingness to pay its preferred's dividends. They also study the nature and provisions of the issue.

Remember, preferred stock is subordinated to all debt issues. This causes its rating to be less than the rating assigned to the firm's debt. (Most preferred stock ratings fall in the "BBB" category.) The easiest way to find out a preferred's rating is to refer to a recent issue of the S&P Stock Guide or ask your broker to do it for you.

Exhibit 9-3 contains the S&P rating system and symbols.

2. *Interest Rate Risk*. Once you have determined that a preferred stock has a good dividend record and a suitable credit rating, the next risk to consider is *interest rate risk*. For most preferreds, this should be your chief concern because interest rates change more often than the quality of an issuer changes.

As we saw earlier, a preferred's value fluctuates with changes in the level of interest rates. While they exhibit wider swings in price than bonds do, they generally are not as volatile as common

Exhibit 9-3
S & P Preferred Stock Rating System and Its Symbols

AAA— the highest rating and indicates an extremely strong capacity to pay preferred dividends.

AA— high quality and capacity to pay preferred dividends is very strong, but not as overwhelming as for issues rated AAA.

A— sound capacity to pay dividends, but more susceptible to adverse effects of changes in circumstances and economic conditions.

BBB— adequate capacity to pay dividends, but, although it normally exhibits adequate protection parameters, adverse economic conditions or changing circumstances are more likely to yield to a weakened capacity to make dividend payments than for A-rated issues.

BB,B & CCC— predominantly speculative with respect to issuer's capacity to pay preferred dividends and, while these issues have some quality and protective characteristics, these are outweighed by large uncertainties or major risk exposures to adverse conditions.

CC— preferred stock is in arrears on dividends or sinking fund payments but is paying current dividends.

C— a non-paying issue.

D— a non-paying issue with the issuer in default on debt instruments.

Source: Standard & Poor's Stock Guide. 1985

stocks. Nevertheless, you should be aware of the risk that their market prices could fall if the level of interest rates rises. Assessing this risk means forecasting the future direction of interest rates.

WHEN SHOULD PREFERRED STOCK BE CONSIDERED FOR INVESTING?

If you desire current, dependable income, stay with money market accounts or high-grade bonds. Preferred stocks are generally less attractive for current income when compared to like-quality investments.

Also avoid low-quality, speculative preferreds that offer high yields. There's a reason for the high yield--their risk is high also!

There are, however, three situations when preferreds may be considered:

Potential Capital Appreciation

If you want to speculate on the direction of interest rates, preferreds can be purchased when you think interest rates have topped out. At this point, you are buying at a relatively low price and a high yield. If interest rates do fall, the preferred's price will appreciate, producing capital gains (refer to the earlier numerical example).

TIP: This strategy should be applied only when the stock is selling far below its par value (at a relatively high yield) and is near the low end of its historical price range.

A CAVEAT: Callable Preferreds. Some preferreds are callable. In these cases, the firm has the right to call (retire) the stock after a certain period of time and at a certain price (usually at a 5-10% premium over par value).

When a preferred's current yield is considerably below the stated dividend yield on par value (i.e., when the preferred's market value is greater than its par value), a firm has an incentive to call in its preferred issue. Reason: The firm can save money by retiring the existing issue and selling a new issue at a lower dividend yield.

Because of this, callable preferred yields will be higher than noncallable preferreds in order to compensate their investors for the risk of having their stock called. But, remember that there will be a cap on any potential capital appreciation.

LESSON: Avoid callable issues when seeking capital gains--they may never materialize.

Preferred in Arrearages

Normally, you should not seek out preferred stock with dividends in arrears, because this is a sign of a financially- troubled company.

Under certain conditions, though, preferred with arrearages may be an attractive investment. If a firm's financial condition is improving, the firm may want to eliminate its arrearages so that it can start improving its credit rating and start paying common stock dividends.

As Exhibit 9-4 indicates, the potential payoff in accelerated dividends and price appreciation has been rewarding. For example, over the 1961-1975 time period, preferreds in arrears averaged a 12.8% total return. This compared very favorably with the 7.9% from common stocks and 3.5% from bonds. Note, however, that the risk was higher with these preferreds.

Exhibit 9-4
Total Annual Returns from All Preferreds with Arrearages, Common Stocks and Moody's Aaa Bonds, 1961-1975

	Preferreds in Arrears	Common Stocks	Aaa Bonds
Average Return	12.8%	7.9%	3.5%
Maximum Return	84.9	36.9	12.2
Minimum Return	-28.9	-24.8	-3.5

SOURCE: R.A. Stevenson and M. Rozeff, "Are the Backwaters of the market Efficient?" Journal of Portfolio Management, Spring, 1979, pp. 31-34.

WARNING: Identifying those preferreds that offer the best chance for superior performance takes special skills. The average investor should avoid these stocks.

Adjustable-Rate Preferreds

One of the newest financial products to hit the market is the adjustable-rate preferred. The dividends on such issues are adjusted quarterly to the current level of interest rates on Treasury securities. Perhaps the best way to participate in these issues is to choose one of the dozen mutual funds that specialize in them.

TERMS TO KNOW
Adjustable-rate preferred
Arrearages
Callable preferred
Cumulative preferred
Current yield on preferred
Dividends in arrears
Interest rate risk
Issuer risk
Noncumulative preferred
Nonparticipating preferred
Par value
Participating preferred
Preferred dividend
Preferred stock
Preferred stock rating system
Sinking fund provisions
Voting rights

EQUITY SECURITIES

10 COMMON STOCKS FOR HIGHEST RETURNS

Chapter Objectives
1. What is a Common Stock?
2. Why Invest in Common Stocks?
3. Fundamentals of Common Stocks

Common stocks are the foundation for all corporations because they represent *owners' capital*. As a shareholder, you become a part owner in a firm "in common" with other shareholders. Because of this, you share in both the good and bad fortunes of a firm, i.e., its profits and its losses. As a result, common stocks offer the *highest returns* but also the *highest risks*.

In this chapter, we cover the basics of common stock investing. Moreover, because common stock is the most complicated security you can study, three additional chapters on common stocks follow this one. There we will consider how to evaluate stocks, and provide ideas on how to select different types of stocks and offer ways to time your purchase or sale of stock. As a suggestion, you may want to read Appendix C "How to Read an Annual Report" as background material before reading these four chapters.

WHAT IS COMMON STOCK?

Where does common stock come from? When a corporation begins operations, its first source of capital funds is from the issuance of common stock shares to the founding owners. These shares are referred to as *equity* or *ownership securities*. As the firm grows, more shares are issued to new owners or stockholders. This contrasts with *debt securities* or *loans* which reflect what capital the corporation owes to "outsiders" such as banks and other investors. As we saw in Chapter 8, these outsiders are called *creditors*.

The equity position of shareholders can best be illustrated by referring to the simplified balance

---

Exhibit 10-1
Simplified Balance Sheet of a Corporation

ASSETS	LIABILITIES
(What it Owns)	(What it Owes)
Current (Short-Term) Assets:	Current (Short-Term) Liabilities:
Cash	Accounts Payable (What it owes
Accounts Receivable (What its	employees, suppliers, etc.)
customers owe)	Short-Term Debt (Loans from
Inventories	banks, etc.)
Long-Term Assets:	Long-Term Liabilities:
Equipment	Bonds and Mortgages (Loans
Buildings and Land	from long-term creditors)

STOCKHOLDERS' EQUITY
(What Owners Provide)*
Common Stock (Paid-In Capital)
Retained Earnings

BALANCE SHEET EQUATION:
Assets = Liabilities + Stockholders' Equity

---

* Note: If *preferred stock* has been issued, it will appear right above "common stock" in the "Stockholders Equity" section.

---

sheet and income (or profit and loss) statement in Exhibits 10-1 and 10-2.

A *balance sheet* depicts the relationship between a firm's *assets* (what it owns) and its *liabilities* and *equity* (what it owes) at a point in time. Common stockholders and creditors both have claims against the assets because they both provided money to purchase the assets. However, the short- and long-term creditors (or debtholders) have *first* claim. This is one reason why the owners are the risk-takers--they are *residual* benefactors, i.e., they're last in line.

Exhibit 10-2
Simplified Income Statement of a Corporation

Line Number	
1	Sales (or Revenues)
2	- Operating Expenses *
3	Net Profit
4	+ Non-Operating Income (Interest and Dividends)
5	− Non-Operating Expenses (Interest on Debt)
6	Pre-Tax Income
7	- Income Taxes (Federal and State)
8	Net Income Available to Stockholders
9	- Dividends
10	Net Income Reinvested (Added to Retained Earnings)

* For example, cost of goods sold, wages, selling and administrative expenses and depreciation.

An *income statement* measures how much a firm has earned over a period of time (its revenues less expenses). It can also be used to point out the "me-last" position faced by stockholders. That is, the creditors also have first claim on a firm's *income*. To see this, notice that the creditors receive their payments first-- employee wages and trade suppliers (Line 2) and then debtholders' interest payments (Line 5). Even the government takes its share of income through taxes (Line 7) before stockholders get anything.

So, after all bills and taxes are paid, whatever income is left over belongs to the stockholders. This doesn't mean you can take it home with you. The reason is because this income is split between *cash dividends* (Line 9), which you do get, and earnings plowed back into the firm as *retained earnings* (Line 10). The latter is a major source of financing for most firms and is used to purchase more assets that will directly benefit

stockholders through the future growth in sales and earnings (and, hence, higher stock prices).

It might also be interesting to point out that this retention of earnings provides the "link" between the income statement and the balance sheet. That is, on the income statement, the income reinvested in the company is the *current year's* retained earnings whereas retained earnings on the balance sheet is the *accumulation of all past years' retained earnings*.

WHY INVEST IN COMMON STOCKS?

The main reason for purchasing stock is for high total return. While highly uncertain, the potential profits (especially from capital gains) can be substantial when compared to other possible investments. As Exhibit 10-3 demonstrates, common stocks have historically outperformed other securities by a wide margin. But remember, there are no promises that this will always be the case.

Exhibit 10-3
Historical Rates of Return, 1929-1979

Type of Investment	Average Annual Compounded Return
Common Stocks	9.0%
Corporate Bonds	3.8%
U.S. Treasury Bonds	3.1%
U.S. Treasury Bills	2.7%
Consumer Price Index	2.7%

SOURCE: R. G. Ibbotson and R. A. Sinquefeld, Stocks, Bonds, Bills, and Inflation: Historical Returns, Financial Analysts Research Foundation, 1979.

Advantages

1. *Capital Growth.* Common stocks appreciate in value because they participate fully in the firm's residual earnings. And, because a stock's market price generally reflects the firm's earnings potential, increasing earnings leads to higher share prices.

So, in contrast to fixed-income securities, stocks can grow in value as the firm prospers. Moreover, earnings and, hence, share prices should keep pace with inflation because a firm's rising costs can be passed on through higher prices for its goods and services.

2. *Rising Dividend Income.* Because dividends are tied to earnings, common stock dividends tend to increase as the firm grows. Of course, they could also decrease or be cut out completely if the firm has financial difficulties. Despite this, there are hundreds of firms that have consistently paid dividends for over 50 years.

    WARNING: Increasing dividends aren't necessarily a sign of a healthy company. Most companies don't like to reduce dividends, even if earnings are headed south. So make sure earnings are also improving along with dividends.

3. *Tax-Advantaged Returns.* Common stock returns are realized primarily through *capital appreciation.* So, by retaining earnings rather than paying them out as (fully-taxed) dividends, a company puts your money to work growing "tax-free" until you sell.

4. *High Marketability, Low Cost.* Most common stocks, especially those traded on major stock exchanges, can be bought and sold in a matter of minutes at a price that is easily obtainable. Transactions costs are modest, and the minimum capital requirements are among the lowest of any traded security. On the latter, most stocks sell for less than $40 per share, and you can buy as few shares as you desire. Compare this with a minimum of $1,000 for bonds or mutual funds or $10,000 or more for money market instruments.

Disadvantages

1. *Highest Risk.* The main disadvantage of common stocks in a word is *RISK*-- business and financial risk, market risk and inflation risk.

As we know by now, high potential rewards only come with higher risk. A stock's value continually fluctuates--both up and down, both short- and long-term-- and sometimes without any apparent rhyme or reason. Moreover, there's no guarantee that dividends will be paid. A bond's interest is a contractual obligation; dividends are not.

Again, stocks represent *residual* ownership of a company whose sales, earnings and dividends are subject to erratic forces-- competition, economic conditions, interest rates , government regulation, etc. This means stock prices and dividends will reflect the effect of these forces on a firm's prospects.

And don't forget the uncontrollable-- market risk. Because stocks' prices tend to move closely together, even high-quality stocks will suffer temporary setbacks in price when investors' overall mood or psychology turns sour.

2. *Low Current Income.* Not only are stocks' *total* returns highly unstable, but their current (dividend) yield is meager by comparison. If you need a high level of current income, you should look to fixed-income securities.

3. A Complex Security. Another drawback not always fully appreciated by newcomers to common stock investing is the complex nature of analyzing and selecting stocks. Because so many factors affect stock prices and because these factors are subject to change, stocks are the most difficult investment to evaluate, plus they require constant monitoring.

FUNDAMENTALS OF COMMON STOCKS

Earnings and Dividends Per Share

Rather than refer to earnings and dividends in *total dollars*, most analysts and investors use *earnings per share* (EPS) and *dividends per share* (DPS). This makes it easier for comparison purposes--over time or across firms.

Fortunately, EPS and DPS are usually reported along with a firm's other accounting information. Referring back to Exhibit 10-2, they are easily calculated as follows:

$$EPS = \frac{\text{Net Income Available to Common Stockholders (Line 8)}}{\text{Number of Shares Outstanding}}$$

$$DPS = \frac{\text{Common Dividends Paid (Line 9)}}{\text{Number of Shares Outstanding}}$$

Types of Dividends

Dividends can be paid in the form of either *cash or additional shares of stock*.

1. *Cash Dividends*. Usually dividends are paid in cash every quarter around the same time every year. However, some companies pay them only semi-annually or annually. How much dividend is to be paid and when is *decided* by management, and is *declared* by the board of directors.

   Also, when a cash dividend is paid, the stock price per share drops automatically by the amount of the dividend. This is because part of the firm's assets or value (its cash) has been paid out.

2. *Stock Dividends*. Occasionally, a firm may pay a *stock* dividend by issuing *additional shares* to stockholders.

   This is especially true for growth companies that prefer to reinvest all their earnings into new investments rather than pay them out as cash dividends.

   Like a cash dividend, a stock dividend also automatically reduces the market value of the stock, BUT for a different reason. A cash dividend reduces a firm's cash resources (assets), while the number of shares remains the same. In contrast, with a stock dividend, assets remain the same, but the number of shares increases. The result is that assets and earnings per

share (and, hence, price) drop because they are spread over more shares.

To see how this works, assume a 100% stock dividend is declared. This means 1 additional share will be issued for every share outstanding. This is also why it's called a *2-for-1 split*--twice as many shares will exist after the stock dividend.

Now, suppose you own 100 shares of a $60 stock, or a total value of $6,000. If the stock splits 2-for-1, this is what'll happen:

	Pre-Split	Post-Split
Shares owned	100	200
Price per share	x $60	x $30
Total value	$6,000	$6,000

Notice that in this case the stock dividend doubles the number of shares but *halves* the price. *RESULT:* You end up with the *same* total value, so you haven't really received anything of "value"--just more shares of a lower priced stock. (Exhibit 10-4 illustrates what happens when different size stock dividends are paid.)

Exhibit 10-4

Effect of Different Stock Dividends

Pre-Split Shares = 100   Pre-Split Stock Price = $60

Stock Dividend	On a Split Basis	Number of Shares	Stock Price
10%	11-for-10	110	$54.54
25%	5-for-4	125	$48.00
50%	3-for-2	150	$40.00
100%	2-for-1	200	$30.00
200%	3-for-1	300	$20.00

So why do firms bother paying stock dividends? Many managers believe a larger number of shares outstanding and a lower price per share improves the marketability and distribution of the stock and, hence, makes it more attractive.

NOTE: Perhaps you have noticed that after a large stock dividend was rumored or announced, the stock price jumped. If you look closer, the reason it did was probably because the cash dividend rate wasn't reduced proportionately--this translated into a larger cash dividend per old share.

The "Ex-Dividend" Date

An important but often confusing part of the dividend payment procedure is the *ex-dividend date*. Let's look at this by means of illustration: "Company XYZ declares a dividend, payable May 15 to stockholders of record April 30."

There are three dates to be familiar with:
1. *Record Date* (April 30). The date when the company "closes its books" to determine which stockholders will receive the dividend.
2. *Ex-Dividend Date* (April 26). The date which actually determines who will receive the dividend. It occurs *4 business days before the record date.*
3. *Payable Date* (May 15). The date on which the dividend is mailed to stockholders--a check if it's a cash dividend and new shares if it's a stock dividend.

A dividend is payable to stockholders of record at the *close* of business on the record date. However, whom these stockholders are is determined four business days *earlier*, on the ex-dividend date. The reason for it being before the record date is because 5 business days are allowed for stock transactions to clear through the system, i.e., for buyers to put up their money and sellers to receive their proceeds.

So, in our example, if you bought the stock before the April 26 ex-dividend date, you're entitled to the dividend. Conversely, if you sold the stock before the ex-dividend date, you would receive no dividend.

When a stock goes ex-dividend, the amount of the dividend is subtracted from the stock's market price. As a result, if you bought the stock on or after the April 26 ex-dividend date, you don't pay for a dividend you won't receive.

Exhibit 10-5 provides an example of how dividend announcements are reported in financial newspapers.

Exhibit 10-5
Dividend Announcements

Dividends Reported July 3

Company	Period	Amt.	Payable date	Record date
REGULAR				
Amerada Hess $3.50pf	Q	.87½	7-31-85	7-15
Bergen Brunswig clA	Q	.08	9-1-85	8-1
Comdata Network Inc	Q	.04	7-23-85	7-16
Houston Industries	Q	.66	9-10-85	8-16
Maine National Corp	Q	.30	9-10-85	8-15
Mark Twain Bancshares	Q	.20	8-8-85	7-19
NWA Inc	Q	.22½	9-30-85	9-13
Pacific Resour deppf	Q	.50	9-15-85	9-3
Pacific Res exchdeppf	Q	.50	9-15-85	9-3
Royal Bank Canada	Q	b.50	8-23-85	7-24
SFN Companies pfA	Q	.30469	7-31-85	7-16
Smith Intl	Q	.08	8-30-85	8-15
Sun Co	Q	.57½	9-10-85	8-9
Sun Co $2.25pf	Q	.56¼	9-20-85	8-9
IRREGULAR				
Snelling & Snelling	Q	.25	7-18-85	7-8
FUNDS-REITS-INVESTMENT COS				
CIGNA High Yield Fund	M	.107	7-15-85	7-5
Delchester Bond Fund	M	h.13	7-15-85	7-8
Houston Oil Royalty Tr	M	.12887	7-25-85	7-15
Sabine Royalty Trust	M	.156	7-29-85	7-15
STOCK				
Carteret S&L Assoc		15%	8-14-05	7-25
Pioneer Fedl S&L Assoc		p	8-1-85	7-19
p-Three-for-two stock split.				
Providence Energy		n	8-15-85	7-25
n-Three-for-two stock split.				

INCREASED

		New	Old	Amounts	
Providence Energy	Q	.61½	.51	8-15-85	7-25

INITIAL

Wickes Cos Inc	Q	.62½	8-1-85	7-15

A-Annual; Ac-Accumulation; b-Payable in Canadian funds; F-Final; G-Interim; h-From income; k-From capital gains; M-Monthly; Q-Quarterly; S-Semi-annual.

* * *

Stocks Ex-Dividend July 8

Company	Amount	Company	Amount
American Can Co	.72½	Iowa-Ill G&E $2.31pref	.58
Appalachn Pwr $2.65pf	.66¼	IPCO Corp	.08½
Appalachn Pwr $3.80pf	.95	Joy Mfg Co	.35
Appalachn Pwr $4.18pf	1.04½	Loew's Companies	.09
Appalachn Pwr 7.40%pf	1.85	• Malartic Hygrade Gold	b.20
Appalachn pwr 8.12%pf	2.03	b-Canadian funds.	
Baruch-Foster Corp	k	New Process Co	.12½
k-3% stock.		PHH Group Inc	.25
BritTelecom'nADR	n	Planning Research	.06
n-Approx. $.606.		Public Sv Colorado	.50
Col & Son Ohio $2.42pf	.60½	Raytheon Co	.40
Col & Son Ohio $3.45pf	.86¼	Sanders Associates	.14
Col&Son Oh $15.25pfOld	3.81¼	Santa Anita Realty	.48½
Col&Son Oh $15.25pfNew	3.81¼	Saul (BF) REIT	.05
Commerical Metals	.09	Scotty's Inc	.13
Ducommun Inc	.20	Sikes Corp clA	.05
EastGroup Properties	.65	Three D Depts clA	.02½
Elcor Corp	.09	Three D Depts clB	.01½
Enserch Corp pfA	2.58	Torchmark Corp	.25
Enserch Corp adlprD	1.46⅞	Torchmark Corp adlpfA2.65	
Enserch Corp deppfE	2.66¼	Van Dorn Co	.23
Friedman Industries	.07	White Consolidtd Indus	.37½
Grow Group	.07½	White Consol Indus pfA	.75
Hi Shear Industries	.12½	White Consol Indus pfC	.75
Hunt Mfg Co	.12½		

SOURCE: The Wall Street Journal, September 21, 1985.

Dividend Policies

Many companies follow a stated dividend policy. Others may not have an explicit policy but their actions imply one. Dividend policies fall into one of 4 categories:

- Regular dividend
- Regular-extra dividend
- Irregular dividend
- Fixed payout ratio

Most companies pay a *regular* quarterly dividend that is fairly predictable. Some firms pay a *regular-extra* dividend, which involves a regular quarterly dividend plus an additional sum (extra) that depends on how profitable they've been during the year. Companies in cyclical industries, such as General Motors, whose earnings fluctuate with the economy tend to follow this policy.

Other firms pay *irregular* cash dividends that have no predictable pattern. For example, real estate investment trusts or closely-held corporations tend to follow this policy. Finally, a firm may maintain a *fixed payout ratio* policy. In this case, a constant *percentage* of earnings is distributed each year.

TERMS TO KNOW

Balance sheet
Cash dividend
Dividend yield
Dividends per share (DPS)
Earnings per share (EPS)
Ex-dividend
Fixed payout ratio
Income statement
Irregular dividend
Net income available to stockholders
Payable date (dividend)
Record date (dividend)
Regular dividend
Regular-extra dividend
Retained earnings
Stock dividend
Stock split

11 EVALUATING COMMON STOCKS

Chapter Objectives

1. How to Classify Common Stocks by Their Risk, Income and Price Performance
2. Understanding Different Common Stock Values
3. Interpreting Stock Market Quotes
4. Two Approaches to Evaluating Common Stocks
5. What to Consider in Evaluating Stocks

This chapter continues our discussion of the fundamentals of common stock investing. We also begin to describe how you should go about evaluating which stocks to consider for purchase (or sale). In particular, we indicate those critical factors that determine a stock's value. This latter discussion will then set the stage for the next chapter, where we develop stock selection or screening criteria for identifying winning stocks.

CLASSIFYING COMMON STOCKS

Individual stocks differ widely in terms of risk, current income and price performance, regardless of general economic and market trends. A convenient way to classify stocks is:

- Income stocks
- Growth stocks
- Defensive stocks
- Cyclical stocks
- "Blue chip" stocks
- Speculative stocks

Income Stocks

If your investment objective emphasizes current income with growth secondary, consider *income* or *high-yielding* stocks. These stocks pay out most of their earnings as dividends. To avoid the unpleasant surprise of a dividend *cut*, however, look for a record of continuous dividend payments. *EXAMPLES:* Electric utilities, real estate and chemical stocks.

Growth Stocks

These stocks exhibit rapid, above-average growth in earnings. A good growth stock is one that has experienced at least a 10%-15% rate of growth in earnings and pays little or no dividend. While their returns come almost exclusively from capital gains, their stock prices are more volatile and high relative to earnings, i.e., high P/E ratios. *EXAMPLES:* Computer, medical services and semiconductor stocks.

Defensive Stocks

Certain companies' earnings and stock prices remain relatively stable through both the thick and thin times. The reason is because they produce *necessary* goods and services. This constant demand for their products "defends" them from economic downturns. *EXAMPLES:* Food, beverage and tobacco stocks.

Cyclical Stocks

These stocks' price performance mirrors the ups and downs of the economy because their profitability is highly sensitive to economic conditions. *EXAMPLES:* Steel, airline and housing stocks.

"Blue Chip" Stocks

These special stocks are highly-visible, industry leaders, usually owning a dominant share of their product markets. They have long, consistent records of earnings and dividend growth that have withstood the test of different economic conditions. *EXAMPLES:* A.T.& T., General Motors and IBM.

Speculative Stocks

These stocks involve great risk, i.e., they offer a small chance for a large gain, BUT a much greater chance that returns will be very low or negative. Low-priced ("penny") stocks and high P/E stocks fall into this category. The risk is that earnings could take a nosedive or even evaporate and this usually translates into dramatic drops in price. *SUGGESTION:* Stay away unless you have the skills, agility and stomach to *trade* these stocks. These aren't stocks you buy and tuck away somewhere.

COMMON STOCK VALUES

Charles Dow (of Dow-Jones fame) once said, "The great mistake made by the public is paying attention to prices instead of values." But what is a stock worth? Saying, "Whatever investors will pay," begs the question. This implies that "rational" investors determine "rational" prices. But, driven by greed (and fear), the market is subject to bouts of excesses--causing excessively over- and undervalued stocks.

Despite this, even rational investors can disagree on a company's future prospects. This means it's difficult to know precisely what a stock's *value* is. To cloud the issue further, analysts and investors often refer to a number of different values--

- Par value
- Book value
- Market value
- "Breakup" value
- Intrinsic value

So, it's useful to examine each of these to see what they mean.

Par Value

This is the face value set on common stock when it's issued. It is usually some low, nominal amount such as $1 or $5. In contrast to bonds, a stock's par value is meaningless (except for accounting purposes). In fact, many companies issue *no-par stock.*

Book Value

This is the sum of the capital paid-in by the owners and (accumulated) retained earnings. It is stockholders' equity found on the balance sheet (refer back to Exhibit 10-1). When used as a measure of value, it's stated on a *per share* basis and tells you how many dollars per share that have been invested by shareholders.

Book value per share will be *less* than market value per share for a healthy, growing firm. This is because book value reflects the *past* (what has occurred), whereas market value reflects the *future* (what will occur). This is why market value is more important. REMEMBER: When you invest in a stock, you're buying future earnings and dividends, *not past* earnings/dividends.

Market Value

This is simply the prevailing market price per share. It reflects the *market's* perception of what a stock is worth, and is an important ingredient in deciding whether to purchase (or sell) a stock.

"Breakup" Value

This is the newest buzzword on Wall St. It's a measure of the *separate* prices that the market would place on the *parts* (divisions) of a company if they were sold off. The idea is to buy stocks where the sum of their parts amounts to far more than the current stock price.

Exhibit 11-1 lists a few stocks that looked attractive when their breakup value was compared to their book or market values.

Exhibit 11-1

COMPANIES WHOSE BREAKUP VALUE MIGHT LEAD TO SELL-OFFS

Company	Breakup value	Book value	Price 6/25/85	Main Business	Possible Divestiture
Adams-Russell	$45	$9	$28	Electronics	Cable TV
Colgate-Palmolive	35	17	26	Household & personal care	Health care, industrial
Crane	55	22	35	Engineering, water treatment	Automation devices
Cyclops	80	50	50	Specialty steel	Retailing
Edison Brothers	42	27	36	Women's shoes	Hardware
Fluor	30	21	18	Plant construction	Mining
General Foods	130	40	82	Packaged food	Bakery, food service
General Host	25	17	16	Specialty retailing	Frozen foods
General Instrument	40	20	16	Electronics	Gambling devices
General Mills	95	28	60	Consumer food	Apparel, toys
Hamilton Oil	25	10	16	Oil & gas production	Refining
National Distillers & Chemical	50	30	32	Chemicals	Insurance, liquor
Parker Pen	25	8	18	Writing instruments, temporary help	Writing instruments
Ralston Purina	75	12	45	Livestock feeds	Restaurants
Revlon	55	28	41	Beauty products	Health care

DATA: BW. BASED ON A SURVEY OF SECURITIES ANALYSTS

SOURCE: <u>Business Week</u>, July 8, 1985, p. 80

Intrinsic Value

This is the most important value. Intrinsic or *investment* value measures what individual investors believe a stock is *worth*, which means this value may or may not be equal to its market price.

Remember, market price is a *consensus* of what most investors think a stock is worth at a point in time. However, there will be other investors who think it's worth more (or less), and these individuals will want to buy (not buy) it. This is why stock prices fluctuate--*the more disagreement among investors, the more prices fluctuate.*

You might be wondering how this can happen? As we said in the last chapter, common stocks are very complex securities that are affected by many, highly uncertain variables. Because of this, investors will differ in their assessments and expectations of the returns from a stock. And, of course, this leads to differing opinions about what a stock is worth.

> MORAL: "Beauty (a stock's value) is in the eye of the beholder."

WHAT STOCK MARKET QUOTES CAN TELL YOU

Vital information on a particular stock can be quickly picked up by referring to its market quotation found in most newspapers. For example, Winnebago, a recreation vehicle manufacturer, had the following stock quotation:

(1)	(2)	(3)	(4)	(5)	(6)	(7)	(8)	(9)	(10)	(11)
52 Weeks				Yld	P-E	Sales				Net
High	Low	Stock	Div	%	Ratio	100s	High	Low	Close	Chg
20⅞	8½	Winnbg	.20	2.1	8	178	10	9⅛	9¾	-¼

Price quotations for stocks are usually given in ⅛s of a dollar (low-priced stocks may be quoted in sixteenths). In the first two columns, the highest and lowest prices during the past 52 weeks are given. Together they help indicate where a stock is currently trading relative to the recent past. In the case of Winnebago, the clos-

ing price of $9.75 (see 9¾ in column 10) tells you it has fallen sharply from its yearly high of $20.875 (20⅞) and is currently trading near its *lowest* price for the year (8½ or $8.50).

The first value after "Winnbg" (Winnebago's abbreviation) is the *cash dividend* paid over the last 12 months, or $.20 per share. If, for example, dividends had been paid quarterly, this indicates a $.05 dividend per quarter.

Column 5 contains the *annual dividend yield,* which is calculated as

$$\text{Dividend Yield} = \frac{\text{Latest year's cash dividend}}{\text{Current stock price}}$$
$$= \frac{\$.20}{\$9.75} = 2.1\%$$

This is the stock's *current yield* based on its current price.

Column 6 indicates the *price-earnings* (P/E) ratio. It's determined by

$$\text{P/E Ratio} = \frac{\text{Current stock price}}{\text{Latest 12 months' earnings per share}}$$

This is an important number because it's a relative measure of value. It measures how much investors are paying for $1.00 in current earnings. For Winnebago, investors were paying a rate of $8 for every $1 in earnings. From Chapter 10, we know that a P/E ratio also reflects the *degree of optimism* investors have with regard to a stock's future. The higher the P/E ratio, the greater the optimism.

Column 7 records the volume (number) of shares traded in round lots (1 round lot = 100 shares). So, 17,800 shares of Winnebago exchanged hands that day. This figure is useful because price changes that occur on heavy trading volume are interpreted as being more meaningful than low volume price changes because more investors "approved" of the price change.

Finally, columns 8-10 provide the day's highest, lowest and closing (last trade) prices.

The last column tells how much the closing price changed from the preceding day's closing price, i.e., it was down $.25 per share.

FUNDAMENTAL APPROACHES TO EVALUATING COMMON STOCKS

A *fundamental analysis* of common stocks involves the study of economic and financial factors that determine a stock's current value and its quality (risk). There are two basic approaches to evaluating common stocks: (1) "top down" and (2) "bottom up."

Top Down Approach

This approach is the more involved of the two, and is the one used by most brokerage firms and institutional investors. Essentially, it involves three steps of analysis:

- National economy
- Industry
- Company

The reason for this approach is that two-thirds of the average stock's price variability is explained by market- and industry-related factors. The remaining third is due to company-specific events.

1. *National economy.* The first step is an examination of the national economy. There is a strong relationship between the economy and the stock market. That is, economic activity affects corporate profits, investor attitudes and expectations and, ultimately, stock prices.

   For instance, if an expansion in the economy is believed to be near at hand, this will lead to investor optimism and higher stock prices. Of course, if an economic downturn is envisioned, the opposite will occur.

   The broader picture is focused on first in order to anticipate emerging patterns that will affect the major components of the economy: personal consumption, investment and government expenditures. Monetary and fiscal policy and the outlook for interest rates are also important.

In many ways, an economic analysis is most useful for *timing* your investments. You need to know *when* to invest as well as *what* to buy or sell.

2. *Industry.* Based on the economic analysis, the next step is to forecast which industries are likely to perform best in such an economic environment. You need to realize that, while all industry groups (and individual stocks) respond to changing economic conditions, they respond in differing degrees. For example, auto and housing stocks tend to perform the best at the beginning of an economic recovery, whereas cyclical and capital-goods stocks usually do best after an economic upturn is well underway.

3. *Company.* Once it's decided that this is a good time to invest and what industries look the strongest, the next step is to select those stocks within the desirable industries that are best. This involves estimating future earnings, dividends and price changes as well as assessing the risk associated with these forecasts. All this leads to an evaluation of what a stock's intrinsic value is, which tells you whether a stock is a potential buy or sell.

Bottom Up Approach

The "bottom up" approach focuses on picking stocks. While attention is paid to the economy and the general outlook for stock prices and interest rates, most of the time is spent looking at companies that make sense--ones that can be bought at an attractive or undervalued price. Timing is of secondary importance because the whole idea is to find undervalued stocks that will turn in above-average performance *regardless of what the market is doing.*

WHAT TO CONSIDER IN EVALUATING STOCKS

Evaluating stocks means analyzing, sometimes overwhelming amounts of, information. As we know by now, your investment decisions should be based on your expectations for the future.

Knowing a stock doubled in price last year means little for deciding whether to buy it today. It's a stock's prospects for the coming year that's important. And, to assess these prospects, you need information.

But what information should you consider? Where do you focus your attention? Below are those factors that determine stock prices.

Earnings Potential

You buy common stocks to earn increased dividends and value. But where does this growth come from? Growing earnings. Both types of returns depend on how profitably a firm operates, and this means *growth in sales and earnings.*

Examine the sales-earnings record for the last 5-10 years. Is consistent growth evident--especially sales? Sales are more manageable and, hence, more predictable, so make sure it's there. As long as sales are growing, earnings will show up if they're not already there. *REMEMBER:* In the long run, earnings growth is limited by the extent to which sales grow.

Besides growth, you need to evaluate a firm's overall *profitability on its sales and investment.* To do this, check out its *profit margin* and *return on equity.*

A *profit margin* (pre-tax income ÷ sales) tells you how much of each dollar in sales is left over after expenses. It indicates how well a company controls its costs. Usually, the higher a firm's margin as compared to other firms in its industry, the more attractive its stock is.

A SPECIAL POINT: Is the profit margin near the lower or upper end of its historical range?

1. *Near the upper end.* Earnings growth will be limited to how fast sales grow. More importantly, there's a greater chance that the margin could shrink before it expands. This will pull earnings growth down.
2. *Near the lower end?* This is a more favorable situation because there's more room for margins to improve. This will give earnings an "extra boost" in addition to that coming from just sales growth.

Return on equity (net income ÷ stockholders' equity) tells you what a firm is earning on its common stockholders' investment. Again, the higher it is, the better. For instance, anything above 10% is considered desirable.

Dividends

Companies can pay any size dividend--from $0 on up. Whatever the level, dividends are strongly tied to earnings. For instance, firms normally don't increase their dividends unless they expect higher earnings. So take an increased dividend as a positive sign--especially when a company raises its dividend on a regular basis.

On the other hand, be cautious of companies that have *reduced* or *eliminated* their dividend payments. This action is usually done only as a *last resort* and suggests financial problems. Examining the 5-10 year dividend record can help here.

Investment Quality

Investment quality covers two aspects: (1) the *quality of earnings* (business risk) and (2) *financial strength* (financial risk). Quality of earnings is measured by the variability in earnings and the uncertainty that a company will continue to experience earnings equal to or greater than past earnings. This variability is greatly influenced by the type of industry the company is in. For example, *cyclical stocks* are characterized by wide variations in reported earnings. *Defensive* stocks have higher earnings quality because of their stability.

Financial strength concerns how liquid a firm is and how much money the company is borrowing (financial leverage).

Liquidity is measured by how much current assets exceed current liabilities (refer back to Exhibit 10-1). *RULE OF THUMB:* Current assets should be twice the current liabilities.

Most companies borrow money to finance their operations. However, the more they borrow, the greater the costs incurred to finance this debt. This makes them a riskier investment, especially if the economy takes a turn for the worse. *RULE OF THUMB:* Stay away from companies that use more than 25% of their total capital to finance assets.

Assessing a stock's investment quality is not necessarily easy. Fortunately, there are several readily available sources that can help you here. The Standard & Poor's <u>Stock Guide</u> ranks a company's *growth* and *stability* in earnings and dividends. <u>Value Line Investment Survey</u> rates the investment quality of the 1,700 stocks it follows in two ways: (1) safety and (2) financial strength. (Exhibits 11-2 and 11-3 describe each service's ranking system). Most university and public libraries as well as brokerage firms subscribe to these two advisory services.

Exhibit 11-2

Standard & Poor's Earnings and Dividend Rankings for Common Stocks

Growth and stability of earnings and dividends are the key elements in assigning the S&P rankings although other considerations may be used to adjust or modify the rankings.

A computerized scoring system is used that is based on per share earnings and dividend records for the past 10 years--a period long enough to measure long-term growth, to provide indications of basic changes in trends, and to encompass the full peak-to-peak range of the business cycle.

Basic scores are computed and then adjusted as indicated by a set of predetermined modifiers for (1) growth, (2) stability within long-term trend and (3) cyclicality. The ranking system makes allowance for the fact that, in general, corporate size is important so minimum size limits (by sales) are set for the various rankings. Exceptions can occur where a score indicates an outstanding earnings-dividend record.

Adjusted scores for each stock are then combined to produce a final score, which is measured against a scoring matrix developed from a large, representative sample of stocks. The range of scores is:

A+	Highest	B	Below Average
A	High	B−	Lower
A−	Above Average	C	Lowest
B+	Average	D	In Reorganization

CAVEAT: A ranking is *not* a forecast of future market price performance. It's an appraisal of *past performance* of earnings and dividends, and relative current standing. Therefore, don't use rankings as market recommendations. Rankings should be used as only part of a complete analysis.

SOURCE: Standard & Poor's, <u>Stock Guide</u>, August 1985

Exhibit 11-3

Value Line's Safety Rank and Financial Strength Rating Systems

1. **SAFETY RANK**--measures total risk, and ranges from "1" (highest safety) to "5" (lowest safety). In contrast to a stock's *beta* or market risk (price stability), the safety rank is more comprehensive, including not only price stability but also financial strength, i.e., financial condition, management competence, earnings variability, etc.

2. **FINANCIAL STRENGTH RATING**--involves key variables that determine financial leverage, business risk and company size. It also contains the judgment of Value Line's analysts concerning factors that cannot be quantified. The ratings range from "A + +" (highest financial strength) to "C" (poorest financial strength).

SOURCE: <u>Value Line Investment Survey</u>, A. Bernhard. <u>A Subscriber's Guide to the Value Line Investment Survey</u>, 1984.

Price/Earnings Ratio

Recall that a stock's *P/E ratio* or *multiple* is its market price divided by its current earnings per share. Because it measures how much people are willing to pay for a company with that level of earnings, it reflects how popular or attractive that stock is with investors. For example, a young, growing firm with a promising future will have a high P/E--perhaps 15, 25 or even 40. Why? Investors expect jumps in the company's future earnings, so they pump up the stock's price. On the other hand, a stodgy, going-nowhere stock will have a low P/E, perhaps 4 or 5.

Two questions: (1) Why is the P/E important in evaluating stocks and (2) what determines the level of P/Es? Regarding the first question, changes in P/E directly impacts stock prices. That is, current price is just the product of a stock's P/E and earnings per share:

Current Price = P/E Ratio x EPS

That is, the P/E ratio translates earnings into value--as the P/E expands or contracts, so does price. More importantly, changes in the P/E and earnings per share are *interrelated*. That is, P/Es also tend to *accelerate* stock prices (in either direction) as earnings per share change.

For instance, if earnings fail to meet expectations, the stock price will fall due to both lower earnings and a lower P/E. The reverse will occur when earnings growth is better than anticipated--that is, higher earnings and a higher P/E will work together to push the stock price higher.

But why does this happen? This leads us to the second question--*the determinants of P/E levels*. In general P/Es increase when:
- the growth rate of earnings are expected to increase
- the portion of earnings paid out in dividends (the dividend payout ratio) is expected to increase
- the riskiness of a stock decreases

In that sense, P/E brings together into one number the three factors we discussed above-- earnings potential, dividends and investment quality.

Also, because most companies have a fairly consistent dividend policy, the variables most likely to affect P/Es are *risk* and *expected growth*. *CONCLUSION:* You should spend most of your time assessing these two variables.

Investor Psychology

Changes in investor psychology also exert a powerful influence on stock prices. Investor optimism is based, in part, on a favorable outlook for business and the economy but it also is based on emotion. Increasing optimism leads to an increasing demand for stock (a bull market), hence, higher prices--sometimes to the point of excessive optimism, when emotion rather than rationality takes over. This is when you want to exit the market. *RULE OF THUMB:* When everybody is talking about their stocks--SELL. Of course, the reverse is true when pessimism dominates (a bear market) and this is the *best* time to accumulate stocks although, psychologically, it's not very easy to do.

But how do you gauge investors' moods? Obviously, you can't go around and ask each investor how he/she is thinking or feeling. Many experts attempt to "read" investors' sentiment by relying on technical analysis.

Technical analysis studies stock market data, e.g., price behavior, volume and other indicators, to determine the demand-supply conditions for a stock or the stock market as a whole. Chapter 13 provides an introduction to some of the techniques used by technicians.

TERMS TO KNOW

Blue chip stock
Book value
Bottom up approach
Breakup value
Cyclical stock
Defensive stock
Dividend yield
Financial strength
Growth stock
Income stock
Intrinsic value
Liquidity
Market value
Par value
Price-earnings (P/E) ratio
Profit margin
Return on equity
Speculative stock
Technical analysis
Top down approach
Volume

12 HOW TO PICK WINNING STOCKS

The ideal stock is one that is a high dividend payer, completely safe and certain to appreciate in value. One problem-- it doesn't exist. However, there are plenty of good stocks around that satisfy at least one of the objectives, but none can meet all three.

In the last chapter we began a discussion of how to evaluate common stocks, with special emphasis on those factors that affect stock prices. In this chapter, we take this knowledge and apply it to finding potentially profitable investment opportunities. Most investors fail to profit from these opportunities because they don't know what to look for (or avoid). Worse yet, some don't take the time to find out. Blind or uninformed investing is a sure shortcut to failure.

To this end, we first describe *where* to look for investment ideas. Next, we provide guidelines and a stock selection format for narrowing your choices to those specific stocks that have the highest potential payoff. Finally, we address what is perhaps the most difficult decision-- when to sell a stock.

SOURCES OF INVESTMENT IDEAS

The secret of finding investment ideas in one word is *READ*. Of course, this takes time, so you need to be interested in following economic and financial news. Once you become adept at accumulating and understanding financial information, you'll find it an immensely interesting subject--especially if your efforts are profitably rewarded!

Investment ideas are everywhere. Items in financial newspapers and magazines may catch your attention. But what do you look for? Exhibit 12-1 provides some clues on things to watch for.

Exhibit 12-1
How to Find Investment Clues

1. *Earnings forecasts or reports on results by company officials.* These often give clues to what's to come and the outlook for various segments of the company's business.
2. *Changes in management.* This is usually a good sign because new blood may "clean house" by redeploying its assets--selling off losing assets or products--and providing new management direction.
3. *Indication of hidden assets.* Has the company sold off a major asset that was carried on the books at a much lower price? If so, there may be other such assets lurking in the balance sheet.
4. *The introduction of new products or manufacturing processes.* These may generate higher profits from enhanced sales or lower costs.
5. *Dividend increases, decreases or omissions.* This usually only occurs if management is confident (worried) about the company's future earnings.
6. *Repurchase by a company of its own stock.* This could lead to higher earnings because fewer shares are outstanding. BUT, it depends on how the repurchase was financed. It's preferable that existing cash was used. On the other hand, if the company had to borrow money to buy the shares, this could squeeze earnings.
7. *Announcement by management that it's looking to merge or sell out.*
8. *Purchase of more than 5% of a company's stock by a financially-strong company or other outsider.* This might be an indication of a potential takeover and higher stock price.
9. *Heavy insider buying.* When officers and directors buy their own company's stock, this is a very positive development for future price increases. After all, who should know more about a company's prospects than the people who run it?

SOURCE: From Street Smart Investing, by George B. Clairmont and Kiril Sokoloff. © 1983 by George Clairmont and Kiril Sokoloff. Reprinted by permission of Random House, Inc. Inc.

You can also followup on a potential stock by looking it up in several of the readily-available investment advisory publications, such as Value Line and Standard & Poor's. Call or write the company for copies of its annual and quarterly reports (refer to Appendix C for how to read an annual report). Exhibit 12-2 contains a "must" list of sources of investment information.

CAUTION: If "everyone" is recommending a particular stock or industry, don't rush out and buy it--no matter how attractive or exciting it appears. Probably everyone has it in their portfolio already. So, you'll be the last one in and with no one left to buy it, there's only one way for it to go . . .

RELATIVE STOCK PERFORMANCE AND ECONOMIC ACTIVITY *

Business Cycles and the Stock Market

Like nature, economic activity moves in cycles--rising periods of prosperity followed by falling periods or recessions. Prosperous times find unemployment low, rising personal income and increasing production, corporate sales and profits. The opposite occurs during recessions.

A first step toward picking winning stocks, then, is to understand the relationship between stock prices and the business cycle. *In general,* the stock market and business activity move together--bull markets occur with rising business activity, bear markets parallel declining business activity.

However, it's important to realize that stock prices are a *leading indicator of changes in business activity.* That is, prices tend to *bottom out* 1-3 months *before* the business cycle does. Similarly, stock prices tend to *peak prior* to an economic recession, sometimes as much as 3-6 months before.

---

*J.B. Cohen, E.D. Zinbarg and A. Zeikel, Investment Analysis and Portfolio Management, 1982, pp. 247-260

Exhibit 12-2

User's Guide to Investment Information

1. **Financial News**

   Newspapers. The Wall Street Journal, Investor's Daily, and the New York Times provide detailed coverage of financial and business-related news as well as extensive coverage of stock quotations. Of particular interest is earnings information both on a *reported* basis and an *expected* basis found in articles on individual companies and industries.

   Barron's, a financial weekly, contains detailed information on securities, the performance of industry groups, in-depth articles on investment ideas as well as regular columns on different segments of the securities markets.

   Magazines. A bi-weekly, Forbes, is an excellent source of investment ideas--one we read on a regular basis. It offers a generous selection of articles on various companies and investment topics, as well as columnists with opinions on specific market segments and activities.

   Other good magazines are Business Week, Financial World and Fortune.

2. **Brokerage Firms**

   Investment information is easily obtainable from brokers, in both oral and written form. Most brokerage firms publish newsletters and research reports on individual stocks and industries. These contain recommendations as well as updated coverage of the economic and business outlook. They also subscribe to various investment publications, including the ones described below, and their use is provided free to clients.

3. **Investment Publications**

   Value Line Investment Survey. This is the largest and best known investment advisory service, which covers 1700 stocks on a regular basis. Besides being a handy reference on financial data, Value Line also *recommends* stock and industry groups to buy. For example, it ranks each company in terms of "timeliness" and "safety." It also ranks the expected performance of over 90 industries from best to worst. This service is *must* reading for the serious investor.

   Standard & Poor's. This advisory service has several publications deserving your attention. The S&P Stock Guide and Stock Reports provide key financial data and statistics on over 5,000 stocks. For specific investment ideas, The Outlook provides weekly recommendations on particular stocks and industries. It also contains special articles, reports on stocks in favor and assessments of the stock market's current performance and its outlook. An excellent source.

The most obvious reason for this is that investors collectively buy (sell) on the basis of what they think is going to happen to business conditions--not what they currently *see* happening.

CONCLUSION: Being able to forecast peaks and troughs in the business cycle should improve your ability to determine major turning points in the stock market.

The Business Cycle and Individual Stock Prices

The next step is to take the relationship between business and stock market cycles and extend it to individual stocks. That is, at different points in the business cycle, certain industries and their stocks tend to outperform the market in general, while others tend to underperform. For example, common stocks in consumer durable goods industries, e.g., autos, housing and appliances, typically perform best during the first year of an economic recovery, peak relative to the market in the second, and underperform as the expansion matures into the third year. The reason is because consumers' pent-up demand for these products is usually satisfied within 1-2 years during an economic recovery.

Also, because the *best* periods for stock market performance are in the latter stages of a recession and the beginning stages of an economic recovery, substantial research has gone into establishing which industry groups (individual stocks) are most likely to outperform the broad market during the early stages of a bull market.

As a convenient reference, Exhibit 12-3 presents the results from a Merrill Lynch study into relative stock group performance over complete business cycles. Exhibit 12-4 presents the same information in graphical form.

Some of the more important findings of this study were:
1. The best performing industries in the *early phase* of a bull market are characterized by

- High (beta) risk, and
- Superior growth qualities or high sensitivity to the expected turning of the business cycle, e.g., credit-sensitive stocks, such as construction and building materials, that benefit from declines in interest rates.

2. The best performing industries during the *middle-to-late phases* are characterized by
- Low (beta) risk, and
- Those more defensive in nature, e.g., utilities, or those that benefit from high factory utilization (that is, greater than 80-82% of manufacturing capacity), e.g., cyclical industries that produce capital (non-consumer) goods used to expand plant capacity.

WARNING: These observations are not hard, fast mechanical rules to follow--they're just *measures of tendency* that have appeared *in the past*. Exceptions are too easy to find. For example, during the bull market that began in 1982, energy and many cyclical stocks did not mimic their "predicted behavior." The oil glut and record foreign imports of manufactured goods totally disrupted the usual pattern these stocks followed in the past.

LESSON: Let the past be a guide only. You still need to assess whether companies' operating characteristics and sensitivity to past business cycles have changed AND whether or not expected events have already been discounted by the market.

GUIDELINES FOR SELECTING INDIVIDUAL STOCKS

Finding winning stocks is not particularly easy. It requires patience, constant diligence, the discipline to stick with established rules for selecting stocks, and often a willingness to go against prevailing opinion.

Moreover, there's plenty of competition facing you. Today, for example, 75% of the trading on the New York Stock Exchange is done by professional money managers of pension and mutual funds. In a sense, then, they have become the market. So, does this eliminate your

Exhibit 12-3
The Business Cycle and Relative Stock Performance

Master Group	Dominant Investment Characteristics	Best Relative Performance	Worst Relative Performance
Cyclical Stocks:			
Credit cyclicals	Sensitive to interest rates--performance best when interest rates low. Most groups building-related.	Early and middle bull markets.	Early and middle bear markets, with the exception of forest products.
Consumer cyclicals	Consumer durables and non-durables. Profits vary with economic cycle.	Early and middle bull markets.	Early and middle bear markets. Exception is hotel/motels.
Capital goods . . . . (cyclicals only)	Many groups depend on capacity utilization.	Middle and late bull markets.	Late bear markets.
Energy . . . . (cyclicals only)	Closely tied to economic cycle.	Early bull markets.	Early bear markets.
Basic industries	Profits depend on industrial capacity utilization. Prices may benefit from supply shortages near economic peaks.	Early and middle bear markets. Economic peaks.	Early or middle bull markets, depending on source of demand for products.
Financial	Interest-rate sensitive, e.g., banks, insurance, and gold mining.	Late bull and late bear markets. Economic troughs.	Early bull markets.
Transportation	Surface transportation.	Early bull markets.	Early bear markets.
Defensive Stocks:			
Defensive consumer . . . . staples	Nonvolatile consumer goods.	Late bear markets.	Early bull markets.
Energy . . . . (defensive only)	Major international and domestic oils. Volatility introduced by OPEC power.	Late bear markets.	Early bull markets.
Utilities	Large liquidity and operating stability.	Late bear markets.	Early bull markets.
Growth Stocks:			
Consumer growth	Combination of growth and defensive characteristics. Several subgroups: offer high yields.	Cosmetics, soft drinks, and drugs: late bear markets. Other subgroups: early bull markets.	Cosmetics, soft drinks, and drugs do not vary in any regular cyclical pattern for this group. Other subgroups: late bear markets.
Capital goods- . . . . technology Capital goods- (growth only)	Linked to capital investment spending cycle, which tends to lags behind the economic cycle.	Early and middle bull markets.	Late bear markets.
Energy . . . . (growth only)	Linked to economic cycle and to OPEC.	Early bull markets but varies.	Varies.

SOURCE: Merrill Lynch, Pierce, Fenner & Smith

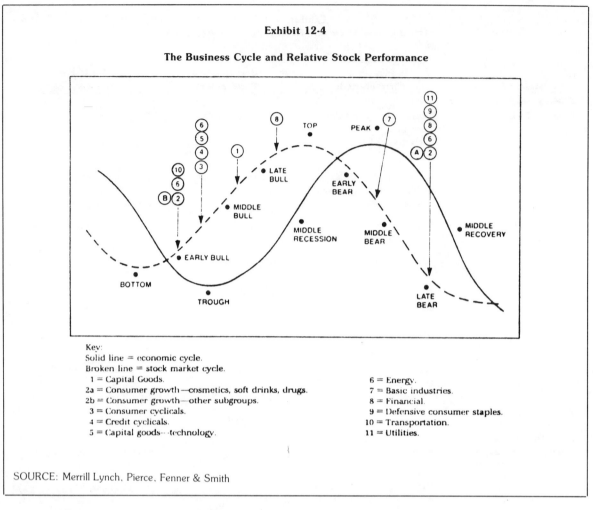

Exhibit 12-4

The Business Cycle and Relative Stock Performance

Key:
Solid line = economic cycle.
Broken line = stock market cycle.
  1 = Capital Goods.
  2a = Consumer growth—cosmetics, soft drinks, drugs.
  2b = Consumer growth—other subgroups.
  3 = Consumer cyclicals.
  4 = Credit cyclicals.
  5 = Capital goods—technology.

  6 = Energy.
  7 = Basic industries.
  8 = Financial.
  9 = Defensive consumer staples.
  10 = Transportation.
  11 = Utilities.

SOURCE: Merrill Lynch, Pierce, Fenner & Smith

chances of finding winning stocks? The answer is a definite NO!

But what you do need to do is stay out of their way. Keep in mind that institutional investors have a very *short-term* orientation. Their return performance is tabulated every quarter, so to keep and attract clients they must aggressively pursue short-term goals.

Also, this orientation breeds a "lemming instinct" that causes these pros to overpay for exciting concepts (who wants to be out of investment fashion?) and then to stampede at the first sign of trouble. What all this means is that you need to adopt a strategy that keeps you out of the way of the thundering herd.

Below, we present several such strategies that should improve your batting average in scoring with stocks. These strategies represent time-tested ideas that have been used by successful investors.

Selecting Out-of-Favor Stocks: The "Sleeping Beauty" Approach

The best place to start looking for undervalued stocks is among those that are "out-of-favor." This is not fast, double-your-money-overnight investing. Rather, it's a long-term strategy that requires patience to bear fruit.

One reason for being out-of-favor is that such stocks have *no visibility* or *sponsorship*. For example, they may be *fallen institutional favorites*, but they could be prime pickings because there's relatively little risk that their deflated prices will decline much further.

Another reason may be that they're too small to attract much attention from institutions. What you're attempting to do is to discover stocks *priced by the market below their intrinsic value--* and to do it before the rest of the world finds out and bids them up.

REMEMBER: To be successful, you must be prepared to wait out the market, which may be slow to recognize a particular stock's merits. In other words, if you buy value stocks right, your chief risk is boredom.

All right, so what do you look for?

1. *Low P/E Ratio.* Undervalued stocks typically have low P/E ratios (less than 7), not only low in an absolute sense, but also relative to the market and its industry. A stock that is priced low relative to the underlying value of the company has the potential for above-average future price performance. One yardstick is that the current P/E ratio be less than 40% of the highest P/E ratio the stock had over the past 5 years.

2. *Dividend Yield.* Preferably, a company should be paying a dividend, and the higher the dividend yield the better (greater than 6%). A high dividend yield serves to buffer a stock from further price declines, plus you can collect income while you wait for the stock to go up. Just make sure a dividend cut is not imminent.

3. *Book Value Per Share.* Market value per share should be less than book value per share. *RULE OF THUMB:* Current stock price is below 2/3s of book value per share.

4. *Liquidity.* It should have a current ratio of two or more. Better yet, an almost sure (but rare) buy is if a stock's price is less than its *net current asset value per share--* a computation that excludes the value of plant and equipment, i.e., long-term assets. A stock's net current asset value per share is current assets minus current liabilities and long-term debt, divided by the number of shares outstanding.

5. *Return on Equity.* Sometimes a firm can have low earnings but still be healthy for the long-term. Check out its 5-year average return on shareholders' equity. The typical stock earns 9-11% on equity, so anything over 10% is a plus.

6. *Sound, Simple Finances.* Ideally, a company should have little or no long-term debt. You want money to go into business expansion, not interest payments. Moreover, low-debt firms are better able to ride out rough times. If debt is more than 35% of shareholders' equity, look elsewhere.

7. *Size.* One way to stay out of the domain of the institutional investor is to stay with smaller firms. Firms with less than $50-$200 million in market value often lack institutional attention yet are large enough to reduce your chances they'll go under. Regardless of size however, you want to screen out stocks that have over 10% institutional ownership of the shares outstanding.

What Have We Learned? Make sure a company is small-to-medium sized, is strong financially, has a good yield, and a reasonable 5-year earnings and dividend growth record. If these check out and the stock has been battered down (low P/E), chances are you will do well.

Selecting High-Yielding Stocks *

A much simpler strategy that's very similar to buying "sleeping beauty" stocks is to focus only on stocks yielding more than 7%-8%. By nature, this strategy makes money because it's a conservative approach that requires patience. Most investors by design or temperament, can't afford to adopt such a strategy. Moreover, this strategy improves your chances of winning for two other reasons:

1. High income stocks have *downside protection.* That is, their price shouldn't fall much farther because this would make their yields even higher. And, remember, there's an upper limit to how far this can

---

* This, for example, is a strategy that has been successfully used by Fidelity's Equity-Income mutual fund as well as other money managers.

go--it's rare that a stock's yield will ever be greater than a bond's yield. On the other hand, this doesn't necessarily mean they don't have upside potential, if you properly select your stocks.

High-yield stocks typically are experiencing problems or at least appear to be--low growth, operating or financial difficulties, unappealing products, etc. That's why they have a higher yield--they are being shunned by investors. This means you are starting with a stock that's already down in price relative to the rest of the market. Thus, such stocks provide you with an opportunity, if you do your homework, to buy only those down-and-outers that are going to improve eventually.

You see, there are two ways such stocks can make you money. First, they are going to improve relative to expectations. Second, even if they aren't going to improve soon, the stock market has already oversold them and discounted the problems or apparent problems. You are starting, almost by definition, with a universe of depressed or cheap stocks.

2. Another reason you can make money is that, compared to a growth stock, your yield is already up around 8%, whereas the average growth stock has an average gross yield of less than 2%. So, you start out at the beginning of the year with a "built-in" 8% return even if nothing happens that year. In other words, you've got a 6% differential over a growth stock year in and year out. And, if you consider the compounding of your income, it's not easy for a growth stock to beat that over the long haul.

But, as you would expect, don't go out and wildly buy everything yielding more than 8%. First, there are certain stocks that perennially carry a high yield, e.g., utility and real estate stocks. Buying just these stocks will give you a poorly diversified portfolio. Second, you need to do some screening. For example, avoid companies with very high debt ratios or those that have had a history of problems. In a nutshell, you want to assess whether things are getting worse or getting better. A high dividend yield can quickly evaporate if a company cuts or eliminates its dividend.

Finally, the high-yield strategy also offers a disciplined rule for selling a stock. A sell decision would be triggered when a stock has run up and the yield has declined to the point where it's below the yield on a stock market index such as the S&P 500. This way you can automatically lock in your profits and recycle them into another slow grower.

To take an example of how this might work, assume you buy a stock yielding 8%. After a period of time, the stock price moves up such that its yield falls to 4%. Note that, if the dividend hasn't changed, this implies a doubling in price or a 100% return.

Selecting Quality Growth Stocks

If you're looking for fast growth in the stock market, you're investing for capital gains, which means your attention will gravitate toward growth stocks.

Growth stocks are those whose sales and earnings have grown at above-average rates (over 15% a year) and whose sales and earnings are still in a long-range phase of expansion. Examples are the computer, hospital management and electronics industries.

REMEMBER: The greater the potential payoff, however, the greater the risk.

Given their risk, is there any way to improve your odds of success? Charles Allmon, editor of *Growth Stock Outlook*, has found an extremely successful method for finding growth stocks. His success is borne out by his having the distinction of being the only investment advisor to outperform the popular market averages *every year* since 1980. To top that, he's averaged a 21% a year gain over the last 10 years. Let's examine his thinking.

His enviable record has been amassed by

discarding the usual (high-flying) growth stocks, such as "hi-techs." He believes there are too few opportunities to buy them at reasonable prices (they've already been discovered by other investors), and too many are like comets--burning brightly for a few years, only to fade into obscurity thereafter.

Instead, he prefers "low-tech," unrecognized growth stocks. To take an example, he likes stocks with special market niches--a company that makes paper forms for computer printers rather than a computer manufacturer. A better computer can always be invented tomorrow, but it's unlikely that someone will reinvent paper. In other words, he likes companies that *support* or *service* high-growth industries rather than those companies in high-growth industries.

Exhibit 12-5 presents the 6 selection criteria he has successfully used to select growth stocks.

Exhibit 12-5

Charles Allmon's Selection Criteria for Quality Growth Stocks

1. *Earnings*--growing by at least 15% a year over the last 3-4 years.
2. *Sales*--also increasing at least 15% annually. Sales growth needs to keep pace with earnings growth; otherwise, profit margins are being stretched--and that can't go on indefinitely.
3. *Return on equity*--usually 20-25%. Occasionally a lower return is acceptable, BUT only if it has been increasing substantially in the last year or two.
4. *Debt usage*--ideally, no long-term debt or as little leverage as possible. A highly leveraged company will have an inflated return on equity which can disguise a deteriorating balance sheet.
5. *Liquidity*--current assets at least twice current liabilities.
6. *P/E ratio*--if a stock passes the first five tests, only buy if the P/E ratio is no more than 15 and, preferably, at a discount to the market's P/E.

SOURCE: Stock Market Innovators, Profiles, Ltd., March 15, 1984.

Avoiding the Losers

Perhaps the real secret to successful investing is not by picking winning stocks buy by *avoiding losers*.

Truly big winners are rare. Besides, you must examine a large number of securities in order to find a few potential high-flyers. This reduces the time and other resources you can devote to researching each security and so increases the chances that you'll make mistakes.

The "loss-avoider," instead of uncovering favorable factors (analysis and brokers have already spread the word on these), looks for harder-to-come-by negative information; that is, he/she looks for reasons *not* to buy a stock. For example, is there heavy insider selling? Has its dividend been cut recently? Debt-to-equity ratio too high? Are institutional investors selling the stock?

On the latter, "following the herd" has often been the right way to go in certain situations. That is, extensive selling of stocks by institutions is usually followed by subsequent price declines. To help you on this, Barron's has a quarterly survey of institutional transactions in which they list the top 50 stocks sold as well as those industries sold the heaviest during the latest quarter.

SUGGESTED STOCK SELECTION FORMAT

Stock selection (or the current buzzword "stock screening") requires you to gather and analyze data and information in some systematic manner. You can think of it as a step-by-step process. That is, you want to organize your decision-making to insure that the relevant data and information is evaluated in a logical and consistent sequence that leads you to a purchase, sale or reject decision.

To help you tie together the various attributes of wining stocks discussed so far, Worksheet No. 7 provides a stock selection format that you can follow in picking stocks. (You may want to make photocopies of the worksheet for future reference.)

The initial screen is used to identify smaller stocks that have little institutional interest. However, you can use this format for larger, better-known stocks simply by skipping the initial screen section. Moreover, you can easily modify this format to reflect other data and information that you prefer to evaluate or to include selection rules of your own design.

DECIDING WHEN TO SELL *

A difficult, yet more important, decision than when or what to buy is *when to sell*. As Charles Allmon, editor of the *Growth Stock Outlook* newsletter, put it: "Any fool can buy stocks. The real test is how much you have left after you've sold."

While there are no easy answers, there are a number of guidelines that successful investors use. Remember, though, they won't do you any good unless you have the discipline to follow through on them--don't second-guess yourself or the market.

Referring to Exhibit 12-6, a checklist is provided of those things to watch for or evaluate.

Exhibit 12-6
Early Warning Signals for Selling Stocks

	YES	NO
1. Have you achieved your investment goals?	☐	☐
2. Has the company's fundamental outlook changed?	☐	☐
3. Is the stock becoming overvalued?	☐	☐
4. Has an economic recovery been in progress for 1-2 years (and/or is the bull market over 2 years old)?	☐	☐
5. Are mutual funds almost fully invested?	☐	☐

If you answer "YES" to 3 or more of these 5 questions, then you need to seriously consider selling.

---

1. *Have you achieved your investment objective?* Setting a goal as to what you expect from a stock should be your *first step*. For example, experts suggest that you sell a stock if it increases 50% in 2 years or doubles in price.
2. *Has the company's earnings or fundamental outlook changed?* Sell if you perceive a deterioration in a company's earnings or fundamental outlook. We say *perceive*

---

* Adapted in part from R. Runde, "How to Tell When to Sell," Money, January 1984.

because if you wait until it's obvious, it's *too late!*

But how do you know a change is occurring? Watch the stock's price behavior. Cut your losses if a stock falls 15-20% from where you bought it, OR it's gone nowhere for the last 2 years. Better-informed investors may be a step ahead of you.

3. *Is the stock becoming overvalued?* Several rules-of-thumb can be used here. Is the P/E ratio significantly higher than its 10-year average, e.g., 30-40% higher? Or, is it at the upper end of its historical range? If so, the stock may have reached its high for the moment.

Another clue that a stock is becoming overpriced is if the ratio of its market price to its book value per share is over 5. Typically, this ratio is between 1 and 3.

4. *Has an economic recovery been in progress for 1-2 years (and/or is the bull market over 2 years old)?* You need to keep up with where the economy is heading. In recent history, economic cycles have tended to follow a pattern of 2 years of growth and about a year of decline.

As we learned earlier, an important indicator of economic progress is the stock market itself. A bull market begins about 1-3 months before a recession ends, on average, and tends to peak before an economic downturn is evident. Remember, we've never had a recovery or recession that wasn't anticipated beforehand by the stock market.

Also, keep an eye on a bull market's *age*. A bull market typically lasts about 2½ years, followed by a 1 to 1½ year downturn.

5. *Are mutual funds almost fully invested?* When mutual funds hold less than 5% in cash, that's a *bearish* indicator. It means that they are already completely into the market. Since fund managers are *trend followers*, a bull market is well under way

by the time they are fully invested. In contrast, when more than 10% of their assets are in cash, it's *bullish* because when they invest that money in stocks, this will push prices higher.

Information on funds' cash position is often reported in the "Abreast of Market" section of The Wall Street Journal as well as other financial newspapers.

TAX REFORM AND COMMON STOCKS

In time, tax reform will benefit common stocks in general. First, economists believe that closing tax loopholes and eliminating tax preferences will mean a more efficient allocation of investment capital to areas of the economy where profits and potential for economic growth are highest. Another benefit is that tax reform should lead to lower interest rates (lower corporate borrowing costs translate into higher profits, plus a lower level of interest rates is always good for stock prices). On the other hand, all this is tempered by a forecast of higher corporate taxes.

As always, there will be winners and losers. *The winners:* Consumer-related companies such as those in retailing, household products, food, tobacco, and newspaper publishing and other media (advertising). The reason: Consumers will have additional disposable income to buy more of their products because of cuts in personal income taxes. Service-oriented companies are winners too, especially because they will see their high tax rates fall. *The losers:* Companies that invest heavily in plant and equipment and are used to low tax rates--aluminum, chemicals, machinery, steel and other companies in basic (heavy) industries.

From an investor's perspective, tax reform's most important provision is the elimination of special tax treatment for long-term capital gains, which increased from a maximum 20% to 28% for those in the top tax bracket. More specifically, all gains--both short and long-term--are taxed at the same rate as your regular income.

One immediate implication of all this is that the smart investor will downplay stocks for potential capital appreciation. Instead, dividends will be sought as intently as potential capital gains. Because of this focus on current income, companies with high cash flow and dividend payouts, especially those with the ability to increase their dividends on a regular basis, become very attractive. This means bank, oil and utility stocks with their high dividend yields will be particularly favored.

Nevertheless, it's not necessarily true that growth stocks will fall into disrepute. Take a look at Exhibit 12-7. Historically, growth stocks have averaged annual dividend yields of about 1% and capital appreciation of about 12%. Compare this with the 5% yield and 2.5% appreciation for more income-oriented stocks. Even though the maximum capital gains rate moved up to 28% from 20% under tax reform, notice that growth stocks may still offer higher after-tax returns than high-yielding stocks (or bonds for that matter). So, over the long run, aggressive growth stocks may retain their advantage over more conservative, high-yield stocks. True, the advantage has been diminished, BUT it's still there. Of course, the choice is yours.

Exhibit 12-7
High-Yield vs. Growth

High-yield stocks are appealing under the new tax bill, but growth stocks still offer highest return.

	AFTER-TAX RETURN		
	Old Law[1]	New Law[2]	% Change
Income stock:			
5% yield			
2.5% annual appreciation	4.50%	5.40%	+20
Growth stock:			
1% yield			
12% annual appreciation	10.10%	9.36%	−7

[1] After-tax return calculated on a 50% tax rate for interest/dividends and 20% for capital gains.

[2] After-tax return based on a 28% tax rate for interest/dividends and capital gains.

SOURCE: "An Appraisal: Money Managers Take a Second Look at the Tax Bill, "The Wall Street Journal (August 25, 1986).

TERMS TO KNOW

Following the herd
"Hi-tech" stocks
Low P/E stocks
"Low-tech" stocks
Net current asset value per share
Out-of-favor stocks
Quality growth stocks
"Sleeping Beauty" stocks

13 PREDICTING STOCK MARKET PRICES: TIMING FOR EXTRA PROFITS

Chapter Objectives

1. To Define What Technical or Market Analysis is and How it Can be Used to Time Your Investments
2. To Familiarize you with the Major Market Indexes Whose Movements Describe Different Segments of the Stock Market and Different Types of Stocks
3. To Learn How to Analyze Market Trends Using Price-Volume Momentum, Investor Sentiment and Market Cycle Theory

---

In Chapters 10-12, we saw how stocks are evaluated in terms of their underlying economic and financial factors. The future growth in company sales, earnings and dividends as well as the future prospects for its industry and the general economy were the important considerations in this analysis.

This particular approach is designed to assess *long-term* values compared to current market prices. It was called *fundamental analysis* because it dealt with fundamental economic factors that determine value.

Another approach is to focus on *timing--when to buy and sell securities*. While you can make money by investing in quality securities--if you're patient--good timing is a way to produce greater profits (smaller losses) sooner.

This chapter explores a timing approach referred to as *market* or *technical analysis*. It is based on the ideas that

- common stock prices tend to move together, and
- these prices are determined by investors' demand for and supply of securities.

PURPOSE OF MARKET ANALYSIS

You have probably heard or read: "The market pulled back sharply today but on light volume" or "After four days of strong advances, the market fell to profit taking."

Such descriptions can be found daily in your newspaper as analysts try to interpret stock market behavior. They are trying to interpret "What story the market is telling." These

statements use market analysis as an underlying basis for explaining market action.

Market analysis' real purpose, however, is *timing--predicting short-term price movements in either individual stocks or the level of market indices* such as the Dow Jones Industrial Average.

This is done by analyzing the day-to-day changes in prices and trading volume, investor sentiment and other technical indicators. So technicians are primarily interested in *price changes rather than price levels* and, more specifically, in *forecasting trends* in prices.

BASIC RATIONALE FOR MARKET ANALYSIS

Investors rarely agree on price (if they agreed, there would be very little trading!). This means prices are determined by the demand for and supply of stocks. And demand and supply are based on how optimistic or pessimistic investors are.

Once an overall mood is established, it's likely to continue for the near term. Technical indicators are used to detect this mood and, thereby, interpret the market's psychology.

Underlying market analysis is the assumption that price changes persist long enough to profit from them. This occurs because investors don't receive or interpret information equally.

For instance, professional investors follow the market daily. They continually look for new information that will affect stock prices.

In that sense, they have an edge on you in

learning of new developments. But, as prices adjust to this new information, they tend to move in a trend. This means market analysis is more useful for *trading* stocks than for long-term investing.

By watching market behavior, technicians try to predict future price changes. What is important is to recognize *quickly* a change in the demand-supply situation and take appropriate action.

Why a change is occurring is *not* important. Rather, the fact that *it is taking place* is all that matters.

To summarize the underlying basis for technical analysis,

- Price changes are determined by demand and supply.
- Fundamental as well as psychological factors affect demand and supply.
- The adjustment to new information takes time and causes prices to move in trends.
- Trends and changes in trends can be detected by studying price movements, trading volume and investor sentiment.

DEFINING THE MARKET'S OVERALL TREND

Market trends are either "bullish" or "bearish." If stock prices are *trending up* overall, this is *bullish* (a bull market). If prices are *falling* overall, this is *bearish* (a bear market).

Bull markets are *favorable* periods for investing. They reflect investor optimism, economic growth and stimulative actions by the federal government.

Bear markets, on the other hand, are *unfavorable* times for investing. They are described by investor pessimism, declines in economic growth and governmental restraint.

From this, we can see that *changes* in market trends are determined by changes in

- Investor sentiment
- Economic activity
- Government decisions to stimulate (slow down) economic growth.

Fortunately, market trends over the last 40 years have been dominated by bull markets,

which tend to be longer in duration (2½—3 years on average), while bear markets last an average of 1½ years.

MEASURES OF MARKET PERFORMANCE: STOCK MARKET INDEXES

To measure the general movements of stock prices, we need to be familiar with the different market indexes that reflect these movements. All market indexes are based on the average prices of the stocks that make up a particular index. There are five general market indexes that are commonly referred to by analysts:

1. Dow Jones Industrial Average (DJIA)
2. Standard & Poor's 500 Composite Index (S&P 500)
3. New York Stock Exchange Composite Index (NYSE Composite)
4. American Stock Exchange Index (ASE Index)
5. NASDAQ OTC Composite Index

Changes in each index describe *different types of stocks and different segments of the market.* For example, the DJIA reflects the behavior of 30 major industrial stocks.

In addition to these general market indexes, there are a number of indexes describing specific *industries* or *types of securities.* Exhibit 13-1 contains a list of these indexes.

DJIA

The oldest and best-known stock index is the *Dow Jones Industrial Average.* The "Dow" is an average of 30 high-quality ("blue-chip") industrial companies.

The 30 stocks' prices are simply added up and divided by a number called the divisor.

When analysts refer to the "market" or "how the market did today," they usually mean the DJIA. While Dow Jones has three other indexes (see Exhibit 13-1), the DJIA is the most commonly cited stock market average.

S&P 500

The *Standard & Poor's 500 Composite Index* is composed of the largest 500 (out of 2100) companies traded on the NYSE--400 industrials, 20 transportations, 40 utilities and 40 financials.

Because this index's stocks represent those issues most widely held by institutions, it is the one most frequently referred to by money managers.

S&P 500 vs. Dow

Although the Dow and S&P 500 indexes tend to move together over time, their movements differ in magnitude. The reasons why are

1. *Coverage.* The S&P index obviously covers a larger number and broader range of stocks.
2. *Construction.* The S&P index is a "true index," whereas the Dow is an average of prices.

   The S&P is a value-weighted index, based on an index = 10 for the 1941-43 time period. That is, the index value is weighted by the number of shares a firm has outstanding as well as the price per share.

   This means relatively large companies such as IBM receive more weight in determining the index value because of their relative importance in the market.

In contrast, the DJIA is *price-weighted* (a simple average) only--each stock has an equal impact on the average. Also, because of stock splits over time, the divisor is not "30" but a much smaller number.

3. *Interpretation.* The S&P index value represents the average price per share of the 500 stocks in the index. For example, a "1 point" change means the stocks' average price changed by $1 per share.

   Also, if the index value is "180," this means the average stock has increased in value from 10 in 1943 to 180, or 1800%.

   However, a "1 point" change in the Dow does not mean $1 in the value of an average share. Rather it amounts to about 10 cents per share.

   While the Dow suffers many weaknesses in its construction and interpretation, it remains the mainstay of "what the market is doing." Remember though that professional investors watch the S&P more closely because it is a better indicator of overall market behavior.

NYSE Composite

The *New York Stock Exchange Composite Index* includes all 2100 stocks listed on the NYSE. It's computed on the same basis as the S&P 500. Its base year is 1965 when the index began with a value of 50.

AMEX Index

The *American Stock Exchange Index* covers all stocks traded on the ASE and is also *value-weighted*. Its base year is 1973 when the index began at 100.

NASDAQ OTC Composite

The National Association of Security Dealers (NASD) publishes an OTC Composite index comprised of over 2,400 common stocks traded in the OTC market. Its base value of 100 was begun in 1971.

Because this index is also *value-weighted*, it's heavily influenced by the largest 100 stocks on the NASDAQ system.

All of these indices are reported on a daily basis in newspapers such as the Wall Street Journal or Investor's Daily and weekly in Barron's Financial Weekly.

ANALYZING MARKET TRENDS

Although there are *hundreds of technical indicators* that can be used in a market analysis, they can be grouped into three categories:
1. Price-Volume Momentum (the "Tape")
2. Investor Sentiment (Contrary Opinion Rules)
3. Market Cycles

Price-Volume Momentum

1. *Relationship of Price and Volume.* Technicians believe that changes in prices and trading volume are critical to predicting the future direction of stock prices, both on an individual stock or general market basis. This relationship can be best summarized as

   - Bullish: Prices decline on low and decreasing volume
   - Bullish: Prices increase on high and increasing volume
   - Bearish: Prices decline on high and increasing volume
   - Bearish: Prices increase on low and decreasing volume

   Essentially, this tells us that *both* bull and bear markets should exhibit *high* and *increasing* volume. Moreover, volume tends to lead price changes--both up and down.

   The rationale for these "rules" is that trading volume is an indicator of investor interest (optimism or pessimism) because volume results from the demand for or supply of stocks. For example, in a strong market, investors are demanding stocks-- and the greater their interest is, the higher the volume will be.

2. *Advance-Decline Line: Market Breadth.* On any day, some stocks go up in price (advance) while others go down (decline). An *advance-decline line* measures the cumulative net difference between the number of stocks advancing and declining over time.

   The logic of monitoring this information is to determine whether the price changes in a stock market average, such as the DJIA, are *also* being reflected by the market as a whole.

   For example, if the DJIA is increasing *and* the number of issues advancing is larger than those declining in price, the market is considered healthy. Moreover, the greater the difference between those advancing versus declining is, the stronger the market. On the other hand, if the Dow is advancing but the number of issues advancing is relatively small, then this means the market is technically weak. In essence, then, the Dow or other market index and the advance-decline line should both be working in the same direction to confirm the overall (primary) trend.

3. *Moving-Average Line.* Another way to detect a potential change in the market's primary trend is to compare a *moving average* of past price changes to current prices. A 10-day moving average is constructed by *summing* the last 10 days' closing prices and then dividing the total by 10. The relationship between the current price and the moving-average price is believed to indicate whether the overall market trend is still intact or is about to change.

   For example, one way to determine the primary (long-term) trend's future direction is to use a *200-day moving average.* If we are in a bull market, this should continue as long as the market averages are above their respective 200-day moving averages. If the current levels of the market averages should fall *below* their moving averages, then this indicates a potential reversal of the overall trend.

   A similar interpretation would be given if we are in a bear market. That is, market indexes' current prices should be below their respective moving averages, whereas a move *above* their moving averages signals a potential market reversal.

NOTE: A moving average can be constructed using *any* number of trading days. For instance, an intermediate-term moving average typically is based on 50 days (10 weeks) of past prices. A shorter-term indicator would be based on a 5- or 10-day moving average.

4. *New Highs and Lows.* An advancing (declining) market normally has an *increasing* number of stocks hitting new high (low) prices compared to their range of prices over the last 52 weeks. At the same time, the number of stocks hitting new lows (highs) should be decreasing.

Many technicians feel that when this typical pattern *diverges* from the overall movement of the stock averages, then the market is ripe for a change in direction in the near future.

Investor Sentiment: The Theory of Contrary Opinion

Investor sentiment indicators help determine whether the majority of investors are bullish or bearish.

A theory related to investor sentiment, known as the *Theory of Contrary Opinion,* says that the majority of investors are wrong *most* of the time. From this, for instance, if most investors are very bullish, you should trade in the opposite direction.

Below are five indicators you can use to assess the relative optimism/pessimism of *different types of investors:*

- Short Interest: Investors in General
- Odd-Lot Short Sales: Small Investors
- Mutual Fund Liquidity: Institutional Investors
- Investment Advisor Bearish Sentiment
- Corporate Insider Buying/Selling

1. *Short Interest: General Public's Sentiment.* Investors *short* a stock when they are bearish about its future prospects. The *total of all shares sold short* is called the *short interest.* Hence, the greater is investors' overall pessimism, the larger the short interest will be.

While such an occurrence would *appear* to be bearish for the market, it's actually *bullish!* The reason is because a short sale assures *future* demand for stock when the short position is covered. (Recall that a short sale eventually *has* to be covered, whereas a long position *never* has to be liquidated.)

What happens is that short sales put a "floor" under how far the market can fall. Moreover, if the short sellers are wrong and the market starts moving up, there will be a mad scramble to cover their shorts (buy stocks back) and this will add even more fuel to the market advance.

This means that when the *level of short interest* becomes *high,* you should become *optimistic* about the market's intermediate to long-term outlook. Conversely, if *short interest* is *low,* this is *bearish.*

Information on short interest is released around the 20th of each month and reported in the Wall Street Journal.

2. *Odd-Lot Short Sales: Small Investors' Sentiment.* To determine the mood of small investors, technicians monitor *odd-lot short sales,* i.e., sales of less than 100 shares. The reason is because the small investor, although generally correct, tends to "overreact" (is wrong) at major market tops and bottoms.

A related view is that the investing public is the last to get into (out of) the market. This normally occurs after *a bull (bear) market has run its course.*

The extent of odd-lot short-sales is watched because
- a short sale is a bearish trade and
- most investors are optimistic and consider short selling too risky.

Therefore, shorting is done only when they are *especially* bearish.

The most common way to measure small investor sentiment is to *divide the total shares sold short by the total shares sold.*

When this *percentage* is *greater than 3%*, small investors are *very pessimistic*. Contrary opinion then states that this is *bullish* for the market. Conversely, when this *percentage* is *less than 1%*, you should be *bearish* because the small investor is *too bullish*.

Information on odd-lot trading is available in the "Market Laboratory" section of Barron's Financial Weekly and in the Wall Street Journal.

3. *Mutual Fund Liquidity: Institutional Investors' Sentiment.* Another contrarian indicator is *mutual funds' cash position*. This is found by taking the *ratio of cash as a percentage of total assets* in institutional investors' portfolios. Over time, this percentage typically ranges from less than 5% to 15%.

Technicians contend that mutual funds (much like odd-lotters) are "wrong" at market tops and bottoms. This is, they hold *high* levels of cash (close to 15%) near the *bottom* of a market cycle--indicating their *bearish* attitude. Of course, this is exactly the point at which they should become bullish.

Conversely, *at market tops*, mutual funds tend to be *fully invested* (less that 5% cash)--indicating their *bullish* sentiment.

Your should then watch for mutual fund cash positions to be at an extreme in order to guide your investing strategy:
- When the cash ratio approaches 5%, begin to liquidate your portfolio.
- When the cash ratio approaches 12%-15%, begin to invest.

This information is a bit harder to obtain. It's often reported in the "Abreast of the Market" section of the Wall Street Journal. Alternatively, many investment advisory services report it as a regular feature in their newsletters.

4. *Investment Advisor Bearish Sentiment.* Another contrary opinion indicator is *investment advisor sentiment*. Technicians say that when *a large proportion* of investment advisory services are *bullish*, this signifies a market top near term, so you should be *bearish*. In contrast, if a large percentage are *bearish*, you should become *bullish*.

Specific levels to watch for are:
- If *more than 50%-60%* of investment advisors are *bearish*, this is a signal that you should become bullish.
- If *less than 10%* are *bearish*, this cautions you to the possibility that the market is topping out.

The *Investors Intelligence* investment advisory service provides an analysis of this index in its service. This information is often reported elsewhere such as in the Wall Street Journal, Barron's and different investment advisory services.

5. *Corporate Insider Buying/Selling: A Non-Contrarian Indicator.* Many technicians believe you should keep an eye on *corporate insiders' buying/selling* of their own firm's stock. An insider is defined as a director or executive officer, but it is also any stockholder who owns 10% or more of the outstanding shares.

Any time an insider buys or sells his company's stock, he or she must report it to the SEC within 10 days after the close of the calendar month. This disclosure is required to protect against fraud, i.e., the use of inside information to speculate in their own stock for profit.

Because insiders know more intimately how a firm is doing, analysts believe that monitoring insider transactions gives excellent clues to future earnings, dividends and stock market prospects. For instance, *net purchases* by insiders are a *bullish* indicator, while *net sales* are *bearish*.

A number of market newsletters cover

insider trading activities:

- <u>Consensus of Insiders</u> (Fort Lauderdale, FL)
- <u>Insider Indicator</u> (Portland, OR)
- <u>The Insider</u> (Fort Lauderdale, FL)
- <u>The Weekly Insider</u> (New York, NY)

Market Cycles

1. *Dow Theory.* One of the oldest and perhaps best-known theories of technical analysis is the Dow Theory, developed by Charles H. Dow in the late 1800s. This theory describes three types of price trends, analogous to the movement of ocean tides:
   - Primary (broad market) movements lasting several years--"tides."
   - Secondary (intermediate) movements lasting weeks or months--"waves."
   - Day-to-day movements occurring randomly within the primary/secondary moves--"ripples."

   The underlying logic is to recognize which way the major trend is going. Realizing that prices never go straight up or down, there will be important intermediate changes in the opposite direction or what is referred to as "corrections." These corrections represent periods in which investors are taking profits.

   However, the important features of this theory need to be kept in mind to provide profitable timing:

   A bullish (bearish) trend is still intact when a new high (low) is reached by the DJIA and is confirmed (soon followed by) a new high (low) on the Dow Jones Transportation Average or vice-versa.

   In other words, these two Dow Jones averages must *act together.* For instance, every recovery or rally that reaches a high point *above* the prior peak must be reached by *both* averages. If this doesn't happen, the primary trend is ripe for a permanent reversal.

2. *The Stock Market and Economic Recessions.* Stock market performance during recessions and the subsequent recoveries appear to follow a predictable pattern:
   - The stock market generally *rises during a recession;* i.e., the market usually turns up while the economy is still deep in recession.
   - *The deeper the recession,* the *more explosive the market's advance after* the recession.
   - The market tends to go nowhere in the following economic recovery.

   As we noted earlier, the average life of a bull market is 2½ years, while the average bear market lasts 1½ years.

   What these observations tell you is that you can
   - Consider selling your stocks, without giving up much potential gains, as much as *eight months before the economy peaks.*
   - Begin buying stocks *12 months after* a recession has begun.

   Of course, your *buy signal* requires no forecasting, but your *sell signal* does presume you know when an economic peak is near at hand. If you don't follow the economy closely, the sell signal may have little use.

3. *Election-Year Cycle.* For over 20 years, it has been documented that politicians tend to create an *expanding* economy in the two years immediately *before* a presidential election. The idea being that a good economy helps to reelect the incumbent party.

   The administration has typically used *fiscal policy* to stimulate the economy so that it expands over the *two-year period prior to the election.* While this can be done in many ways, the more common methods have been to *increase spending* or *cut taxes.* Moreover, the *Federal Reserve* has also contributed implicitly to this endeavor by *increasing the rate of growth in money supply.*

On the negative side, fueling the economy this way often results in freeing *inflationary* pressures *after* the election. This means that in the post-election period, the administration and Congress apply the brakes by stressing a *stringent* fiscal policy. The result is usually a *recession*, with the economy hitting bottom in the second year following an election.

Because the stock market is a *leading* indicator of the economy, there has been a strong correlation between a *four-year* stock market cycle and the *four-year presidential election cycle*. That is, the stock market has tended to

- advance strongly in the second year *before* an election
- continue to increase in the year *before* an election, and
- *peak* near the election in November, and
- *fall* for the *next two years*.

Exhibit 13-2 presents the annual investment results from investing in the DJIA over the four-year cycle for the last 20 years.

4. *Bellwether Stocks*. A stock market saying holds that "as GM goes, so goes the country." This is an example of using a *bellwether stock* to predict future stock price changes.

The idea is that a few major stocks such as *Exxon, GM, IBM* and *Merrill Lynch* are highly reliable in reflecting the current state of the stock market. That is, the price behavior of these stocks tends to track closely the overall movement in the market.

More importantly, market analysts believe that the overall *strength (weakness)* in these stocks foretells future market directions. For example, in a bull market, when a bellwether stock does not reach a new yearly high within 3-4 consecutive months, a market top is near. The reverse of this holds for bear markets--if the stock fails to make a new low for 3-4 months,

a market bottom is near.

Exhibit 13-2

Annual Investment Results from Investing in the DJIA Over the Four-Year Presidential Election Cycle

Date (Month's End)	DJIA	2 Years Before Elections	1 Year Before Elections	1 Year After Elections	2 Years After Elections
October 1963	755	28.1%			
1964	873		15.6%		
1965	961			10.1%	
1966	807				-16.0%
1967	880	9.0%			
1968	952		8.3%		
1969	856			-10.1%	
1970	755				-11.7%
1971	839	11.0%			
1972	955		13.9%		
1973	957			0.1%	
1974	665				-30.4%
1975	836	25.6%			
1976	965		15.4%		
1977	818			-15.2%	
1978	792				-3.2%
1979	816	2.9%			
1980	924		13.3%		
1981	852			-7.8%	
1982	992				16.3%
1983	1225	23.5%			
Average 1962-83		16.7%	13.3%	-4.6%	-9.0%
Years with Gains		6	5	2	1
Years with Losses		0	0	3	4

SOURCE: F. C. Allvine. "Presidential Elections and the Stock Market: Will the Cycle Hold?" AAII Journal, June 1984 , pp. 9-12.

A WORD OF CAUTION

Never rely on only one or two indicators for your buy-sell signals. Rather, use a consensus of a number of indicators to guide your market timing.

Any indicators will produce a false or no signal on occasion. If an indicator turns bullish, for instance, *double-check it by looking at the other indicators* to see if they confirm this change.

For example, Stan Weinstein, a highly-regarded technician and publisher of the popular Professional Tape Reader, uses 49 different technical indicators to forecast market directions.

Remember, you have time--significant changes in the market do not occur overnight.

TERMS TO KNOW

ASE Index
Advance-decline line
Bellwether stocks
Corporate insiders
Dow Jones Industrial Average
Dow Theory
Election year cycle
Fundamental analysis
Market breadth
Moving average line
NASDAQ OTC Composite Index
NYSE Composite Index
Odd-lot short sales
S&P 500 Composite Index
Short interest
Technical (market) analysis
Theory of Contrary Opinion

14 AN INTRODUCTION TO STOCK OPTIONS

Options are not bought for the usual benefits offered by other securities, e.g., interest and dividends. Rather they are purchased to acquire the right to *subsequently* buy or sell securities. (In that sense, they are an alternative to investing in a security.) The reason for doing this is that an option's expected return is greater than the underlying security (and so is its risk). As we'll see shortly, options can be used in a number of different ways:

*   to speculate in an attempt to grab a quick profit
*   to earn extra income on securities you own
*   to hedge existing positions

In today's market, you'll find options on a wide variety of securities--common stocks, stock market indices, Treasuries and commodities. In this chapter, though, we'll focus only on *stock* options that are listed on an exchange such as the Chicago Board Options Exchange (CBOE).

This may seem rather narrow but two reasons prompt us to do this: (1) almost all of the option trading volume is concentrated in stock options and (2) the basics of option trading are the same regardless which type of security you are dealing with.

Below, we introduce the *language* of options trading. At first, it could be overwhelming, but it's really not that complex after a little study. Next, the *mechanics* of options trading are presented, including the advantages and disadvantages of option trading.

Remember, though, options normally are not for the typical investor. While options trading can range from the most speculative to the very conservative, they do require a *thorough* understanding and careful weighing of their risks and potential rewards. In fact, at the very least, we suggest you master the basics of common stock investing before plunging into the world of options.

WHAT IS AN OPTION?

Listed options are *contracts* that give the holder the right to buy or sell a *prespecified* security at a *prespecified* price by a *prespecified* date. As the word "prespecified" indicates, all contract terms are standardized except for the price you pay for the option.

*   Prespecified security--*what* can be bought or sold and is referred to as the *underlying security*.
*   Prespecified price--the *price per share* paid for the stock if the option contract is exercised and is referred to as the *exercise* or *strike* price.
*   Prespecified date--the *expiration date*, which tells how long before the option expires.

There are two types of options:

1. *Call options* give the owner the right to *buy* 100 shares of a specific stock at a specific price.
2. *Put options* give the owner the right to *sell* 100 shares of a specific stock at a specific price.

While puts and calls differ only by the words "to buy" and "to sell," they are very distinct investments, and are used for entirely different

Exhibit 14-1
Effect on Options' Values When Different Variables Change

Type of Option	Investor Demand Increases (Falls)	Stock Price Increases (Falls)	Stock's Volatility Increases (Decreases)	Time to Expiration Increases (Decreases)	Interest Rates Rise (Fall)
Call Option's Value	Rises (Falls)	Rises (Falls)	Rises (Falls)	Rises (Falls)	Rises (Falls)
Put Option's Value	Rises (Falls)	Falls (Rises)	Rises (Falls)	Rises (Falls)	Falls (Rises)

purposes. For example, *calls* in effect are an expression of the buyer's optimism (bullish)--you buy calls if you expect stock prices to rise. Conversely, *puts* are bearish investments--you expect stock prices to fall.

OPTION TERMINOLOGY *

1. *Option Buyer (Holder or Owner).* The individual who obtains the *right* to exercise. Note that this is a right, *not an obligation.*
2. *Option Seller (Writer).* The individual who is *obligated*, if and when he or she is assigned an exercise notice, to perform according to the terms of the option contract.
3. *Exercise (Strike) Price.* For a *call*, the price per share at which the holder can *purchase* the underlying stock from the option writer. For a put, the price at which the holder can *sell* the underlying stock to the option writer. Which exercise prices are available depends on the stock price; that is, a new option *begins* to be traded once the underlying stock trades within $2 of the exercise price.
4. *Expiration Date.* Stock options expire on the Saturday following the third Friday of the expiration month. If an option reaches this date without being sold back or exercised, it ceases to exist ("expires worthless"). Expirations are based on a 3-month calendar cycle, e.g., January-April-July-

October. The longest lived option ever traded is 9 months.

5. *Premium.* The price paid by the buyer to the writer of an option. It's set in the marketplace by investors' demand and supply. Other variables that determine an option's value are
   • the relationship between the exercise price and the underlying stock's current price.
   • the volatility of the underlying stock.
   • the remaining time to expiration.
   • current level of interest rates.

Exhibit 14-1 tells you what happens to the value of an option when each of these variables change.

REMEMBER: Option premiums are simply and entirely a *non-refundable* payment for the right to buy or sell shares of a stock-they don't give you ownership in anything.

EXAMPLE: "Buy an IBM July 120 call at 5." This says you can buy a call option contract for $5 an option (i.e., $500 per contract) that gives the right to *purchase* 100 shares of IBM stock at $120 a share, regardless of what IBM's current market price is. This option will expire on the Saturday after the third Friday in July.

6. *"In-the-Money" Option.* A *call option* is "in-the-money" whenever its exercise price is *below* the current stock price. Conversely, a *put* option is "in-the-money" whenever its exercise price is *above* the current stock price. Such options are said to have *intrinsic value.*

---

* Adapted in part from "Characteristics and Risks of Standardized Options," Chicago: The Options Clearing Corporation, September, 1985.

7. *"Out-of-the-Money" Option.* An "out-of-the-money" *call* has an exercise price that is *above* the current stock price, while an "out-of-the-money" *put's* exercise price is *below* the current stock price. Such options have *no intrinsic value.*

HOW TO READ OPTION QUOTES

Let's now refer to Exhibit 14-2 to see how to read Ford's option quotes and to help you understand the various terms discussed so far. First, the current (closing) stock price was 44¾ or $44.75. Next, we have
1. *Exercise Prices.* The Ford options are offered with *two* different exercise (strike) prices: $40 and $45. (Exercise prices are set at $5 intervals.)
2. *Expiration Dates.* Each exercise price has 3 expiration months: September, December, and March. Note that, altogether, 12 different calls and puts are available.
3. *Premiums.* The Sept 40 *call's* premium is $4.75 per option (or $475 per contract), while the Sept 40 *put* is selling for ⅛ or $0.125 per option.

Exhibit 14-2
How to Read Stock Option Quotes

Trade Date: September 18
Options Exchange: CBOE

Option & NY Close	Strike Price	Calls-Last			Puts-Last		
		Sep	Dec	Mar	Sep	Dec	Mar
Ford							
44¾	40	4¾	5½	6¼	⅛	¾	1⅛
44¾	45	¾	1⅝	3	½	2	r*

*"r" means "not traded"

Some Observations on Option Pricing

First, notice that for a *given exercise price* (reading across the rows), the premium steadily increases from September to March. This occurs because of an option's time value. The *time value* of an option is that portion of an option's premium that represents what investors are will-

ing to pay in hopes that the option will increase in value as the stock price changes before the option expires. *And,* the farther away from expiration, the *greater* a put or call option's time value will be.

Second, for a given *expiration date* (reading down a column), a *call's* premium *decreases* but a *put's premium increases.* The reason is that the 40 call is "in-the-money" (has intrinsic value) but the 45 call is "out-of-the-money" (has no intrinsic value). With the puts, just the opposite occurs.

COMMISSIONS

Option commissions are determined as if you were trading a common stock. For instance, if you bought an option contract selling for $4 an option, your commission cost would be based as if you bought 100 shares of stock at $4 per share. Refer to Chapter 17 for further discussion on brokerage commissions.

LISTED OPTION EXCHANGES

Exchange-listed (negotiable) options began trading in 1973 on the CBOE. (Before then, only "over-the-counter" options were available, where option contracts were non-standardized and individually negotiated between the buyer and seller. This "market" still exists today for the non-listed options but it's very illiquid.)

The instant success of the CBOE led other exchanges to begin option trading (AMEX, NYSE, Pacific and Philadelphia). Today, over 400 common stocks have options traded on them.

THE OPTIONS CLEARING CORPORATION

Options are not issued by individual corporations. Rather, they are bought and sold through The Options Clearing Corporation (OCC). While the exchanges are used to match orders of buyers and sellers, the OCC is responsible for seeing that the option contracts are satisfied. This frees buyers and writers from one another. That is, you don't have to know whom you sold to or bought an option from.

For example, a call *writer* can terminate his/her obligation to deliver stock merely by buying back a call to offset the obligation. At the same time, however, the buyer can *still retain* all his rights--the OCC guarantees them.

WHY BUY OPTIONS?

Advantages

The major advantages of buying puts and calls are their speculative appeal in
- leveraging potential investment returns
- limiting potential losses
- reducing the required investment

A Call Option Example

To illustrate, let's say you are bullish on Delta Airline's stock, currently $40 a share. You could: (1) invest $4,000 in 100 shares or (2) invest only $400 to buy a Delta June 40 call, assuming a $4 premium.

Referring to Exhibit 14-3, let's see what risk and rewards these two strategies offer. If the stock rose to $50 before the option expires, you would make $1,000 on your stock investment for a 25% return. In contrast, you would gain $600 on your call option for a *150% return. The reason for this much higher return is that you needed less capital to buy the option in order to participate dollar-for-dollar* in the stock's appreciation.

A WORD OF CAUTION: A stock must appreciate enough to offset an option's premium before any profit is earned. In our example, the stock must increase 10% to $44 just to break even.

But, what if the stock ended up at $40 or below? Your option expires *worthless*. That is, you would lose 100% of your money, while your loss from buying the stock outright would be much less.

This example points out an important principle--the more leveraged an investment is, the greater the risk that a large percentage of it will be lost. In the case of options, as we just saw, you could lose everything. On the flip side, though, the more leveraged the investment is, the greater the potential reward--if you're right.

A final point. Notice that your *dollar* losses are limited to the option premium paid (or $400 in this example)--regardless how far the stock price falls. With the stock, your *dollar* losses continue to mount as the price falls.

Disadvantages

Major disadvantages of buying puts and calls are:
- No benefits of stock ownership
- Limited lives

For the price of the option, the only benefit an option buyer receives is the privilege of participating in a stock's price changes. Moreover,

---

Exhibit 14-3
How Options Affect Your Potential Risk and Rewards

Stock Price = $40

Call Option Premium = $4
Put Option Premium = $4

Delta's Stock Price at Option Expiration	STOCK Invest $4,000 in 100 shares		CALL Invest $400 in a June 40		PUT Invest $400 in a June 40	
	Profit (Loss)	Percent Return	Profit (Loss)	Percent Return	Profit (Loss)	Percent Return
$50	$1,000	25%	$600	150%	−$400	−100%
$45	$500	13%	$100	25%	−$400	−100%
$40	$0	0%	−$400	−100%	−$400	−100%
$35	−$500	−13%	−$400	−100%	$100	13%
$30	−$1,000	−25%	−$400	−100%	$600	150%

this right is good only until the option expires.

Remember, options are short-lived, i.e., they are "wasting assets" that have no value after expiration. Even if the stock price stands still, an option will lose value (its time premium) as it approaches expiration. On the other hand, if you had purchased the stock, you could continue owning it in the hope of realizing a profit.

WHY WRITE OPTIONS?

Advantages

Major advantages of writing options are:
- To earn extra income
- To hedge risk

The *most conservative option strategy* is to write call options against stocks you own (referred to as *covered option writing*). In doing so, you earn returns from the premiums you receive in addition to the stock's dividends and price appreciation.

NOTE: Naked options can also be written in which the underlying stock is not owned. However, naked option writing involves considerably more risk than covered option writing. In fact, it's the *riskiest* option strategy you can follow. Here's why. If the stock price rises and the call is exercised, the option writer must purchase the stock in the open market and deliver it to the buyer at the (lower) exercise price. Theoretically, then, your losses could be unlimited.

RULE OF THUMB: Write options on stocks when the total annual cash return--dividends plus call premiums minus brokers' commissions — is 1½ times the current 52-week T-bill rate.

Option premiums can also be used to offset part or all of your losses in a stock. For example, say you buy 100 shares of a $50 stock and write a 50 call for $4 an option. The stock can fall as much as $4 (to $46) before your losses begin. Moreover, if the option expires without being exercisable, you can write another option to generate more income, i.e., you can use the 100 shares over and over again to cover the writing of options.

Disadvantages

The major disadvantage of writing options is the foregone opportunity to benefit from an increase in the stock. That is, you give up the chance to profit from the stock's appreciation above the exercise price. Should such an increase occur (causing the option to be in-the-money as expiration approaches), your option will be *exercised against you*. One way to avoid this is to buy back an offsetting option prior to being assigned an exercise notice. Of course, you'll suffer a loss this way because you'll pay more for this option than for the option you initially wrote.

Exhibit 14-4 gives a summary of different option strategies classified by their risk profile.

Exhibit 14-4
Summary of Options Strategies by Risk Category

LOW-RISK STRATEGIES
1. Write call options on stocks you own.
2. Write put options on stocks you are willing to purchase now at current market prices.
3. Use part of dividend and interest income from your portfolio to buy call or put options.

HIGH-RISK STRATEGIES
1. Purchase put and call options.
2. Sell call options without owning the underlying stock.
3. Sell put options for speculation.

OTHER THINGS TO KEEP IN MIND

1. It's usually advisable to take your profits by acquiring an offsetting option rather than exercising it—your brokerage commissions and capital requirements will be less.
2. While you may be tempted to purchase an out-of-the-money option because little investment is required, there's only a small chance it'll ever become profitable. Most options expire worthless.
3. Put buying can be a conservative investment if it's used to *protect a profit* in an existing stock position. A put offers "insurance" agains a near term decline in stock price because you can always exercise it and sell the stock to the writer at the

higher exercise price OR sell the put and use the profits to offset your stock losses.

4. Most importantly, buying options to achieve increased leverage can be a profitable strategy IF your price expectations are realized within the allowed time. However, the possible loss of your *entire* investment makes this investment appropriate for only those individuals who understand and can afford the risks involved.

TERMS TO KNOW

At-the-money option
Call option
Covered writer
Exercise price
Expiration date
In-the-money option
Intrinsic value
Leverage
Naked writer
Option buyer (holder)
Option seller (writer)
Out-of-the-money option
Premium
Put option
Strike price
Time value of an option

OTHER POPULAR
INVESTMENTS

15

PROFIT FROM REAL ESTATE INVESTMENTS

<table>
<tr><td>

Chapter Objectives

1. Are Real Estate Investments for You?
2. Why Invest in Real Estate?
3. The Investment Merits of Different Types of Real Estate Investments
4. Guidelines and Suggestions for Selecting a Real Estate Investment

</td></tr>
</table>

Real estate has been a popular form of investment for both the small and large investor. Good reason--it's been a profitable investment. For instance, many people have watched their home purchased years ago turn out to be their most successful investment. But future success is not guaranteed. Knowledge, hard work and lots of patience are the first prerequisites if you want to profit from real estate. And, despite the drastic impact of the 1986 tax reform on real estate, opportunities in real estate still exist, plus it's an essential ingredient in a well-balanced portfolio.

In this chapter, we look at the investment merits of real estate and devote our attention to five ways to play the game:

- Home ownership
- Residential rent property
- Real estate investment trusts
- Real estate partnerships
- Master limited partnerships

Specific guidelines, tax features and other factors to consider are also presented. Remember, though, real estate values are cyclical and just because real estate has been one of the best investments in the past does not mean this trend will continue.

ARE REAL ESTATE INVESTMENTS FOR YOU?

You have doubtlessly seen ads or heard stories about getting rich (quick?) in real estate. You'll find the basic idea of how to invest successfully in real estate simple but not easy to apply. Furthermore, the new tax laws have dramatically altered the relative advantages and attractiveness of real estate. Below we examine

those advantages that are uniquely combined in this type of investment.

Tax Advantages

Real estate used to be a "tax-motivated" investment because it offered tax incentives that no other investment could offer. Essentially, it had the dual advantages of lowering taxes while increasing wealth through extensive tax deductions and a lower, preferential tax rate on its largest source of income--capital gains. Operating, mortgage interest, and other carrying costs were fully tax-deductible. Perhaps more importantly, property (except for land) could be depreciated for tax purposes while its market value appreciated. Most of these advantages have now been either reduced or eliminated such that real estate decisions are once again based on economic rather than tax reasons.

Perhaps the most major change is the reclassification of rental income as "passive income" instead of as "investment income." Briefly, there are three income categories for tax purposes:

- *Regular income,* i.e., salary, wages, tips and bonuses
- *Investment income,* i.e., interest, dividends, and capital gains/losses
- *Passive income,* i.e., rents, royalties and other income from business activities where you aren't regularly involved in management

Essentially, this change means that interest, property taxes and other "passive" expenses or losses incurred in a real estate venture must be applied against passive income. Any excess losses, however, can be carried over to future

Exhibit 15-1
Pooled Real Estate Funds' Risk and Returns Compared to the S&P 500 and the CPI Inflation Index, 1975-1983 [a]

Year	Pooled Real Estate Funds			S&P 500 Stocks			Consumer Price Index
	Unrealized Appreciation	Income Return	Total Return	Unrealized Appreciation	Income Return	Total Return	Total Return
1975	1.3%	8.6%	9.9%	4.0%	4.3%	8.3%	9.1%
1976	2.4	8.8	11.2	18.4	3.8	22.2	5.8
1977	3.1	8.9	12.0	-3.7	4.6	0.9	6.5
1978	7.7	9.6	17.3	-2.2	5.3	3.1	7.7
1979	10.9	9.7	20.6	7.3	5.5	12.8	11.3
1980	8.8	9.3	18.1	15.3	5.3	20.6	13.5
1981	7.7	9.0	16.7	7.8	5.2	13.0	10.4
1982	0.0	8.5	8.5	-6.5	5.8	-0.7	6.1
1983	3.9[b]	8.4[b]	12.3	34.0	4.4	38.4	3.2
Average	5.1	9.0	14.1	8.3	4.9	13.2	8.2
Standard Deviation	3.8	0.5	4.2	12.8	0.7	12.5	3.2

[a] All returns are pre-tax.
[b] Data available for first three quarters was annualized.
SOURCE: N. Schloss, "Realty Reality: A Look at the Alternatives," AAII Journal, April 1984, pp. 10-14.

income. (As we'll see later, there are a few exceptions to this.) This further means that tax-motivated investments such as limited partnerships or "tax shelters" have been blown away because salary and wages cannot be sheltered with passive losses--a concern largely affecting the wealthy investor.

In addition, a lower tax bracket reduces the "value" of any deductions that you are entitled to but increases the "value" of current income. Finally, the preferential tax treatment of capital gains/losses is gone--they are all treated as regular income, with no distinction made between short-and long-term.

BOTTOMLINE: This should make you focus more on the economics rather than the tax implications of real estate investments. This is why *income-oriented* real estate will be the main benefactor of tax reform.

High Total Returns

Real estate offers an opportunity to hedge inflation. Income- producing property can provide a steady income to the extent rental income ex-

ceeds maintenance and financing costs. In addition, its value will generally appreciate with inflation. Exhibit 15-1 compares the *pre-tax* returns and risk of real estate with stocks and inflation from 1975 through 1983. Real estate provided a very favorable total return of 14.1% on average. Its total return exceeded inflation in *every* year while stocks achieved this performance in only 5 of 9 years. Notice also that the risk or variability in returns (as measured by standard deviation) was much less for real estate than that associated with stocks. Of course, these results were attained during a period of high inflation--something we may or may not see again.

Diversification

Exhibit 15-1 also illustrates another advantage of real estate. Note how its returns tended to be *unrelated* to what was happening in the stock market. This means your investment portfolio's risk-return performance could be *improved* by including real estate as an alternative investment.

Leverage

Real estate is one of the most leveraged investments available--80% to 90% of the purchase price can be borrowed, compared with only 50% for stocks. This allows you to control an investment that far exceeds your cash investment. Of course, the new tax law has placed severe restrictions on the deductibility of mortgage interest as well as other expenses that has reduced the advantages of leverage. More will be said on this in the next section.

WARNING: While leverage is a powerful tool for increasing wealth, don't *overextend* yourself. (In fact, tax reform pushes you in the opposite direction.) Excessively leveraged real estate investments have proved disastrous for some investors--one only has to look at what happened to (former) developers and lending institutions in the Southwest during 1986-87!

RESIDENTIAL PROPERTY
Home Ownership

Even after tax reform, *one of the best (and largest) investments for most people is still purchasing their own home.* The new laws continue the deductibility of mortgage interest and property taxes on your primary residence. True, these deductions may be worth less to you if you're in a lower tax bracket, because the after-tax cost of owning your home will rise. But, don't let this keep you from buying a home--just be certain that you can afford it in your new bracket.

TIP: Because mortgage interest deductions are worth less, take a closer look at 15-year, "fast-pay" mortgages--you'll slice in half the interest expenses you'd eventually pay.

Moreover, the new tax law leaves untouched certain benefits when you sell. That is, you can defer taxes by rolling over the sales proceeds into a new home within 24 months if it costs as much or more than your current home. Also, you're still entitled to a one-time $125,000 capital gains exclusion if you're over age 55.

CONCLUSION: Buying a home should be your first venture into real estate.

Residential Rent Property

After home ownership, *residential rent properties* such as single-family, duplex and apartment houses are your next best, moderate-risk investment. Unfortunately, tax reform weighs very heavily on this type of investment and makes things more complicated. For one, depreciation is now spread over $27\frac{1}{2}$ rather than 19 years. Also, the size of your deductions now depends upon *your income* and whether or not you're an *active landlord*. For instance, mortgage interest, property taxes and other expenses can be written off up to the amount of your rental income plus any other "passive income" you have. Beyond that, you can deduct up to $25,000 of the house's annual expenses or losses against your salary and investment income (interest, dividends, etc.) *IF*

1. *Your adjusted gross income does not exceed $100,000.* (For every $2 in additional income between $100,000 and $150,000, you lose $1 in deduction. Over $150,000, any losses exceeding your passive income cannot be deducted.)
2. *You own at least 10% of the rental property.*
3. *You actively manage the property.* ("Actively manage" means, for example, you write the checks and help in selecting tenants.)

But what if you don't own 10% or let someone else manage? Only expenses or losses that tally up to the sum of the property's rental income and other passive income can be deducted. Losses are greater than this? The excess losses can be carried over so long as you still own the property and used in years when you have passive income, including the year you sell.

And this has been referred to as a "tax simplification" plan?

CONCLUSION: The emphasis should be on buying property that generates a positive cash flow, i.e., rents exceed costs, or expect a cash drain that will wipe out your budget. On a brighter note, while the reduction or elimination of tax benefits has taken the lustre off investing in rent property, the supply of rental housing will decline relative to demand as construction of rental property falls off. This means rents will go up, increasing cash flow and after-tax returns. However, don't expect property values to increase as fast.

TIP: Equity in your home exceeds that in your rent property? Think about getting a second mortgage on your home and using the funds to pay down your rent property's mortgage quicker. Why? (1) You can fully deduct the interest on the new mortgage. (2) With higher equity in your rent property, expenses will be smaller and, hence, cash flow goes up.

Before reading further, we suggest that you first answer the questions in Exhibit 15-2. If you can't answer "yes" to all five questions, then rental property may not be for you. However, as we'll see shortly, there are other ways to participate in real estate that involve less capital and much fewer hassles.

Some DOs and DON'Ts with Rental Property

1. *DO* learn how to analyze real estate before you jump in. Successful investing takes knowledge, effort and ability to estimate cash flows. It's not the same as buying your own home.
2. *DON'T* buy the first house you see. Look for pockets of growth, and a structurally-sound house in a good neighborhood. Start in your own area, especially if this is your first time out. Plan on checking out dozens of homes before finding the one that'll make you money. An experienced broker who knows the area and whom you can trust is a strong plus.

Shop around (and bargain) for the best price--the lower the cost is, the greater the return. Avoid, if possible, properties with negative cash flow, i.e., expenses exceed rents. Negative cash flow only works during high inflation (when rents increase faster than expenses) OR appreciation more than recovers the steady outflow of cash.

Exhibit 15-2

Questions to Ask Yourself Before Investing in Residential Rent Property

YES	NO		
___	___	1.	*Do you have at least $5,000-$15,000 that can be committed for several years?* Rent property requires a higher down payment than a home (usually 20%-30%), and is a very illiquid investment.
___	___	2.	*Do you plan to stay in the same geographic area in which the prospective rental investment is located?* Real estate needs frequent attention and management.
___	___	3.	*Do you have the time and expertise to manage property effectively?* For instance, rental property can be very time-consuming--maintenance, finding new tenants, rent collections, recordkeeping and bills to be paid. Of course, a property manager can be hired but this will reduce your income 6%-10% a year, plus you may not qualify as an "active landlord."
___	___	4.	*Can you shoulder the risk found in real estate investing?* High leverage and low liquidity add risk not found in other investments.
___	___	5.	*Are you in a high tax bracket?* The higher your tax bracket, the greater the tax benefits received from any tax write-offs.

SOURCE: Adapted from Ben Branch. Investments: A Practical Approach, pp. 497-498. Published by Longman Financial Services Publishing, Inc., a Longman Group USA Company. © 1985 by Longman Group USA Inc. Adapted by permission.

---

3. *DO* arrange easy financing terms. Monthly mortgage payments as well as other expenses must fit your budget. Keep interest, downpayments, closing costs, points, etc. to a minimum. Depending on how fast the owner wants to sell, *seller financing* often beats the terms offered by more traditional sources. But, rest assured that the property's price will include this benefit.
4. *DO* manage the property yourself to maximize your returns. This means keeping professional help (and their fees) to a minimum. But, it also means a lot more

headaches--late night calls, finding tenants and evicting unwanted ones, collecting back rent, fixing a leaky pipe--the list goes on and on… True, a property manager can be hired to do all this, but the 6%-10% fee can erase thin profits.

5. *DON'T* overspend on repairs and improvements. Avoid homes that need major facelifts, the payoff is not there--unless you're a handyman. Stick to minor, cosmetic repairs--new paint, curtains or light fixtures. Remember, any improvements must be justified by their incremental returns. RULE: Expect a $2-$5 gain for every $1 spent.

6. *DO* keep an eye on governmental actions or policies--they can have a major impact on values, both favorable and unfavorable. Examples: property tax increases, changes in zoning, provision of new city parks or recreational facilities, location of new schools, arterial improvements, etc. All will affect property values.

REMEMBER: Successful investing comes more from aggressive bargaining skills and an ability to upgrade than from what you buy. Luck plays a part, but nothing substitutes for hard work and doing your homework.

COMMERCIAL PROPERTY
Real Estate Investment Trusts (REITs)

Under tax reform, perhaps the next best realty investment is a REIT (pronounced "Ree-it"). In fact, they're the current rage on Wall Street. Why? They came out the big winner under tax reform because they never had any tax benefits to begin with. So, they're more competitive now with other real estate investments that lost their benefits. Moreover, your *REIT's earnings represent investment income* rather than passive income, and you'll keep more of the income because of a lower individual tax rate.

What exactly is a REIT? By definition, it's a trust or corporation that participates in the ownership and/or financing of real estate. For you, it's an *indirect* investment in real estate through publicly-traded shares (most trade on the New York Stock Exchange). Much like a mutual fund, REITs pool shareholders' monies and invest them in a diversified portfolio of real property. They either invest directly in property *(equity REITs),* make loans to developers or building owners *(mortgage REITs),* or both *(hybrid REITs).*

Their major benefits are:
- *liquidity* that's not available with most other real estate investments,
- *diversification,*
- *smaller capital requirements,*
- *professional management,*
- *high current yield*--95% of their taxable income is paid out as dividends to avoid double taxation.

Choosing a REIT *

1. *Current Yield.* Consider first what current yield you desire. Yields typically average between 7%-13% compared to 3%-4% on the typical stock. Equity REITs, being safer and more conservative, yield the least; mortgage REITs, the most (in 1986, 11%-13%).

   Equity REITs, however, have more potential for growth because they share in property appreciation and higher rentals. Being lenders, mortgage REITs miss out on this.

   TIP: Check the REITs' annual reports to see where they get money to pay dividends—from regular cash flow is preferred. If proceeds from selling property or mortgage refinancing are being used, watch out!

2. *Inflation Outlook.* Expect inflation to rekindle itself? Go with equity REITs because, as inflation accelerates, their income and holdings will appreciate and the greater

* J. Lipman. "Real Estate Investment Trusts Cultivate Fresh Image and New Crop of Investors," The Wall Street Journal, June 18, 1985.

your returns will be. But, plan on a minimum 3-5 year commitment of your investment to realize these returns.

Expect inflation to remain low or fall? With lower inflation, interest rates fall. This encourages developers to take out more mortgages. The beneficiary--mortgage REITs. While equity REITs benefit, too, they don't depend on falling interest rates for their profitability. What they really need to bolster earnings/dividends is higher inflation.

Not sure where inflation is going? Hedge your bets by looking at two other types or REITs:

- *Participating mortgage REITs* add "equity kickers" to their loans that let them share in rental income and property appreciation.
- *Hybrid REITs* take a balanced approach, investing in both mortgages and real property.

3. *Safety.* Disregarding inflation, you may prefer equity REITs because they're relatively safe (it's *usually* better to own than to lend). Mortgage REITs are not for the weak of heart. If borrowers default, you lose.

4. *Diversification.* Read the annual report closely. What do they own? Where's it located? Apartments and shopping centers were big in 1985 and early 1986. BUT, you want a diversified portfolio both in terms of asset type and geographical location. *WARNING:* Avoid "blind pools" where properties are unidentified as to type of location.

5. *Break-Up Value.* Compare break-up value with its stock price. Many REITs conduct annual appraisals. Look for it in the annual report or ask for it. The better REITs often trade at 10%-20% discounts from break-up value. If less, you may be overpaying. Beware of REITs selling at more than a 25% discount. Poor management or properties may be the reason.

TIP: You should be cautions in dealing with newly-formed REITs, especially those put together by managers previously in the real estate syndication business where tax write-offs were foremost. It's preferable that the REIT have been in existence for at least 10-15 years—these have weathered both the good and the bad times.

Real Estate Limited Partnerships (RELPs)

The stereotype of a RELP is a "tax shelter for the super wealthy." This arose because the primary motive for forming many RELPs before 1987 was to generate generous tax deductions to offset income of wealthy investors in high tax brackets. While this was not always the case, tax reform has destroyed those RELPs that were tax-motivated. That is, tax reform has made them the biggest losers by eliminating or reducing most of their deductions and by reclassifying whatever income they earned as passive income. Nevertheless, it's still worthwhile to discuss them, especially since the *new* RELPs emphasize *economics* and *current income* rather than tax benefits.

RELPs pool investors' money to purchase commercial property such as apartments, shopping centers, office buildings, etc. An occasional partnership is formed to invest in non-income producing properties or to buy mortgages.

There is an individual or firm, called the *general partner,* with *unlimited* liability, who assembles and manages the properties. The general partner sells participation units to investors, called *limited partners,* i.e., their losses are limited to their investment. These investors then share in the income and any capital gains when the assets are sold (usually in 5-10 years). In addition, tax deductions for depreciation, interest, taxes, maintenance expenses and so on are passed along to the investors.

Are RELPs for You?

Capital Requirements. Public programs are registered with the S.E.C. and pool money from thousands of investors. Minimum investment:

$2,500-$5,000, or $2,000 for Individual Retirement Accounts. *NOTE:* Tax deductions amount to less than 10% of the total returns so these were not hurt much by tax reform. *Private programs* were designed more for the wealthy, with substantial tax write-offs being their main attraction. Sorry, these have largely disappeared. Minimum investment: $10,000-$100,000.

Returns. Tax reform has made estimating future returns an exercise in "crystal balling." Historically, though, the general partners and sales people have done well--taking 20%-35% off the top. But what about the limited partners?

In recent history, RELPs have yielded cash and tax benefits totaling 20% or more a year after taxes. This figure, however, assumed a high tax bracket and reaches back to the heady inflation days of the '70s, when *any* real estate deal did well. The low-inflation '80s and the new tax laws aren't going to be as generous.

Fees also will hit you heavily at the front-end as well as at the back-end. You'll often end up with only 75%-85% of your original investment working for you. Tack on annual management fees of 5%-6% and you can see that a RELP has to be *very lucrative* before you earn more than a low-risk investment such as Treasury securities.

Risks. Real estate values move in cycles, with short-term price moves deviating from the long-term trend. Yet, who's to say that high inflation won't rear its head again and make real estate the darling of the investment world. Low inflation, on the other hand, is generally not kind to real estate--and disinflation would be disastrous.

Perhaps the *biggest risk is illiquidity.* If you want out, you'll have to find a buyer. Even if you find one, expect to sell at a *30% discount* if you've been in only a few years. Why? It takes time to recoup the heavy up-front costs. While this discount diminishes with longevity, you may still end up with an overall loss if you get out prematurely.

NOTE: Public programs are easier to sell than private ones. Also, RELPs fashioned primarily to generate income are generally more easily resold.

Choosing a RELP *

Good economics, with tax benefits secondary, lead you to the best RELP. Seek advice from a professional such as an accountant or lawyer who is knowledgeable in this field. He/she can quickly weed out the garbage, so a couple of hundred dollars for an opinion is well worth the price.

Next, familiarize yourself with the prospectus. Here's what the experts suggest you look for:

1. *"Summary Section"*--See what properties have already been purchased. Check to see if the area is overbuilt and who the tenants are. Stay away from "blind pools" of unidentified or unpurchased properties. You want to know what specific properties your money is invested in.

2. *"Use of Proceeds Section"*—Here, the various fees are detailed. Avoid overpaying by staying within the following guidelines:
    *   *Up-Front Costs:*
        Sales commissions: 7%-10% of investment
        Legal and accounting fees: 1%-3% of investment
        Organizational and finder fees: Up to 15% of investment
    *   *Annual Costs:* Management fees equal to 5%-6% a year of cash flow
    *   *Back-End Costs:*
        Sales commissions: 3%-6% of sales price
        Profit Sharing: 10%-33% of any gains may go to the sponsor

    Needless to say, the smaller these percentages the better. For instance, under 20% for total up-front fees is preferred, and 8%-10% is ideal. Keep the general

---

* J. Lipman. "Real Estate Syndication Investors: Look Beyond the Pretty Pictures," The Wall Street Journal (February 2, 1985).

partner's profit sharing to under 25% and only after you have received a minimum return, e.g., 6% as a limited partner.

3. *"Conflicts of Interest" Section*--Are fees being paid to groups related to the sponsor? These will run higher than usual. *Avoid partnerships that mix their funds with those of other programs.*

4. *"Risks" Section*--Can the sponsor delay cash distributions (you'll still be taxed as if you had received them) or can you be tapped for future payments? "Tax risks" involve possible I.R.S. challenges or audits. For instance, if the I.R.S. thinks the purchase price is overstated, you may lose deductions. Make sure a reputable law firm has evaluated the tax aspects.

   RULE OF THUMB: The thicker the risks section, the more problems you'll likely have.

3. *"Financial Results" Section*--Previous returns should at least equal the return given by investments with similar risks. Insist on an independent source supporting rental income projections and verifying any statements made by a broker.

TIPS: Tax reform will favor income-producing partnerships. Yields of economically-sound programs should be 8%-11%. Remember, though, this will be passive income. While income programs will be the "hot item" with newly-formed partnerships, again stay with general partners or sponsors whose managers have been in business more than 10 years. Experience is a plus, especially with today's real estate industry. Avoid unseasoned types of partnerships such as parking lots. Let them establish a track record before you invest your hard-earned money.

RELPs vs. REITs

In the past, RELPs have offered higher potential rewards *after taxes* because of their tax benefits. But, it's a totally new game under tax reform. It's anybody's guess as to what will happen now. In contrast, REITs' returns are more diversified and predictable. With careful selec-

tion, their dividend and price appreciation can produce pre-tax returns of 15%-20%. Also, income from REITs is investment income whereas RELPs' is passive income, but REITs cannot pass along tax losses to their shareholders while RELPs can.

Partnerships usually dissolve within 10-15 years, selling their properties and distributing the proceeds. REITs normally have an unlimited life.

REITs offer liquidity. When you want to get out, just sell your shares of stock. Partnerships tie up your money for years, with little recourse but to wait it out or sell at a loss in the secondary market. In a few words, *RELPs are illiquid.*

The only costs involved with getting into a REIT are brokerage commissions when you buy the shares. As noted earlier, RELPs have management and up-front fees that can significantly reduce long-term returns.

Finally, REITs don't have minimum purchase requirements ($1,000-$2,000 will typically buy you 100 shares) or impose minimum financial standards that may lock you out of RELPs.

Master Limited Partnerships (MLPs)

This year's investment spotlight is clearly on real estate MLPs. The first MLP was put together in 1981 by an oil company that rolled up a number of existing oil and gas partnerships into a single, or "master" partnership and then offered it as a publicly-traded limited partnership. And this is one of the major advantages over traditional real estate partnerships--you can get your money out of the deal any time you want because they are listed on a stock exchange, where it trades just like a stock, usually for $20 or less a unit. (Perhaps they should be called "publicly-traded limited partnership" rather than "master limited partnership.")

So why are MLPs so popular? You get some of the tax advantages available to partnerships, yet your investment is liquid and easily sold. Also, many of the newer MLPs are being done as initial public offerings and are being designed to generate income rather than shelter it from taxes.

There are three basic types of MLPs:

1. *"Roll-Up" MLP*--A combination of a number of *existing* partnerships. You may want to watch out for these. Roll-ups tend to be last-ditch efforts to salvage loans or troubled properties from foreclosure and limited partners from unpleasant tax consequences due to tax recapture. You should examine these offerings carefully. The tax considerations are complex. Also, the properties could be marked up by the MLP sponsors before they are sold, plus you're stuck with the organizational fees (up to 5% of the equity value). My advice: Leave them alone unless you know what you're getting into.

2. *"Roll-Out" MLP*--A spin-off of a corporation's existing assets to its shareholders. Currently, this is being done by firms that have large real estate holdings such as restaurants, hotels and nursing homes. The corporation then leases the real estate from the partnership, providing a high current yield to the owners. For instance, Pillsbury formed Burger King Investors in 1986, which bundled up $85 million worth of Burger King real estate leases into an MLP and sold the MLP units off to its shareholders.

3. *"Roll-In" MLP*--New units offered periodically as an initial public offering, and the proceeds are invested in real estate. Future offerings then provide additional capital for expansion.

CAVEATS: MLPs, like RELPs, can be laden with fees. Property acquisition fees can run 5%-6% of equity, and MLP sponsors often charge 7%-8.5% front-end commissions on the units. Because of this, *initial* investors in an MLP may watch the value of their shares drop after the closing of the initial offering. Better to wait and buy your MLP units after they begin to trade in the aftermarket. Another potential cloud: MPLs currently avoid corporate taxation (double taxation), but if conversion to MLPs turn into a massive tax avoidance problem, Congress could change its mind and eliminate this tax-free status.

Are real estate MLPs for you? It's still too early to tell exactly how they'll fare as an investment vehicle. You may want to give them some time to establish a track record and become better understood by investors.

MLPs vs. REITS *

Which one is best for you? As usual, the answer is not easy. MLPs and REITs are similar in that both are publicly traded, both escape double taxation (only cash distributions paid to unit holders are taxed) and both are treated very favorably under tax reform when compared to RELPs. Other considerations are:

1. MLPs are less restricted in the types of investments and activities they can engage in.

2. Yields on recent MLPs are higher than most REITs. But this can change, so carefully compare the relative yields before you purchase. Also, part of your yield with both can be a return of capital rather than income. This will obviously affect your taxes.

3. You may feel more comfortable with a REIT. They are run by independent directors or trustees. (NOTE: Under the new tax law, REITs are given more freedom to manage actively the properties they own, rather than farming out management to independent contractors.) An MLP's managing partner, however, has complete control over most operational and payout decisions with few restrictions. This requires a heightened awareness on your part. Moreover, there is a tinge of potential abuse with a roll-out MLP because a corporation sells you its real estate *at its price* and then tells you how much rent it will pay.

4. An MLP's earnings is *passive* income: a REIT's is *investment* income so the tax

* From B. Vinocur. "Master Partnerships, REITs Both Gain from Tax Reform," <u>Barron's</u> (October 20, 1986), p. 78.

consequences are very different. *SUG-GESTION:* If you're already in a limited partnership or rental property that has passive losses, these can be used to offset an MLP's passive income.

5. MLPs are able to pass along tax losses to its investors; REITs cannot do this.
6. MLPs are more complicated in nature and require more of your time. One surprise to watch for is that it's possible that you'll be liable for taxes even though you haven't actually received a cash distribution from the partnership.
7. MLPs are largely unproven investments with little history for comparison purposes. REITs, on the other hand, are better understood because they've been around for 25 years.

OTHER REAL ESTATE INVESTMENTS

Still interested in real estate but want the least risky approach? Consider:
- Real estate CD investments
- Unleveraged RELPs
- U.S.-backed partnerships
- Triple-net leases
- Government-subsidized housing developments
- Rehabilitated real estate

Real estate CDs are discussed in Chapter 6, while the rest are described in Exhibit 15-3.

TERMS TO KNOW

Back-end fees
Blind pools
Carrying costs
Depreciation
Equity REIT
Front-end fees
General partner
Hybrid REIT
Illiquidity
Investment income
Leverage

Exhibit 15-3
Low-Risk Real Estate Investments

1. *UNLEVERAGED RELPs.* Stimulated by tax reform, they are the latest development in RELPs wherein properties are purchased with all or mostly cash. They are designed to generate *income* and deemphasize tax write-offs or spectacular returns. Their newness as an investment vehicle makes their returns hard to quantify. But, buying property with all cash should produce better deals and, therefore, more for your money. No debt service means higher cash distributions. Could be a good investment for your IRA--see Chapter 18.
2. *GOVERNMENT-BACKED MORTGAGE PARTNER-SHIPS.* These partnerships invest in federally-insured or guaranteed mortgages. Very safe because the government insures against default or foreclosure risks. Yields in 1985 were about 10%.
3. *"TRIPLE-NET" LEASE PARTNERSHIPS.* The safest RELP where the general partner acquires retail stores or office buildings and leases them for 5-30 years. Escalation clauses keep rents in line with inflation. The "triple nets," taxes, insurance and maintenance, are paid by the lessee so you don't shoulder the unpleasant surprise of higher expenses. The usual tax deductions are not there, but the payout should be about 10% a year.
4. *GOVERNMENT-SUBSIDIZED HOUSING DEVELOP-MENTS.* These have some tax advantages, and the federal government guarantees the rents.
5. REHABILITATED REAL ESTATE. Investment in a certified historical structure or a commercial building over 30 years old will get you all the normal benefits of a real estate investment *plus* a tax credit equal to a percentage of the rehabilitation costs.

Limited partner
Master Limited Partnership (MLP)
Mortgage REIT
Negative cash flow
Participating mortgage REIT
Passive income
Passive losses
Private offering
Property manager
Public offering
Real Estate Investment Trust (REIT)
Real Estate Limited Partnership (RELP)
Regular income
Rehabilitated real estate
Triple-net lease
Unleveraged RELP

16 SIMPLIFYING INVESTMENT DECISIONS WITH MUTUAL FUNDS

Chapter Objectives

1. What is a Mutual Fund?
2. Are Mutual Funds for You?
3. Benefits and Costs of Investing in Mutual Funds
4. Types of Mutual Funds
5. How to Select Mutual Funds

Mutual funds are the best way to simplify your investment decisions. Why? Because they relieve you of the time-consuming chores (and worry) of managing your investments. With a mutual fund, you "hire" a professional to:

- Research/evaluate/monitor the outlook for the economy, financial markets and different securities, and
- Make all the buying and selling decisions you're too busy or uncomfortable to make.

Throw in to boot the diversification that's difficult to attain on your own, especially if you have limited funds.

Despite this, you need to be aware of what you're getting into. This chapter covers the basics of mutual funds. You'll learn about their benefits and costs, and the different types of funds available. We'll also suggest things to consider and how to select the mutual fund(s) that best fit your investment objectives.

WHAT IS A MUTUAL FUND?

A mutual fund (MF) is an investment company that pools individual investors' money and invests it in a diversified portfolio of securities that matches its investment objectives. Most MFs invest in bonds and stocks, but they are not limited to those securities.

Just like a corporation, mutual funds issue shares of ownership which fluctuate in price with the underlying value of the fund's securities. Unlike a corporation, which invests in *real* assets such as plant and equipment, MFs invest in *financial* assets such as common stocks. So, your investment gains or loses value just as it would if it were in individual securities.

A distinguishing feature of MFs is that they *continually issue new shares* and *buy them back when redeemed.* (This is why they are also referred to as *open-end investment companies.*) The daily value or price of these shares is calculated by summing the market values of the portfolio's securities and any cash they hold, and then dividing this figure by the total number of shares outstanding. This is referred to as the *net asset value* (NAV) and is quoted daily in major newspapers' business section.

ARE MUTUAL FUNDS FOR YOU?

One way to decide whether or not MFs are for you is to think about the following questions:

1. *What is the size of your current investment portfolio?*
   If you have less than $10,000-$20,000 in securities or investable funds, then MFs may be the best route for you. In general, the smaller your portfolio, the more attractive MFs become because the expense and monitoring costs of managing individual securities are disproportionately high when smaller dollar amounts are involved. In addition, it's very difficult to diversify your holdings with less than $20,000.

2. *How much time and effort can you devote to following general economic and market trends or analyzing different investment alternatives?*
   Properly managing a portfolio of individual securities takes time—at least an average of one hour per day. For the typical investor, this is not always possible, so think

seriously about having your investments managed professionally by a mutual fund manager.

3. *How much can you afford to set aside each month for investment purposes?*
Most of us can't find more than $100-$200 a month to invest. This means we would have to discipline ourselves to save this much money for at least a year just to buy one bond or 100 shares of a stock. On the other hand, most MFs let you invest as little as $100 per transaction.

This provides several advantages. First, your money starts to work for you right away with a diversified holding of securities. Second, with a regular, monthly investment in a MF, e.g., arranging for an automatic withdrawal from your checking account, you will benefit from *dollar cost averaging*. That is, if you invest a constant dollar amount each month, you end up buying *more* shares as market prices fall and buying *fewer* shares as prices rise. In effect, you avoid having to worry about "timing the market."

Clearly, there are other considerations, such as the psychic reward or excitement of managing your own investments, that come into play. But, for most investors, MFs are a very viable alternative that give you a wide diversity of investment options that can't be duplicated very easily on your own. In a few words, think about what MFs can offer you, given your personal situation.

WHAT BENEFITS DO MUTUAL FUNDS OFFER?

While mutual funds have many benefits, the two main ones are:
- Instant diversification
- Professional management

Instant Diversification

Each fund usually invests in a broad-based portfolio of different securities across industries. This enables an investor with limited capital to spread his/her risk over more securities than would be possible if individual securities were purchased. This diversification makes a fund's overall performance and volatility less sensitive to individual securities' behavior.

Professional Management

Fund managers are highly-qualified specialists who devote full time to their job of managing money. Besides their investment skills, they have expertise in accounting, economics and finance. So, for a relatively low cost, you're freed of the time, effort and complexities of managing your investments and, perhaps, you lend a little more rationality rather than emotion to your investing. Remember, the fund manager can't deviate from the fund's investment objectives.

Exhibit 16-1 briefly describes some of the other benefits.

Exhibit 16-1

Other Benefits from Investing in Mutual Funds

1. FLEXIBILITY makes for easy buying and selling of shares on a regular or irregular basis. You can invest any dollar amount, subject to the fund's minimum requirement, because you receive fractional shares (to 3 decimal places) not available elsewhere.
2. AUTOMATIC TRANSFERRALS of money from your bank account to the fund or automatic withdrawals (called systematic withdrawal plans) from the fund can be made on a regular basis.
3. AUTOMATIC REINVESTMENT of dividends and capital gains distributions at no charge.
4. SWITCHING PRIVILEGES if the management firm (called an investment advisory company) offers a "family of funds." This allows you to move all or part of your money back and forth between money, stock or bond funds, usually with a simple (800) phone call and at no charge.
5. SIMPLIFIED RECORDKEEPING eases your tax preparation. Periodically, you'll receive statements describing your shareholding and income received to date, as well as Form 1099 detailing your taxable income. Quarterly reports are also sent to apprise you of income, expenses, portfolio holdings and performance.

WHAT ARE THE COSTS OF INVESTING IN MUTUAL FUNDS?

Load vs. No Load Funds

Buying a mutual fund can cost you *nothing* or *as much as 8½%* of its share value. In the case of *load funds,* you're charged a front-end fee or commission. The reason is because it's compensation for brokers, insurance agents and other salespeople who actively sell fund shares. These people also provide services such as financial advice, help in establishing an investment plan and selection of a fund they believe will produce satisfactory results.

With a *no load fund,* no commission is charged. Shares are purchased directly by mail from the fund. This cuts out the middleman and saves you money. No loads attract investors largely through advertising.

EXAMPLE: Assume a mutual fund's NAV is $10.00 a share, and you have $1,000 to invest. If it's a no load, you buy 100 shares ($1,000 ÷ $10) and 100% of your money goes to work for you immediately. On the other hand, what if there's an 8% load? You only buy 92 shares ($920 ÷ $10) because 8% or $80 comes off the top first.

Why buy a load fund? As you see, load fees can be quite costly. Since the relative performance and expenses of both types of funds are comparable, why should you bother with a load fund?

One reason is *lack of knowledge.* The general public typically knows very little about how MFs work or which ones to buy. Salespeople help fill this knowledge gap, but their effort needs to be rewarded by a sales commission.

Another reason is that *buying no loads requires you to do your own research and monitoring* of MF performance. Many people don't have the inclination or time to do this. Nevertheless, as you'll see, these tasks are relatively simple once you understand the basics. Besides, saving $50-$85 per thousand dollars would seem to be well worth the effort.

Management Fees

Whether you buy a load or no load, you'll have to pay a management fee. This compensates fund managers for their professional services as well as operating expense such as mail, recordkeeping and office costs. Typically, the fee is 0.5%-1.5% of the fund's NAV and is assessed monthly on a pro rata basis.

Performance

Performance is measured *net* of management fees and other expenses. To just cover these, mutual funds have to *outperform* the market by 2-3 percentage points.

Their record in "beating the market" is not encouraging. The average fund tends to *underperform* the market, especially in down markets. So, you may or may not view this as a "cost." This also means you need to monitor your funds' performance relative to other, similar mutual funds.

Of course, you need to ask yourself whether you could do better more cheaply and with less risk. Carefully selected funds have and can beat the market average--sometimes with less risk. More on this later.

Why do MFs rarely outperform the market? Beating the market is difficult for money managers because of their dominant position. For example, they own 50% of the common stocks and can account for as much as 75% of the trading volume. This produces intense competition among talented managers who all have the same information. It's tough to beat yourself! Also, because of their size, their trading can adversely affect prices, and they have to narrow the universe of securities to large capitalized firms (most can't own more than 5% of a firm's existing securities). As mentioned, another reason is that just to "breakeven" they have to overcome their fees and expenses.

"Hidden Costs" or When is a No Load not a No Load?

The surest way to lackluster performance is to buy a fund with fees that are a continual drain on earnings. Even a so-called no load fund may have cleverly-disguised ways to squeeze one or more fees out of you.

Exhibit 16-2 contains some of the more popular ways of inserting a sales charge. The best defense against such excesses is to be an alert investor, so watch out for them--you could be "nickeled and dimed to death" if you're not careful.

Exhibit 16-2

"Hidden Costs" to Avoid if Possible

1. REDEMPTION, SURRENDER OR BACK-END CHARGES: A redemption fee is levied whenever you sell shares. It ranges as high as 5% of the shares' NAV and can be on a sliding scale the longer you hold the shares.
2. CONTINGENT DEFERRED SALES CHARGES: Perhaps a bit less worrisome, these are fees assessed whenever you sell shares before a specified time period, which is based on when you bought the shares. This is usually applied to just your original investment but it could also apply to increases in NAV from dividends and capital gain distributions.
3. 12b-1 PLANS: The latest twist for so-called no loads that's perfectly legitimate. Here, your fund assets are tapped periodically for a "distribution expense," referred to as a 12b-1 Plan. This additional expense is just a disguised sales charge that helps to pay for advertising and sales literature.
4. OTHER COSTS: Other items to check on are "one-time account start-up fees," "account maintenance fees" and "transfer agency fees." Just like the others, these can be avoided.

GENERAL TYPES OF MUTUAL FUNDS

Let's now look at the various types of funds which are categorized below by *investment objective* and *types of securities* held. They are also presented from the riskiest to the least risky investment. (Exhibit 16-3 gives you an idea of the asset size managed by different funds. Notice that the newest mutual fund concept—money market funds—is by far the largest type.)

Common Stock Funds

These funds can be subdivided into 3 categories which differ primarily on the level of risk assumed:

Exhibit 16-3
Asset Size of Different Types of Funds
(Billions of Dollars)
YEAR END

INVESTMENT OBJECTIVE	1983	1984
Aggressive Growth	18.7	18.8
Growth	25.9	25.9
Growth & Income	29.3	32.7
Balanced	3.1	2.9
Income	8.8	19.4
Bond	11.3	13.0
Municipal Bond	14.6	21.0
Option/Income	1.9	3.4
Total	**113.6**	**137.1**
Money Market	162.5	214.5
Short-term Municipal Bond	16.8	29.1
Total	**179.3**	**243.6**
Grand Total	**292.9**	**308.7**

SOURCE: J. Horowitz, "The Mutual Fund Explosion," Personal Investor, May 1985.

- *Aggressive Growth.* These shoot for maximum gains with no emphasis on current income. The riskiest type of fund, they invest in small, promising companies or concentrate in certain industries--often amassing spectacular profits in bull markets but falling steeply in down (bear) markets. They may also borrow funds to finance their investments, and some attempt to time market swings.
- *Growth.* Emphasis is on long-term growth with some income. Typically, they hold stocks of older, larger firms and avoid speculative tactics such as leveraging their investments with borrowed monies.
- *Growth-Income.* Emphasis is on a balance between good appreciation and income that tempers wild fluctuations in NAVs. They invest in seasoned, high dividend-paying stocks such as public utilities.

Balanced Funds

These combine investments in common stocks, bonds and preferred stocks to provide good dividend and interest income plus some growth. Also referred to as *income funds*, *equity-income funds* or *total return funds*.

Bond Funds

These invest in corporate and government bonds to yield safety and current income rather than growth. While historically considered to be a conservative investment, rollercoaster interest rates in the 80's have added considerable risk to their performance.

Money Market (Cash Reserve or Liquid Asset) Funds

These invest in short-term, high-quality securities such as T-bills and bank CDs to provide high current yield and safety of principal. They offer special services such as checkwriting privileges. Because they are more sensitive to changing market conditions, their yields may be higher or lower than comparable bank money market or CD accounts, and they're *not* federally insured against losses.

Exhibit 16-4 provides a description of other, specialized types of mutual funds.

GUIDELINES FOR SELECTING THE BEST FUND FOR YOU

Investment Objectives

Knowing your investment goals will help screen out most funds. (There are over 1500 funds to choose from!) A fund's objective (its risk/return plan) needs to fit your objectives and should be *clearly stated* in its prospectus. If not, then look for another fund.

Registration

Is the fund registered with the S.E.C. and registered to sell its shares in your state? If not, keep looking.

Keep it Simple

The more speculative funds tend to average more return over the *long haul* (5-10 years) but when you consider risk, a bond or growth-income fund tends to do better. In other words, the small incremental returns of a high-risk fund versus a more conservative fund may not be worth the sleepless nights.

Exhibit 16-4
Specialized Mutual Funds

1. INDEX FUNDS--the best way to "buy the market." An index fund attempts to mimic (but not beat) a specific market index's performance, such as the S&P 500. This is done by buying the stocks in the index in the same proportion as the issues are weighted in the index.
2. SECTOR FUNDS--a way to concentrate on certain types of stocks. These funds narrow their focus to specific industries such as hi-tech, energy-related, computer stocks, etc. Of course, by doing so, they eliminate one of the main advantages of mutual funds--diversification.
3. GOLD FUNDS--a popular fund with many investors. Gold provides diversification because it tends to move countercyclically to other financial assets. It also is a good hedge against inflation. These funds can be in gold mining stocks, gold bullion or other precious metal stocks.
4. INTERNATIONAL FUNDS--another good way to diversify and improve performance. These funds invest in foreign issues such as Japanese or West German stocks and, thereby, broaden your investment alternatives. While their performance has been above-average, they introduce additional risks such as currency controls, foreign exchange-rate fluctuations, etc.
5. MUNICIPAL BOND FUNDS--a way to earn tax-free income with what are otherwise illiquid securities. Most invest in long-term municipal bonds but a few specialize in short-term munis. This eliminates the often wide fluctuations in longer term bond prices, but you sacrifice yield.
6. OPTION/INCOME FUNDS--these funds write put and call options for extra income. These can be conservatively managed (write calls on their portfolio's securities) or speculative (buying and selling options without taking an offsetting position in the stocks). Their performance to date has been mediocre at best.
7. GINNIE MAE FUNDS--want to invest in mortgages? These funds invest in GNMA (Ginnie Mae) mortgage-backed securities. Besides a fixed return higher than long-term bonds, monthly payments ("pass-throughs") of interest and principal can be used to reinvest in new shares or you can have them paid out on a regular basis.

Performance

Over a given quarter or year, certain funds will have the "hot hand" because they're in the right securities or industries. But, as market conditions change, the funds that do best tend to rotate. For example, 1984's top performing funds were conservative *income* funds, a sharp reversal from 1983 when *growth* funds were hot.

So, don't be led astray by their latest

performance--you may end up forever chasing *last year's* "manager of the year." Remember, mutual fund investing is long-term investing. That is, it's not a 100-yard dash, rather it's an endurance contest, a test of stamina or staying power. That's why you want to look for *consistency* in performance and continuity of the people managing the fund.

So, your first step is to focus on their 5-10 year track record. (Exhibit 16-5 lists the best funds for the latest 10 years.) You want a fund that's done relatively well consistently in several up *and* down markets. Of course, the ideal fund makes good money in rising markets and preserves their gains in down markets. But, there are very few funds that can do that consistently.

Exhibit 16-5
Top Performing Mutual Funds, 1974-1984

		Total Return
1.	Fidelity Magellan	1784%
2.	Penn Mutual	1476%
3.	Lindner Fund	1342%
4.	Evergreen Fund	1275%
5.	Twentieth-Century Growth	1223%
6.	Twentieth-Century Select	1194%
7.	American Capital Income	1158%
8.	Sequoia Fund	1149%
9.	Oppenheimer Special	1098%
10.	American Capital Pace	1090%

However, there is a way to *check out a fund's performance in both types of markets.* To do this, look at Forbes magazine's annual survey of mutual funds (usually a September issue). Forbes assigns a rating, A + through F, to each fund's performance during an up market and during a down market. For instance, Fidelity Magellan Fund has an "A + " for up markets and an "A" for down markets over the last 3 market cycles--an exceptionally good performance.

To help you get started, though, Exhibit 16-6 contains the latest Forbes' "Honor Roll" of funds for "all seasons." These funds finished in the top half of the pack in both bull and bear markets, plus they delivered good performance over the long term, averaging 20% or better annual returns.

Other fund rating services that are easy to get your hands on are:

- Barron's "Quarterly Survey"
- Money magazine's "Fund Watch"
- S&P's Stock Guide
- United Mutual Fund Selector
- Wiesenberger's Investment Companies, 19xx

Most or all can be found in your local library, or try your broker.

Don't forget, though, *past* performance is not necessarily a good predictor of *future* performance.

Minimize Fees and Expenses

Avoid load funds if possible and funds that have "hidden costs" (refer again to Exhibit 16-2). Look for funds that have *low expense ratios*, e.g., less than 0.75% of NAV, and *low turnover ratios* (the average is about 30%-40%). "Turnover" tells you to what degree securities were bought or sold during the year. For example, a 100% turnover ratio means the entire portfolio was "turned over" once. This frequent trading usually adds little to performance, and you have to pay the brokerage fee.

HOW TO SELECT A MONEY MARKET FUND

As Exhibit 16-3 indicated, *money market* funds have quickly become the dominant type of fund in the industry. Also, because most individuals' first venture into mutual fund investing will be with a money fund, let's take a few minutes and examine the special features of this popular investment and offer some tips on how to sift through the 300 money funds from which you can choose.

Minimum Investment

The initial investment requirement can be as high as $50,000; however, most funds range from $1,000 to $5,000.

Yields

Yields are determined by two factors:

Exhibit 16-6
Forbes' 1985 "Honor Roll" of Mutual Funds
1976-1985

FUND	PERFORMANCE Up	Down	PORTFOLIO STRATEGY	AVERAGE ANNUAL TOTAL RETURN
Acorn Fund	B	A	Small company growth	20.6%
Amcap Fund	B	A	Growth	21.5
American Capital Pace Fund	B	A+	Aggressive growth	27.5
American Capital Venture Fund	B	A	Aggressive growth	24.9
Evergreen Fund	A+	B	Growth	26.4
Explorer Fund	A	B	Small company growth	20.7
Fidelity Destiny Fund	B	A	Growth	22.1
Fideltiy Magellan Fund	A+	A	Growth	33.3
Growth Fund of America	B	A	Growth	22.3
Janus Fund	B	A	Aggressive growth	20.9
Loomis-Sayles Capital Development Fund	A	B	Growth	22.7
Mass Cap Development Fund	A+	B	Growth	23.8
NEL Growth Fund	A	B	Growth	22.2
Nicholas Fund	B	A+	Growth	25.4
Over-the-Counter Securities Fund	B	A	Small company growth	23.4
Pennsylvania Mutual Fund	B	A	Small company growth	22.6
Pioneer II	B	A	Growth-income	20.7
Scudder Development Fund	B	A	Small company growth	20.8
Sigma Venture Shares	A	B	Small company growth	22.7
Tudor Fund	A	B	Aggressive growth	21.5
Twentieth Century Select	A+	B	Growth	28.0
United Vanguard Fund	B	B	Growth	21.0

SOURCE: Reprinted by permission of Forbes Magazine, September 16, 1985. © Forbes Inc., 1985.

- Type of securities held
- Average maturity of these securities

1. *Security Type.* Most funds hold a diversified portfolio of government securities, bank CDs and commercial paper. Some funds buy only Treasuries--these offer the highest safety but lowest yield. Others emphasize highly-rated debt (called "prime" paper) of banks and corporations. Still others go for riskier but higher-yielding investments such as repurchase agreements, bankers acceptances and Eurodollar CDs. (There are even funds that invest in short-term, tax-exempt securities). Check a fund's prospectus to determine its investment policy and objectives. Is maximum safety or maximum yield stressed? Better yet, look at a few quarterly reports and see what they *actually* purchase. A few funds are rated for quality by Standard & Poor's Corp.

NOTE: Given the excellent safety record of money funds so far, you probably don't have to be overly concerned about the risk differences.

2. *Average Maturity.* Another factor that influences a fund's yield is the *dollar-weighted maturity* of its securities. Typically, the longer the maturity, the higher the yield but the less quickly the fund's yield will respond to changes in the market.

The average maturity also may say something about a fund's risk. Generally, shorter maturities have less risk and lower yields.

Where can you find this information? Monday's <u>Wall Street Journal</u> contains a list of those money funds over $100 million in size. Referring to Exhibit 16-7, you can get the average maturity and the latest (annualized) seven-day yield.

The seven-day yield is the rate earned during the latest seven-day period, without adjustment for compounding. You may also run across the 30-day yield. This is figured similarly but uses more days and is less sensitive to changing market rates. If, for instance, interest rates are falling, a fund's seven-day yield will be less than its 30-day yield.

Convenience and Flexibility

What types of service does a fund provide? Does it have checkwriting privileges? What's the minimum amount of the check you can write? (Check amounts may vary from no to $500 minimums, depending on the particular fund.) How easy is it to buy or redeem shares? Is it done by check, telephone, wire or letter? Can you switch your funds into a stock or bond fund (preferably by phone)? Are there any fees for this privilege? Are there limits on the number of switches allowed per year? What's their policy on signature guarantees? Do they offer *private* insurance against losses? Only a few do this.

TAX REFORM AND MUTUAL FUNDS

The main effect of tax reform on mutual funds has been the introduction of new products tied to the tax bill or the use of tax concerns as a marketing tool for existing funds--for instance, pushing funds that invest primarily in service-oriented stocks, one of the main benefactors of tax reform.

Beyond that, lower marginal tax rates increase the after-tax yields on income funds for most investors. This, of course, makes them more attractive. Taxation of capital gains at ordinary income rates enhances both income and growth-income funds compared with growth funds.

On a more subtle note, the Tax Reform Act requires mutual funds to distribute most of their realized earnings on a *calendar* year rather than a *fiscal* year basis. This means that, by the end of the calendar year, a mutual fund is required

---

Exhibit 16-7

MONEY MARKET MUTUAL FUNDS

Friday, July 12, 1985

The following quotations, collected by the National Association of Securities Dealers Inc., represent the average of annualized yields and dollar-weighted portfolio maturities ending Friday, July 12, 1985. Yields are based on actual dividends to shareholders.

FUNDS	AVG MAT.	AVG YLD.	FUNDS	AVG MAT.	AVG YLD.
ActvAsst GovSc	60	7.26	LordAbbet Cash	28	6.75
AlexBCash Gvt	27	7.38	LuthBrMon Mkt	43	7.09
AlexBCash Prm	30	7.10	ManCshActTr a	34	6.75
Alliance Capital	45	6.98	MAP GovtFund	50	6.68
AllianceGvt Res	27	6.76	Mariner Cash	31	7.41
Alliance TaxEx	52	4.63	Mariner Govt	25	7.53
AmCap Resrv a	21	7.05	Mariner TxFree	43	4.45
Am Genl MM a	19	7.15	MarinerUS Trs	50	7.42
Amer Natl MM	16	7.02	MassCashMgt a	34	7.20
AMEV Money	28	6.81	MassMtl Liquid	27	6.94
AutomCash Mgt	40	7.38	McDonald MM	37	6.85
AutomGvt MTr	54	7.49	MerrLGovtFd a	(z)	(z)
Babson Prime	(z)	(z)	MerrLInstFd af	(z)	(z)
BenhamCal TF	84	3.69	MerrLRdyAst u	54	6.82
BenhamNatl TF	77	4.69	MerrLRetRsv a	57	6.56
BirrWilson MFd	31	6.39	MidwstGrp TF	67	5.00
BLC Cash Mgt	19	6.61	Midwst Incm Tr	43	6.70
Boston Co Cash	50	7.33	Midwst IT Cash	40	6.76
BostonCo Mass	79	4.31	MnyMgtP Govt	29	6.50
Bull&Bear DRs	22	6.71	MnyMgtP Pr	33	7.02
CalvrtSocInv af	40	7.09	MoneyMkt Instr	67	7.08
Calvrt TF MM	95	4.94	MoneyMktMgt f	46	7.11
CAM Fund	17	6.55	Money Mkt Trst	39	7.54
CapCash MgtTr	25	6.95	MorganKeegn f	42	6.96
Cap Preservtn	52	7.06	MuniCashRsv c	63	4.90
Cap Preservtn 2	4	6.86	MuniFundInv c	51	4.38
CardGovt SecTr	37	7.37	MtlOmCash Res	39	6.82
CarngieGov Sec	25	6.82	MtlOmMny Mkt	32	7.20
CarnegieTax Fr	21	4.00	Natl Cash Resv	43	6.58
CashAssett Tr	29	7.02	NEL Cash Mngt	61	7.17
Cash Equiv MM	(z)	(z)	NEL TxEx MM	85	4.47
CashEq GovSec	(z)	(z)	NEL US Govt	91	7.36
CshMgt TrAm a	15	7.17	NatlGovt Fund	22	6.95
Cash Rsv Mgt a	63	7.31	NatlMMkt Fund	28	7.07
CentenniMM Tr	39	6.80	NatlTax Exmpt	69	4.10
CignaMM Fd b	50	7.29	Nationwide MM	42	7.23
CimcoMM Trst	32	7.34	NeubrgBer Gov	44	6.86
CMA GovtSec a	53	6.08	Newton Money	33	6.69
CMA MnyFd a	52	6.80	NLR Cash Port	34	7.15
CMA Tax Ex	62	4.31	NLR Govt Prt	26	7.02
Col Daily Inc af	29	6.95	NuveenTaxEx c	47	4.56
Colonial MnyM	22	6.56	Nuveen TaxFr	25	4.34
CommMnyF a	43	7.31	Oppn Mny Mrkt	37	7.09
Comp Cash M a	26	6.79	Oxford CshMgt	10	7.20
Current Interest	38	7.06	PacHrzGov MM	83	7.49
CurrentInf USG	36	7.12	PacHrzMM Prt	24	7.39
Daily cash Fd1	39	7.07	PacHrz TaxEx	68	3.85
Govt	29	6.70	PaineWb Cash f	34	7.26
			Parkway Cash		

SOURCE: The Wall Street Journal, July 15, 1985.

---

to distribute 97% of its ordinary income for the calendar year and 90% of its capital gain net income for the period covered by the preceding November 1 through October 31. If a fund has historically made its distributions during January, for example, it will be required to pay two distributions during a single year in order to comply with the new law. Without going into the details, this will make compliance a very difficult job for mutual fund managers and will make your tax reporting more complicated.

TERMS TO KNOW

Automatic reinvestment plan
Automatic (systematic) withdrawal plan
Bond fund
Common stock fund
Contingent deferred sales charge
Dollar-cost averaging
Ginnie Mae fund
Gold fund
Index fund
International fund
Load fee
Management fee
Money market fund
Mutual fund
Net asset value
No load fund
Open-end investment compnay
Redemption or surrender fee
Sector fund
12b-1 plan

ADDITIONAL
CONSIDERATIONS

17 CHOOSING A BROKER OR OTHER INVESTMENT ADVISOR

Chapter Objectives

1. Things to Consider Before Selecting an Investment Advisor
2. How to Select an Investment Broker
3. Description of Services and Fees of: Full-Service Brokers, Discount Brokers, Professional Investment Managers, Investment Newsletters, Bankers and Financial Planners

Investment advisors can play an important role in designing and implementing your investment program. The extent to which you should consider them depends on

- How much time you can devote to your investments.
- How much confidence you have in researching, analyzing and making your own investment decisions.
- The size of your investment portfolio.

Because there are a variety of different advisors to choose from, your response to these considerations will lead you to the one(s) that most suit your needs.

In this chapter we discuss the following investment advisors, their services and fees:

- Investment brokers
- Professional investment managers
- Investment newsletter advisors
- Bankers and financial planners

Some, such as professional managers, can help all the way from originating investment ideas to transacting buy/sell orders. Others, such as financial planners, simply help you to design a general (model) portfolio mix, e.g., 20% savings, 50% stocks, 20% bonds and 10% insurance annuities.

Because you pay fees for an advisor's services, your portfolio's size becomes an important consideration. As a guideline,

- If your investments total less than $20,000, you can make your own decisions with what you've learned in this guide.
- If greater than $100,000, professional management becomes a viable alternative.

However, it's in the "gray area" of $20,000—$100,000 that your decision about an investment advisor becomes difficult. Below we offer suggestions to consider before deciding.

Remember, you should conduct your search carefully and thoroughly. Once an advisor is chosen, you'll also want to reserve the right to approve any trade. The ultimate decision should be yours--after all, it's *your* money!

CHECKLIST OF POINTS TO CONSIDER IN SELECTING AN ADVISOR *

Comfort Factor

The "comfort factor" is the single, most important consideration. You need someone that you can trust and "believe in." If ever in doubt, switch advisors.

Basic Investment Philosophy

You need an advisor whose investment philosophy matches yours in terms of goals, investing style, risk-return attitude, etc. This can be determined through a personal interview and/or by reading promotional literature and reports. Discuss with him/her the type of investments they held during different market cycles, his/her approach to selecting a particular security, etc. For example, do they use a "top down," "bottom up" or a "market timing" approach (refer to Chapters 11 and 13).

---

*Adapted from C. C. Hardy, Dun & Bradstreet's Guide to Investments (29th edition), Harper and Row, 1984.

Investment Experience

Ideally, you want someone with at least 10 years investing experience and preferably over 40 years of age. It's important that they have gone through several market cycles, especially the '73-'74 bear market (debacle!). Let the younger people learn with somebody else's money.

Historical Performance

While past performance is not necessarily a clear indication of the future, you do want an advisor with a good track record. But, what is "good?"

No one can consistently outperform the market year-to-year but, on average, they should have realized 12%-15% per year over the last 5-10 years. (Note: If they claim a goal of making over 20% per year, walk away-- they're taking on too much risk!)

You may also want to take time to check their actual holdings or recommendations. An advisor should make this available upon request.

- Where did the gains come from--a few big winners or were they spread out over a number of securities? If their recommendations work out 60% of the time, they're ahead of the average investor.
- Did they buy stocks near their lows and sell near their highs? Check their losing trades to see if the reverse occurred.
- Were losses due to general market conditions (bear market) or to poor selections?
- How long did they typically hold individual securities-were they trading often (high turnover), or did they tend to buy for the longer term?

Fees

You can easily do some shopping here. Investment brokers charge you commissions. Take their commission schedule and determine the cost for different size trades, e.g., 100 shares at $20, 300 shares at $10, etc. Pick dollar amounts that you expect your orders to be.

Professional advisors usually charge 1%-3% of your asset value. Subscriptions to investment newsletters normally run from $75 to $500 per year, although they can be higher.

In addition, find out if there are any other charges that are (may be) assessed and the conditions under which they are increased.

Clientele

It's best to deal with an advisor whose clients are similar to you in terms of age, income, objectives, etc. For instance, if you are 50 and planning for a retirement fund, don't use an advisor who has younger clients who are speculating in options.

Documentation

To what extent do they provide reports on your portfolio's performance? Do you get monthly or quarterly reports? How detailed are they? Are the reports prepared so as to simplify the preparation of your tax forms? Ask to see a sample copy.

INVESTMENT BROKERS

Your investments most likely will be purchased through a brokerage firm such as Merrill Lynch or Fidelity Brokerage Services. Within this firm, you will have a broker (referred to as an account executive) who services your account.

Always keep in mind that brokers are sales people first because their income comes from commissions on your buy/sell orders. The degree to which a broker provides investment advice depends on whether he/she is a full-service or a discount broker.

Full-Service Brokers

Individual investors typically use full-service brokers. The reason, as their name implies, is because they offer a wide variety of services, including free research reports, investment ideas and advice. In fact, these brokers are the major source of investment advice for the average investor. (Refer to Exhibit 17-1 for questions to ask your broker before buying a stock.)

They may also make suggestions on how to establish or change your portfolio to best fit your goals. Related to this, it's advisable to be certain that your broker knows exactly what kind of investor you are, e.g., investment goals, the degree of risk you'll tolerate, the amount of money you want to start with, etc. Moreover, this information will largely determine the kind of service a broker will provide. Remember: Brokers are paid for making trades--not for giving good advice.

It's a fact of life that the larger, more active accounts receive the most attention. If you only have $2,000, don't expect much. Brokers may have as many as 200 customers, yet less than 10% of these receive most of the broker's attention. Despite this, a good broker wants to develop future business. If you intend to build a steady investment program, a broker is going to show more interest in your account.

Selecting a Full-Service Broker

Friends and associates may have suggestions. (Note: Don't pick a friend to be your broker-- business and friendship don't mix well.) It's a good idea, though, to check out 3 or 4 brokers first. Your phone directory or newspaper ads can give you a start on brokerage firms in your area.

Visit with the branch manager to see if the firm can service your needs. "Cold calls" like this usually result in a junior broker being assigned to you. That's both bad and good: They're likely to be *inexperienced* (*not* necessarily incompetent, because all brokers must pass a battery of tests to be licensed) but they'll work harder because they're trying to build business.

If you have a sizable account, you can ask for a more senior broker. Even then, don't assume the broker is an expert. It's almost impossible these days to be an expert on all aspects of investing. (Exhibit 17-2 describes why.) Besides, his/her recommendations are based on research done by analysts, and most brokers usually can only afford to follow a handful of stocks at any one time.

Just don't forget that a successful relationship means developing a rapport in which trust and confidence in a broker are paramount. If you feel anything less than this, take your account elsewhere.

Exhibit 17-2
Exploding Growth in New Investment Products Overloads Brokers

Many brokers feel overwhelmed these days because of the proliferation of new investment products--ranging from stock index options and futures to sophisticated tax shelters.

Even though they may not fully understand the risks and rewards of the new products, brokers tend to push them because they carry fat commissions or because aggressive product managers are applying pressure. *RESULT:* Problems for brokers and their customers. Investors find themselves in investments unsuited to their needs *and* sometimes end up complaining to authorities or suing.

The genesis of this broker overload goes back to the late 1970s and early 1980s, when surging inflation and interest rates led investors to do more comparison shopping. Brokerage houses responded by introducing more new and repackaged products, like annuities and CDs. Deregulation also forced them to sell the latest and widest range of investments to stem the loss of clients to banks or insurance companies.

As a result, the days of specializing in a handful of products, usually stocks and corporate or municipal bonds, are gone. Brokers are now expected to be experts across the entire investment spectrum--from mutual funds and stock options to insurance and stocks and bonds.

The outcome has been the development of "generalists" rather than specialists who are *conversant* with most products (enough to sell them) but who don't understand every product well.

SOURCE: S. McMurray, "Big Increase in Investment Products Creates Problems for Brokers, Clients," The Wall Street Journal, December 24, 1984, p. 19.

Discount Brokers

Most *discount brokers* are strictly "no frills, order takers" who earn a straight salary. By eliminating the extras, though, hefty cuts in commission costs are made possible--up to 50%-75% less than their full-service counterparts--but no investment advice is given.

Should you use a discount broker? The answer depends on your investment behavior. If you buy fewer than 100 shares and/or deal in low-priced stocks, discounters save you nothing because of their minimum charges (see Chapter 5). Savings don't usually occur unless you trade in more than $2,000-$3,000 amounts.

Full-service brokers are the right choice if you are inexperienced in investing. If you are not interested in following the market closely or you want someone to tell you what to buy and when to sell, stay with a full-service broker.

As Marty Zweig, editor of the Zweig Forecast newsletter, put it:

"Figure out the premium that you're paying to a full-commission firm, and then consider what you're getting for your money. Is it hand-holding privileges, access to the new issues market, your relationship with the specific broker? The handholding, for example, may be very important to you. If you require it, then you'll have to pay for it."

If you decide to go with a discount broker, choose one with a local office so that any problems can be settled in person. Also, choose one who offers the kind of business you need--e.g., deals in bonds, unit trusts, mutual funds and IRAs, and offers money-market interest rates on idle cash.

Finally, trying to save a few dollars by shopping around may be a waste of time for most investors. Reason: If you trade 5-10 times a year, there won't be much difference across firms.

INVESTMENT TIP: Using a discount broker doesn't mean going it alone. One approach is to subscribe to an investment advisory newsletter for your investment ideas (see below). The commission dollars you save with a discounter in just a few trades will pay for the advice from the newsletter.

PROFESSIONAL MONEY MANAGERS

Mutual Funds

Mutual funds are professionally-managed portfolios of securities which handle all your investment chores. When you buy shares in the funds, you become an indirect owner of the securities.

There is a mutual fund designed to meet almost any investment objective. They are especially attractive for investors with limited funds to invest.

The costs and fees you can expect to pay are:
- A *one-time sales commission* of 6%-8% if it is a "load" fund.
- *Management fees* of .25% to 1.5% of your net asset value annually, but paid pro rata on a monthly basis.
- *Administrative costs* such as operating expenses and brokerage commissions. Usually these amount to less than 1% of your net asset value.

Records of your dividends and capital gains (FORM 1099) as well as quarterly/annual reports on performance and security holdings are provided. Refer to Chapter 16 for a more detailed discussion of mutual funds.

Professional Investment Managers

Individual advisors or management firms are available to manage your investment portfolio. These professional money managers follow changes in the tax laws, market and economy in order to help you meet your investment objectives.

Their clientele is usually small in numbers. Because they are smaller, they have greater trading flexibility and bring a more personal touch in comparison to a mutual fund. Your account is custom-designed to match your investment philosophy, tax situation, and so on.

Your manager will open a brokerage account in your name (some managers are also licensed brokers). Two types of accounts can be designated:
- *Discretionary account*--gives the manager power of attorney to decide what to buy or sell without consulting with you.
- *Nondiscretionary account*--requires the manager to act only with your permission.

The broker mails you a confirmation slip for each trade and a monthly statement on your security holdings and their value.

Some managers also send out reports on stocks they purchase as well as on their economic or market outlook. Most offer personal consultations on the risk and rewards of different investment opportunities. A few even publish advisory newsletters.

Their fees run higher than a mutual fund, usually 1%-3% a year. The biggest drawback is most managers will not handle an account that's less than $100,000.

Obtaining performance information is difficult because managers are not required to divulge publicly the results for their individual accounts. However, there are a few sources of performance data. Exhibit 17-3 contains a list of three such sources.

INVESTMENT ADVISORY NEWSLETTERS

Many investment services publish newsletters dealing with both stock market timing and selection. Subscriptions can be obtained for $75-$500 a year.

Because it is a relatively simple matter to start a newsletter, there are literally *hundreds* from which to choose. (Your "junk mail" has probably contained its share of their advertisements.) More importantly, most tend to be of low quality--more interesting than profitable.

A good source to help you filter out the chaff from the wheat is a five-year old newsletter rating service:

Hulbert Financial Digest
643 S. Carolina, S.E.
Washington, D.C. 20003
(800) 227-1617, Ext. 459

For $135 a year, HFD monitors nearly 75 of the more popular advisory newsletters and dispassionately ranks them on performance, clarity of language and portfolio size. (Recently published is the first HFD Annual Review of Investment

Newsletters, Reston, $16.95, which profiles the newsletters and suggests techniques of utilizing them.)

Exhibit 17-4 presents the long-term performance of the top 5 newsletters HFD has followed for at least five years. As a guideline, for 1983, the average length of the holding period and number of positions closed out as well as the percentage of closeouts which were longer than one year are also included. These are important considerations in determining the different approaches taken by each newsletter (trading vs. a buy-and-hold strategy) and the impact on *after-tax* performance.

OTHER ADVISORS

Bankers

Bankers (trust officers) often provide investment advice to their customers. This usually stems from their investing funds held in trust. Traditionally, because of their training and fiduciary responsibility, they have been very conservative and produced poor performance records.

Increasingly, competition has forced many banks to upgrade their investment services. Now, you can find banks that have established

Exhibit 17-4
Performance of Top 5 Newsletters Followed
By The Hulbert Financial Digest
(July 1980 through February 1985)

	Total Performance	1983		
		Holding Period (Days)	Number Closed Out	Percentage Long-Term*
1. Growth Stock Outlook	187.6%	285	14	29.6%
2. Green's Commodity Market Comments	153.5%	N.A.	N.A.	N.A.
3. Value Line OTC Special Situation Survey	143.4%	1 Year	6	66.7%
4. Zweig Forecast	121.6%	70	99	1.0%
5. Market Logic	118.2%	292	1	0.0%
S&P 500 Composite Index	99.8%	--	--	--

* In 1983, long-term for tax purposes was defined to be more than one year.

SOURCE: The Hulbert Financial Digest, April 1985.

special departments to provide financial counseling and portfolio recommendations. This is usually made available only to well-heeled customers with large deposits of over $100,000.

Financial Planners

The complexities of building personal assets has spawned a new professional: *personal financial planners*. If you haven't already heard from someone anxious to be your personal financial planner, the odds are growing that you soon will. An estimated 250,000 men and women now call themselves financial planners. They may work for a bank, a brokerage firm or other respected financial services firm, or they may be independent consultants.

There are two types of planners: those who work for a *flat fee* and those who work largely for *commissions*. "Commission" planners derive their income by selling you insurance, annuities, tax shelters, etc.

CAUTION: Their advice tends toward your buying more of what they sell, and be wary of "know-it-all" types. No one individual can be thoroughly schooled in, among other things, all aspects of taxes, life and health insurance, stocks and bonds, trust funds, pensions and real estate.

"Fee-only" planners operate independently. While more expensive, they have less self-interest. Hourly fees run $50 to $150. If they charge a flat fee it'll run $750-$1,000 on the low side, for example, for a basic financial plan for a homeowning family with a household income of $75,000. Expect to pay one-third as much annually for updating your plan.

Financial planners offer a variety of services--evaluating your current financial situation, setting financial goals given your income, assets and needs, giving tax advice, and providing very *broad* investment recommendations. What investment advice you do receive may be largely self-serving. That is, you will hear recommen-

dations that lean toward load mutual funds and universal life insurance--high commission products. You're not likely to find no-load funds or bank CDs mentioned. Exhibit 17-5 describes what you can expect to get from a financial planner.

Exhibit 17-5
What to Expect from a Financial Planner

A typical financial plan will include the following:
1. A balance sheet and analysis, including an asset allocation breakdown that relates to your risk preferences and needs.
2. A projection of income taxes.
3. A projection of cash flow.
4. Long-term accumulation plans for children's education, retirement, etc. as well as a statement of your goals.
5. A life and health insurance analysis.
6. Estate and tax planning.

The plan should also identify weaknesses in your financial picture, such as inadequate cash flow, unnecessary tax payments and the wrong kind of insurance or investments, and it should recommend specific improvements. Finally, the plan should include recommendations for implementing the program.

SOURCE: M. C. Scott, "Financial Planners: An Individual Investor's Guide to the Industry," AAII Journal, July 1985, pp. 13-17.

Unfortunately, *anyone* can call himself or herself a financial planner (an industry badly in need of regulation). Some are good, others are terrible. *TIP:* If you decide to seek out a planner (they *are* a convenient, "one-stop shopping" advisor), stick with a *Certified Financial Planner* (and ask friends to recommend planners whose work has pleased them). With a C.F.P., you have someone who has demonstrated a certain level of skills and experience in financial planning and investments.

Exhibit 17-6 gives a list of four organizations that will provide referrals to members in your local area.

TERMS TO KNOW

Account executive
Certified Financial Planner
Discount broker
Discretionary account
Financial planner
Full-service broker
Investment broker
Investment newsletter
Non-discretionary account

18 PLANNING FOR A PROFITABLE RETIREMENT WITH IRAs

That comfortable, financially secure retirement you've been planning may demand more savings on your part than you think. Otherwise, uncertain future inflation and Social Security benefits may deny you your retirement dreams.

In 1981, the federal government expanded the existing *Individual Retirement Account (IRA)* provisions to make it an "every man's retirement plan," not just for those who were not covered by any other type of retirement plan. Although the Tax Reform Act of 1986 made IRAs less attractive for some people, they can still be a very important part of retirement planning.

This savings plan offers two important incentives: (1) *tax savings* (for some taxpayers) and (2) *accelerated growth in income from tax-free compounding.* While it is easy to understand, brokers and financial institutions have tended to confuse the issue with their heavy advertising and numerous IRA products. This chapter examines the basic features and advantages of an IRA program, provides ideas on managing your IRA account, and discusses how tax reform has affected your IRA decisions.

BASIC FEATURES OF AN IRA
Who's Eligible?

Anyone gainfully employed under age 70½ can set up and contribute to an IRA. If your spouse is unemployed, a *Spousal IRA* can be established for him or her. And, you can't be too young-- even children with earnings can start an IRA.

How Much Can You Contribute?

Maximum contribution is $2,000 a year, assuming you earned at least this much. If you earned less than $2,000, the most you can fund is 100% of your earned income. This rule also applies to your spouse if he/she is also employed. So, a maximum of $4,000 can be invested in IRAs each year by employed couples.

If you or your spouse is *unemployed* and you file a joint tax return, $250 a year can be contributed to a Spousal IRA, or a maximum of $2,250 between the two.

NOTE: The $2,250 can be divided between IRA and the Spousal IRA however you like-- so long as neither account receives more than $2,000 a year. And, if the unemployed spouse starts working later, the *same* IRA account may be used.

For purposes of determining your maximum contribution, "earned" income includes wages, salaries, business earnings, *etc.* It also includes alimony payments received, but *investment income* such as interest and dividends doesn't qualify.

You have from January 1 to April 15 of the *following* year to make your IRA contributions. If you file your tax return early, you can claim a tax deduction (if you are eligible--see below) even if you haven't yet made the contribution. In any case, you *must* make your contribution by April 15, even if you have a filing extension on your tax return.

Are Contributions Tax Deductible?

From 1982 through 1986, the federal income tax laws provided that all contributions to an IRA were fully deductible on your IRS Form 1040. After passage of the Tax Reform Act of 1986, the rules were changed to limit deductions in some cases. Beginning with contributions made for 1987, several factors must be considered to determine how much is deductible:

1. *Married.* If *NEITHER* spouse is an active participant in an employer-sponsored retirement plan or a Keogh plan, then *both* are eligible to make *fully deductible* contributions to an IRA. If either spouse participates in another plan, you can still deduct all contributions if your adjusted gross income is less than $40,000.

   Between $40,000 and $50,000, the IRA deduction is reduced by 20% of adjusted gross income in excess of $40,000, until only *non-deductible* contributions can be made at income levels above $50,000.

2. *Single.* You can *fully deduct* your IRA contribution if you are *not* an active participant in an employer-sponsored plan or a Keogh plan. If you do participate in another plan, you can still deduct all contributions if your adjusted gross income is less than $25,000.

   Between $25,000 and $35,000, the deductible contribution decreases by 20% of adjusted gross income in excess of $25,000, until only *non-deductible* contributions can be made at income levels above $35,000.

NOTE: You are considered an active participant in an employer-sponsored retirement plan whether or not your benefits are vested. However, if you do not meet your plan's eligibility requirements because you are too young or haven't worked at the job long enough, you are *not* considered an active participant. In that case you can still make deductible IRA contributions.

Even if the new rules limit the amount of your tax deduction, remember that you can still make *non-deductible contributions* to your IRA for the difference between the allowable deduction and the maximum $2,000 annual contribution.

Distributions: When, How Much, and How Taxed?

WHEN? Withdrawals can be made at any time and are *taxed in the year withdrawn.* They can be made monthly, quarterly, etc. or a lump-sum amount can be received. However, depending on your age, certain restrictions may apply.

1. *Under Age 59½.* A 10% penalty or excise tax is imposed because this is considered an early withdrawal. There are, however, two exceptions. You may use the funds before 59½ without penalty if you become permanently disabled. The penalty is also waived if you elect to withdraw the money in equal installments over your lifetime, such as through an annuity.
2. *Age 59½ − 70½.* No restriction. In fact, you can elect to *continue to make contributions* in this age category if you continue to earn income each year.
3. *Over Age 70½.* No further contributions can be made, and you *must* begin withdrawals by *April 1 of the year after age 70½ is reached.* Otherwise, a very stiff penalty is assessed by the IRS. A *50% excise tax* on what is called "excessive accumulations" will be due on money that should have been withdrawn but wasn't. (I ask you, is that not a big enough incentive to encourage withdrawals . . .?)

HOW MUCH? In general, the minimum withdrawal is based on the owner's life expectancy. Specifically, though, one of three options (if they apply) can be selected to find the minimum amount. (We're focusing on "minimum" because some people may not need the money for living expenses and/or may want to leave something behind for a spouse or a child.)

1. *Holder's Life Expecancy.* The minimum withdrawal is found by dividing the IRA's value by the owner's life expectancy. For

example, a man aged 70 has a life expectancy of about 12 years, so *at least* 1/12th of the IRA's value must be taken out in the first year.

A SPECIAL NOTE: IRA holders may recalculate their life expectancy *each* year and adjust withdrawals accordingly. In effect, this extends the withdrawals over a longer period by reducing the yearly withdrawals.

2. *Owner-Spouse Life Expectancy.* Another option that may allow you to spread out the withdrawals is to use the *combined* life expectancy of the IRA owner and the owner's spouse. By taking into account both spouses' life expectancy, withdrawals may be stretched over a longer period (assuming, of course, that the spouse is younger than the owner). Again, life expectancy can be recalculated yearly.

3. *Owner-Child Life Expectancy.* If the beneficiary is a child or a grandchild instead of a spouse, the combined life expectancy of the owner and child can be used. This will make withdrawals even smaller and extend them farther into the future. BUT, "life expectancy" can't be recalculated each year.

What happens to an IRA when the owner dies? It becomes part of his/her estate for tax purposes. While unlimited assets can be left to a spouse without estate tax liability, an estate valued at more than $600,000 that is left to others is taxable. Also, withdrawals from inherited IRAs by an heir are taxed as ordinary income.

HOW TAXED? To determine how much of your withdrawals is subject to taxation, you must first add together the balance in all your IRA accounts. The total amount is then divided into two pieces: (1) Non-deductible contributions, and (2) Deductible contributions and untaxed earnings. Withdrawals are treated as if they come proportionately from each component. Taxes will apply only to the part that is allocated to *deductible contributions* and untaxed earnings.

EXAMPLE: You have accumulated a total of $100,000 in your IRA accounts, including $20,000 of contributions for which you received no tax deduction. That means 20% ($20,000 ÷ $100,000) of your total IRA balance is allocated to non-deductible contributions. If you make a $10,000 withdrawal, 20% or $2,000 will not be subject to tax.

In the example above, the $2,000 not subject to income tax is also not subject to the 10% penalty if your withdrawal is made before age 59½.

SUGGESTION: To help you keep track of non-deductible IRA contributions, consider maintaining a separate "non-deductible IRA" account for these contributions. This will simplify matters when you calculate the tax on withdrawals.

The Tax Reform Act also added a new *excess distribution penalty* which must be considered. If you receive a taxable distribution of more than $112,500 in a year, you'll owe a 15% tax on the excess.

IMPORTANT ADVANTAGES OF AN IRA

By 1986, 35 million households owned IRA accounts totaling $260 billion. From a government survey, major reasons given for opening an account were in order of importance:

- to generate current tax savings
- to plan for retirement
- to defer taxes on earnings

Let's examine each of these advantages.

Saving on Current Taxes

To the extent you can deduct IRA contributions before taxes, you get to reduce your taxable income. This cuts you federal tax bill and, depending on your state laws, it can also reduce your state income taxes. (Of course, if you make a "non-deductible IRA" contribution, there's no immediate tax savings because it's done with after-tax dollars.)

For instance, say you are in the 28% marginal tax bracket. A $2,000 deduction for your IRA contribution will save you $560 (0.28 × $2,000) in tax. In effect, the government picks up $560 of your contribution.

Planning for Retirement

An IRA's contributions and tax-deferred compounding of earnings can make a regular $2,000 contribution grow to a sizable retirement fund. Even if you are age 55 or 60, it may be wise to start an IRA.

Exhibit 18-1 illustrates the nest egg that can be accumulated when an IRA is started at different ages. For instance, let's say you're 40. If you contribute $2,000 annually, you'll make total contributions of $50,000 by age 65. Now, if these funds are invested at 10% interest, your IRA will be worth $216,364.

Exhibit 18-1
Annual Retirement Income From an IRA

Age IRA Started	Deposits to Age 65	Value at Age 65	Annual Retirement Income Over 15 Years
25	$80,000	$973,704	$116,379
35	$60,000	$361,887	$ 43,253
40	$50,000	$216,364	$ 25,860
55	$20,000	$ 35,062	$ 4,191

(Assumes a 10% annual return, and does not consider the loss of purchasing power due to inflation.)

Furthermore, if you elect to have a 15-year distribution schedule, this retirement fund will generate $25,860 in income per year. If the payments are scheduled over a period less than 15 years, your annual income will be even higher.

Tax-Deferring Your Earnings

Perhaps the best way to illustrate the advantage of tax-deferred earnings is to compare IRA investments with a non-IRA (taxable) investment. Exhibit 19-2 illustrates the amounts which can be accumulated over various periods by making a $2,000 (pre-tax) contribution to a fully-deductible IRA account, a non-deductible IRA account and a non-IRA investment.

Exhibit 18-2
IRA vs. Non-IRA Investments

Years	Fully-Deductible IRA	Non-Deductible IRA	Taxable Investment
10	$ 35,062	$ 25,245	$ 21,531
20	$126,005	$ 90,724	$ 64,683
30	$361,887	$260,559	$151,171

NOTE: Assumes an annual contribution of $2,000 in pre-tax dollars (or $1,440 in after-tax dollars), an earnings rate of 10% annually, and a marginal tax rate of 28%.

Compare the non-deductible IRA with the taxable investment. Even though both investments must be funded with *after-tax* dollars, the rate of accumulation is much faster in the IRA, which amounts to $260,559 after 30 years. After the same period, the taxable investment accumulates only $151,171 because its earnings must be reduced each year by 28% for taxes. This clearly shows the substantial power of *tax-deferred earnings*.

CAVEAT: As we have seen, an IRA can accumulate retirement funds at an *accelerated* rate because its earnings are not taxed until withdrawn. If your tax bracket during your retirement years is *less than* during your working years, an IRA is *always* superior to an equivalent taxable investment. But, if your rate becomes *higher* during retirement, then a non-IRA investment may be preferred. More on this later.

MANAGING YOUR IRA INVESTMENTS

Two Types of IRAs to Consider

The kinds of investments you may put your IRA money in depends on which type of IRA you open.

1. *Product-Oriented Plan.* This plan is usually limited to savings accounts, bank CDs or mutual funds. Savings institutions and investment companies sponsor this type of plan.

2. *Self-Directed Plan.* This plan offers you more options than a product-oriented plan, where your choices are limited to those offered by the institution. With a self-directed plan, you can choose from a wider array, including stocks, bonds, mutual funds, annuities, real estate and mortgage securities. They are offered by brokerage firms and many banks.

Both plans are very simple to establish--have your money ready and just sign a preprinted form. Nevertheless, costs and other considerations may push you one way or another.

Product-Oriented Plan

This involves minimal costs and hassles. *Savings* and *CD accounts* have low, if any, administrative fees plus they offer a fixed return, backed by federal insurance. A major disadvantage is a penalty for early withdrawal (we are not referring to the excise tax assessed by the federal government).

Mutual funds offer you a range of investments from money markets, stocks and bonds to specialty or sector funds such as high technology and gold. They offer professional management and good diversification. They charge annual management fees (and perhaps set-up and surrender fees). Operating expenses and commissions also come out of your income. Many investment companies now offer a "family of funds" that allows you to switch between funds as economic and market conditions change.

Fixed- and Variable-Rate Annuities frequently have been fee-heavy and produced unimpressive returns. Comparing different annuity plans is difficult, too. Surrender charges can be 6%-10% if you close your account before a certain date. Another thing is that the tax-deferred income feature of annuities is wasted (see below).

Self-Directed Plan

If you like to make your own decisions, a *self-directed plan* may suit you. It provides greater flexibility and the opportunity to maximize your

returns. The major drawback is that brokerage firms charge the highest set-up and maintenance fees for an IRA ($30-$75). Brokerage commissions must also be paid; otherwise, there are few restrictions.

A Word on Tax-Advantaged Investments: The Case of "Oversheltering." About the only investments that don't make sense for an IRA are those that are appealing because of tax advantages--tax-exempt municipal bonds (munis) or limited partnerships. Because IRAs are sheltered from taxes, any tax advantages or write-offs are wasted. Worse still, all income will be taxable when withdrawn, including tax-free yields.

Where to Invest?

Except for collectibles, life insurance and precious metals, you have many choices of what to invest in. Like choosing a wine, picking the best IRA investment is largely personal preference.

NOTE: Under the 1986 Tax Reform Act, the ban on collectibles in an IRA was altered to allow investments in gold or silver coins issued by the U.S. government.

Exhibit 18-3 gives you an idea where your fellow IRAers are putting their money.

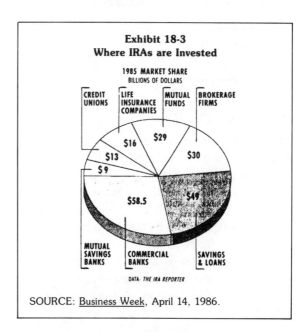

Exhibit 18-3
Where IRAs are Invested

1985 MARKET SHARE
BILLIONS OF DOLLARS

CREDIT UNIONS — LIFE INSURANCE COMPANIES — MUTUAL FUNDS — BROKERAGE FIRMS

$16 $29 $30

$13

$9

$58.5 $49

MUTUAL SAVINGS BANKS   COMMERCIAL BANKS   SAVINGS & LOANS

DATA: *THE IRA REPORTER*

SOURCE: <u>Business Week</u>, April 14, 1986.

As you can see, the biggest share of IRAs is being funneled into product-oriented plans of savings institutions. As a further suggestion, you may want to ask yourself the 3 questions found in Exhibit 18-4 before you decide where to invest.

Exhibit 18-4
Questions to Ask Yourself Before Deciding on Where to Invest Your IRA

Your Age?

The closer to retirement you get, the less risk you should take. If you are under 50, you can afford riskier but potentially more profitable investments that emphasize capital growth. If your investments should go awry, you have more time to recoup your losses. If close to retirement, preserving capital is most important, so stay conservative. Refer to Exhibit 18-5 for some helpful guidelines.

Also, older persons shouldn't tie up funds for *long* periods (e.g., a 20-year bond) because it'll take years to produce their returns. If this is your only retirement plan, remain ultra conservative regardless of age.

What Other Investments Do You Have?

If your non-IRA assets are mostly in the stock market or growth mutual funds, *diversify* by placing your IRA into high-income investments such as CDs, fixed-income securities or bond funds. Remember: *All* your assets should be considered, *including your other retirement plans.*

What's Your Investing Expertise?

GUIDELINE: If you don't understand an investment, leave it alone. This is especially true as more and more complex (risky) IRA products hit the market. Prime items to view very cautiously are options, commodity futures and limited partnerships. As you become more informed and gain confidence, you'll have more choices.

Exhibit 18-5
Guidelines for IRA Selection by Age Bracket

Under Age 30

It's possible to ignore an IRA here if you are in a low marginal tax bracket and have little disposable income. Use any funds for capital growth potential, especially home ownership.

Age 30-40

Invest in a diversified portfolio of common stocks such as a no-load fund. Avoid bonds and/or preferred stock investments-- zero growth potential. Avoid non-dividend paying stocks. Try to combine *both* growth and income. For example, stick to investments that are expected to generate ⅔s capital appreciation and ⅓ current income.

Age 40-50

Similar to the last age group. However, if you expect to begin taking distributions at age 59½, shift to an 80% equity, 20% debt portfolio. Some high-yielding common stocks such as public utilities can be substituted for the 20% debt portion.

Age 50-60

As the age of allowable distribution approaches, increasingly shift toward fixed-income investments to reduce risk and to provide income for cash distributions. Depending on how close you are to the first distribution, 50%-80% of your portfolio should be in common stocks. Fixed-income investments with short- (1-3 years) to intermediate-term (3-8 years) maturities should account for 10%-25% of your portfolio.

Over Age 60

Nearly 100% of your IRA should be in current-income investments with 40%-50% in short-term investments and the remainder in 3-5 year maturities. This strategy provides safety and maximum current income.

SOURCE: G. W. Perritt and L. K. Shannon. The Individual Investor's Guide to No-Load Mutual Funds. Chicago: Investment Information Services Press, 1985.

The Tax Reform Act of 1986 will probably affect the types of assets you put into your IRA. Prior to reform, it did not make sense to put growth stocks or similar investments into an IRA. That was because you lost the benefit of the favorable long-term capital gains tax rate if income on these investments was taxed as withdrawals from an IRA account.

Since tax reform eliminates favorable tax treatment of long-term capital gains, it makes growth stocks or mutual funds more attractive for your IRA.

TIPS FOR YOUR IRA

There are a number of things you'll want to keep in mind with regard to your IRA:

1. You can open an IRA with just $1 (most plans, however, may require a larger minimum amount). Contributions can only be made *in cash.*

   You don't have to contribute *every year* if the cash is not handy. However, it's possible to *borrow* your contribution through a short-term personal loan. Even if your loan rate is 13%-15%, you can come out ahead. For example, you'll get the tax deduction on the IRA contributions (if you qualify) and the tax-deferred interest it earns. Also, if you itemize deductions, you may be able to deduct some or all of the loan's interest charges (subject to the investment interest limitations--see Chapter 19).

2. An alternative way to fund your IRA is to claim an income tax deduction for an IRA *before* actually making the contribution. This will work if your tax return is filed early and a large refund is expected before the April 15 deadline for contributing to an IRA.

3. If you qualify to deduct your IRA contributions, amend your W-4 form with your employer. Claim two *extra* exemptions and put the extra take-home pay in your IRA. Remember: You need the discipline to follow through on this strategy or else you'll end up owing taxes.

4. Don't "overcontribute" to your IRA. If you do, it'll cost you a 6% excise tax on this excess unless you remove it before filing your tax return.

5. You can't *borrow from* your IRA, but you're permitted a *once-a-year use* of your IRA money *without tax penalty*. (This is referred to as a *Rollover IRA.*) But, you must reinvest this money into an IRA *within 60 days* or it'll be treated as an early withdrawal and subject to penalty and tax. *If you don't take possession of your IRA money,* any number of switches can be made from one account to another.

6. You may open as many IRAs as you like-- just don't exceed the allowed deduction each year.

7. It makes the most sense to contribute to your IRA as early as possible (January 1 is most preferred!). Why? The timing can make a substantial difference--tens of thousands of dollars upon retirement. Exhibit 18-6 gives you an example of why

it pays to invest early. *MORAL:* Don't habitually fund your IRA just before April 15 of the following year.

8. IRA contributions may be deductible on your *state* tax return. This varies by state, so you'll need to check on it.

9. Make sure you keep track of what is in your IRA(s). Some people open a new account every year. After a while, that can become confusing. (Worksheet No. 8 is an IRA financial record form you might want to use to help you keep track of your yearly IRA contributions.) Also, require regular reports from the institution that holds your money. If there's an error, all you will have for proof are the records you keep.

Exhibit 18-6
Why It Pays to Contribute Early in the Year

Value of an IRA Account at Retirement (Age 65)
When a $2,000 Annual Contribution is Made Every:

Current Age	January 1	June 1	December 31	Following April 15
35	$361,886	$345,429	$328,988	$319,548
45	$126,005	$120,274	$114,550	$109,989
55	$ 35,062	$ 33,467	$ 31,874	$ 29,195

NOTE: Assumes contributions earn 10% annually.

SOURCE: Investment Company Institute

THE IMPACT OF TAX REFORM ON IRA DECISIONS

Before the Tax Reform Act of 1986, IRAs offered such advantages that they were almost always a part of smart retirement planning. But tax reform eliminated some of the advantages, and makes the decision more complicated.

The reduction in tax rates decreases the value (advantage) of a tax-deferred return relative to a taxable return. Moreover, the fewer tax brackets significantly reduce the chances that your future income will be taxed at a lower marginal rate upon retirement. It's also possible that by the time you withdraw your retirement savings, marginal rates could have been *increased* by Congress--they've done it before.

If you continue to use an IRA, tax reform affects the types of investments to consider. We have already discussed how the elimination of favorable tax treatment for long-term capital gains now makes growth stocks and similar investments suitable for inclusion in a retirement account.

But perhaps the biggest issue arising out of tax reform is whether or not you should continue to contribute if you get *no tax deduction*.

While tax-deferred compounding of earnings is still the biggest advantage of IRA accounts, the loss of tax deductions makes the decision to contribute a more difficult one. You must now compare a nondeductible IRA with other tax-advantaged investments.

Tax-exempt municipal bonds (or mutual funds or unit trusts that invest in them) offer tax-free income without the early-withdrawal penalty. Depending on their yield, these could be a better deal, especially if you are near retirement.

You should also contrast a nondeductible IRA contribution to a deferred annuity or a single-premium life insurance contract (see Chapter 7). These contracts have the same tax-free buildup as IRAs, but there are no limitations on the amount that can be invested. With these investments, however, you should watch out for heavy fees. You may also give up the opportunity to self-direct your investments.

Under the old tax rules, you could sometimes justify an IRA investment even when it was possible that the funds would be needed before retirement. An IRA investor could often withdraw funds after 5 or 6 years and still come out ahead of an unsheltered investment, even after paying taxes and the 10% penalty. But with the combination of lower tax rates and the loss of tax savings from a deduction, it now takes the IRA account much longer to breakeven. Exhibit 18-7 gives some examples of the breakeven point both before and after tax reform.

Exhibit 18-7
IRA vs. Taxable Investment
Years to Breakeven

(Interest Rate Equals 10%)

Tax Bracket (Old vs. New)		Old Tax Law	New Tax Law (1)
TOP	(50% vs. 33%)	5 years	11 years
MIDDLE	(34% vs. 28%)	6 years	11 years
LOW	(20% vs. 15%)	8 years	16 years

(1) Assuming the taxpayer gets no deduction for his IRA contribution.

As the exhibit clearly demonstrates, an IRA was not a short-term investment even under the old rules. Without a tax deduction, it can no longer be considered a good intermediate-term alternative.

IRA investors must also consider whether they should make early withdrawals from existing accounts. Lower rates in 1987 and even lower rates in 1988 make this less expensive than before. Early withdrawers give up the benefit of tax-deferred earnings, in addition to the 10% excise tax. But if you strongly believe tax rates are going to increase, this option could be beneficial.

One group of taxpayers will find IRAs more attractive under the new rules. Before tax reform, people entitled to lump-sum payouts from company pension or profit-sharing plans could compute their tax as if the amount had been paid out over 10 years instead of all at once. Now, 10-year forward averaging has been replaced by 5-year averaging except for those who were 50 or older on January 1, 1986. This means more people will want to "rollover" their distributions into an IRA, which is a tax-free transaction.

Also, the new tax law imposes an additional 15% tax on lump-sum distributions in excess of $562,500. You can avoid this by rolling the money into an IRA, and then making annual withdrawals of $112,500 or less.

TERMS TO KNOW

Deductible IRA
Fixed-rate annuity
Individual Retirement Account (IRA)
Non-deductible IRA
Product-oriented IRA plan
Rollover IRA
Self-directed IRA Plan
Variable-rate annuity

19

HOW 1986 TAX REFORM AFFECTS YOUR INVESTMENT DECISIONS

Your objective in investing is to make a profit. But, the tax laws determine *how much* profit you get to keep. That is, smart investors measure returns in *after-tax* dollars, especially when they evaluate alternative investments which are treated differently under the tax code.

To make wise investment decisions, you must have at least a fundamental understanding of the federal income tax system. But, if you haven't taken the time to learn much about it, don't worry--many of the rules just changed. On October 22, 1986, President Ronald Reagan signed into law the most sweeping revision of the federal tax code since 1954.

The Tax Reform Act of 1986 reduces individual tax rates to the lowest levels since Calvin Coolidge was president 60 years ago, and curtails more tax deductions, credits and exemptions than any previous tax bill. Individuals will have to rethink a host of economic decisions, from owning a home vs. renting, to setting up bank accounts for children, to planning for retirement. Tax reform also changes the basis for making investment decisions.

In this chapter, we examine the basics of tax reform, help you to determine how much your taxes are likely to increase or decrease, discuss how tax reform affects your investments, and explore the tax-saving strategies which survived or emerged from tax reform.

THE BASICS OF TAX REFORM

While a comprehensive review of the Tax Reform Act of 1986 is beyond the scope of this discussion, we are going to examine those basic elements which have a significant impact on most taxpayers, and especially those which affect the more common investment decisions.

Rates, Deductions and Exemptions

Under the old system, tax rates ranged from 11% to 50%, and were broken into 14 taxable income brackets (15 for single filers). When the new rates take full effect in 1988, there will be only two brackets plus a surtax for higher income taxpayers. In the 1987 "transition year" there will be five rates ranging from 11% to 38½%. Exhibit 19-1 lists the new rates.

The standard deduction (which may be taken instead of itemizing deductions) is increased from $3,670 to $5,000 for joint filers and from $2,480 to $3,000 for single returns.

The 1986 personal exemption of $1,080 is increased to $1,900 in 1987, $1,950 in 1988 and $2,000 in 1989. Thereafter, exemptions will be indexed for inflation. However, the personal exemption will be phased out for high income taxpayers in 1988.

Interest on Municipal Bonds

Interest earned on "essential purpose" municipal bonds is still free of federal income taxes. But interest on certain "private purpose" bonds (such as those issued to finance sports stadiums, convention centers, industrial parks and pollution control facilities) is no longer excludable if the bonds were issued after August 7, 1986.

Capital Gains/Losses

Prior to tax reform, 60% of long-term capital gains was excluded from taxable income. That meant the maximum rate for such gains was 20% (40% of the gain taxed at the maximum rate of 50%). In 1987, the maximum rate on long-term gains jumps to 28%, and thereafter there will be no distinction between long and short-term gains or losses. All capital gains will be taxed at the same rate as your ordinary income, such as wages, interest and dividends. That rate could be as high as 33%--the regular top rate of 28% plus the 5% surtax that will apply to some people. Net capital losses can be used to offset ordinary income, but only to the extent of $3,000 per year.

Tax Shelters

"Passive" losses, which investors in limited partnership tax shelters often incur, can no longer be used to offset ordinary income. Passive losses, which typically are losses in investments where you are not involved on a day-to-day basis, will only be able to offset passive income from other similar activities. Unusable passive losses can be carried forward for use in offsetting passive income in future years, or to be deducted when the investment is eventually sold.

Investments held as of the October 22, 1986 signing date of the tax bill get a break. The curbs on their passive losses are phased in so that 35% of losses not offsetting passive income are disallowed in 1987, 60% in 1988, 80% in 1989, 90% in 1990 and 100% thereafter.

Interest on Consumer Loans

Consumer interest generally includes all non-business interest other than investment interest (see below). It includes, for example, interest on an automobile loan and credit card interest incurred for personal expenses. The new law disallows all consumer interest deductions with the exception of tuition and medical expense loans. These limits are phased in so that 65% of the disallowed interest is still allowed in 1987, 40% in 1988, 20% in 1989, 10% in 1990, and none thereafter.

Investment Interest

Borrowing to make an investment, including buying stocks on margin, is trickier under the new law. You will be able to deduct such interest only to the amount of your investment income, including dividends, interest income and capital gains. Under the old law you could deduct up to an amount $10,000 more than your investment income. The new cap applies not only to new borrowings, but also to interest paid on debt incurred prior to the new law. The new limits are phased in over five years just as the limits on consumer interest.

Special Provisions for Homeowners

The new tax code preserves the cherished tax advantages of homeownership. Homeowners not only get to keep a number of valuable tax breaks, they also get a chance to borrow against the equity in their homes and get additional deductions for interest expense that would otherwise be disallowed.

Unlike interest on consumer loans, interest on a home mortgage is still fully deductible. Also deductible would be interest on a second mortgage or a home-equity loan, such as a revolving credit account that is secured by your home. You can raise cash with a second mortgage to, for example, buy a car, redecorate the home, make investments, or pay for other personal expenses. Interest is deductible on debt up to an amount equal to what you paid for the home, plus the cost of improvements. The deduction applies to loans on both your principal home and a second residence.

For example, let's assume you paid $85,000 for your home, and spent $15,000 on various improvements. The home is currently worth $125,000. You would be able to fully deduct interest paid on loans secured by the home, to the extent that such loans do not exceed $100,000 ($85,000 plus $15,000). There is, however, one exception allowed under the new rules. If you borrow to pay for education or medical expenses, then the interest is fully deductible on loans up to an amount equal to the value of the home, or $125,000 in our example.

A special provision of the new law helps people who previously borrowed against their homes and currently have loans that exceed the new limits. This provision allows an interest deduction on loans outstanding before August 17, 1986, for up to the value of the home, regardless of how the funds were used.

A number of other homeowner tax breaks are also preserved under the new rules:
- Real estate taxes are still fully deductible
- You may still defer profits on the sale of a home if you buy another home of at least equal value
- There is still a one-time exclusion which allows people over age 55 to exclude up to $125,000 of the profit on sale of their homes.

Individual Retirement Accounts

The new tax code retains the deduction of up to $2,000 each for contributions to Individual Retirement Accounts (IRAs), provided that neither the taxpayer nor the taxpayer's spouse is an active participant in an employer-sponsored retirement plan. Even if the taxpayer or the spouse is an active participant in a plan, the deduction for contributions to an IRA might still be allowed if adjusted gross income does not exceed certain limits.

See Chapter 18 for more information on IRA accounts.

Miscellaneous Provisions

The Tax Reform Act of 1986 also repealed or modified a number of other commonly used provisions of the old tax law. Among the more significant are the following:
- repealed the regular income averaging provisions
- repealed the two-earner deduction for working couples
- repealed the dividend exclusion
- repealed the investment tax credit
- repealed the deduction for state and local sales taxes
- increased the amount of nondeductible medical expenses from 5% to 7.5% of adjusted gross income
- made charitable contributions and moving expenses deductible only for those who itemize
- changed the rules for miscellaneous itemized deductions, allowing only the amount

which exceeds 2% of adjusted gross income

- changed the rules to require that unreimbursed employee travel and transportation costs, outside salesmen's expenses, union dues, costs of business periodicals, tax preparation fees, uniforms, and job-related education expenses will be deductible only as miscellaneous itemized deductions, subject to the 2% floor

ESTIMATING YOUR TAXES UNDER THE NEW RULES

There are both winners and losers under the new tax law. A majority of individuals will pay less after the new rates are in full effect in 1988, and millions of poor people will pay no taxes at all. But for many middle-income taxpayers, the lower rates won't compensate for the loss of many deductions and exclusions. Large numbers of taxpayers will find their tax burden higher than ever, especially those who made extensive use of the shelters available under the prior tax code.

To help you estimate tax reform's effect on your personal tax situation, turn to Worksheet No. 9. This worksheet will help you estimate your taxes for the 1987 transition year and for 1988 after the lower rates take full effect.

HOW TAX REFORM AFFECTS YOUR INVESTMENTS

The new tax law significantly affects how individuals make investment decisions. Generally, there is now greater emphasis on investments that produce income, and less emphasis on investments that produce tax losses. Investors can spend more time worrying about real financial matters, and less time about how to beat the tax law.

The effect of tax reform on your investments will, to some extent, depend upon how it affects the economy as a whole. And this is a highly uncertain and hotly debated issue. The new code shifts much of the tax burden from individuals to corporations, and eliminates or reduces many provisions that were designed to encourage a variety of economic goals. Proponents contend the economy will become more efficient in the long run because the marketplace, not the tax code, will shape investment decisions. Critics argue that an already weak economy will sink into recession in the short run.

But whatever happens to the economy, there are a number of observations which can be made about the effects of tax reform on the various types of investments.

Stocks

Tax reform will likely benefit the market for equity securities by increasing their attractiveness relative to other types of investments. Stocks have become more attractive as compared to real estate investments, which were particularly hard hit by tax reform. With the new law treating short- and long-term gains the same, many investors will turn to stocks for short-term gains, rather than to real estate which primarily offers the potential for long-term appreciation.

The virtual elimination of tax shelters should also benefit the market for equities. Some of the money investors previously channeled into these shelters will undoubtably find its way to the stock market.

The *immediate* impact on individual stocks will differ, depending on the firm's profitability, previous tax rate and dividend policy. However, the following general guidelines should hold true:

1. High-dividend stocks, such as utilities, international oils and foods, benefit because the tax on dividends declines, both in absolute terms and in relation to the tax on long-term capital gains.
2. Volatile, low-yielding stocks, such as computer software, semiconductors and biotechnology, are less attractive because their primary appeal is the potential for long-term capital gains, which now offer no advantage over ordinary income.
3. Consumer-oriented businesses, such as retailing, advertising, brokerage and household products will benefit because their effective tax rates will decrease under

the new tax laws. This will tend to boost earnings and increase share prices.

4. Companies that serve the real estate industry will suffer.
5. Capital-intensive industries, such as chemicals and electrical equipment, will suffer tax increases, and thus reduced earnings.

Real Estate

The attractiveness of real estate investments has been drastically reduced under tax reform. The lengthening of depreciation schedules, loss of the investment tax credit and extension of the "at risk" rules cut into potential returns, especially for limited partnerships. The new limits on passive losses and investment interest deductions don't help either.

See Chapter 15 for a detailed discussion of real estate investments.

Tax-Exempt Bonds

Owners of tax-exempt municipal bonds will likely see their investments affected by both positive and negative factors. Munis are one of the few sources of tax-free income left. Given the elimination of many deductions, investors could have a greater proportion of their income subject to tax than ever before. This might increase the demand for these investments. Also, the supply of munis may be reduced because the issuance of tax-exempt bonds for most private purposes has been eliminated. Both of these factors could tend to push prices upward (and yields downward).

On the other hand, the lowering of tax rates makes tax-free income inherently less valuable. It is hard to predict the net effect of all these variables.

Corporate and Treasury Bonds

These investments may be the only clear winners under tax reform. Elimination of the tax break for capital gains now puts income investors on an equal tax footing for the first time since 1921. Bonds also benefit from the lower rates which increase after-tax returns.

Mutual Funds and Unit Investment Trusts

The primary advantages of these investments (professional management, diversification, etc.) are in no way affected by tax reform, but investors may want to rethink their selection of funds. With the elimination of favorable taxation for capital gains, income and growth-and-income funds become more valuable in relation to those primarily oriented toward long-term capital appreciation.

Life Insurance/Annuities

Insurance products were virtually untouched by tax reform. They offer a means of deferring income as long as possible--until the taxpayer/insured dies. Even then, the proceeds, which include the tax-deferred earnings, pass to the named beneficiary free of federal income taxes. See Chapter 7 for a detailed discussion of how insurance contracts can fit into your financial plan.

TAX-SAVING OPPORTUNITIES

Although the 1986 Tax Reform Act eliminated or reduced many tax-saving opportunities, there are still a number of techniques that can help you retain more of you investment earnings. In this section we will discuss how you can use these strategies to reduce or postpone income taxes. Also, you can bet that sharp tax strategists will find innovative new ways to deal with tax reform--so watch for them in the financial press.

A Note on Your Marginal Tax Rate

An important number for you to know is your *marginal* tax rate. It's important because this is the tax rate applied to each additional dollar of income earned from a potential investment. We're *not* talking about the *average rate* on your adjusted gross income before the extra income.

To illustrate, let's take an example. Assume you're planning to purchase bonds that will increase your 1987 interest income by $1,000.

If your taxable income is $30,000, what will be your

- Average tax rate *before* the bond purchase?
- Marginal tax rate?
- Additional taxes owned on the interest income?
- Average tax rate *after* the bond purchase?

Referring back to Exhibit 19-1 (and assuming you file a joint return), your 1987 taxes would be $4,640 ($4,080 plus 28% of the $2,000 excess over $28,000). This means your *average* tax rate is 15.5% ($4,640 divided by $30,000). The *additional* income, however, will be taxed at your *marginal* tax rate of 28%, not your *average* rate of 15.5%. So, your taxes will increase by $1,000 × 0.28 = $280, for a total tax of $4,920. Note that your new average tax rate is 15.9% ($4,920 divided by $31,000).

It is your marginal tax rate that is most relevant for your investment decisions. This is the rate to use when the tax consequences of different strategies are considered.

Deductions

Investment-related expenses, except for commissions, can be treated as part of your *miscellaneous itemized deductions*, which in the aggregate can be deducted to the extent they exceed 2% of adjusted gross income. Commissions are subtracted directly from the sales proceeds of an investment-- reducing taxable gains or increasing tax-deductible losses.

A checklist of deductions to keep track of includes:

1. Safe deposit rentals
2. Newspapers and magazines related to investments such as Wall Street Journal, Forbes and Money
3. Investment advisory subscriptions
4. Investment advisor fees
5. Postage and telephone calls used to manage your investments
6. Service charges for financial data bases such as The Source and the Dow Jones News/Retrieval
7. Investment software for your personal computer

8. Travel expenses such as trips to check on real estate investments (be sure to keep a detailed diary of these)
9. Interest on loans for investment purposes such as margin debt or mortgages on real property. (Note: There are limitations here. You can deduct such interest only to the amount of your investment income, including dividends, interest and capital gains. This limitation is being phased in over five years, and the interest not offset by income is carried over to the next tax year.)

In addition, you should reduce your tax withholding if you expect a sizable tax refund, e.g., from deductible losses, an increase in the number of your dependents or any other source. This is done by increasing the number of exemptions claimed on your W-4 form (see Exhibit 19-2). It takes only a few minutes to do this.

Conversions

Converting fully-taxed income from CDs or money funds to tax-exempt or tax-advantaged investments achieves two benefits: (1) taxable income and thereby taxes are reduced and (2) income earned on the new investment produces more spendable (after-tax) dollars.

1. *Tax-Exempt Municipals.* Buy federally tax-exempt municipal bonds, which can be bought directly from brokers or purchased as shares in a mutual fund or unit trust (refer to Chapter 16). For example, for someone in the 28% marginal tax bracket, a tax-free yield of 10% is equivalent to a 13.9% yield on a fully-taxed investment.
2. *Treasury Securities.* Treasury bills, notes and bonds are exempt from state and local income taxes. Taxpayers who reside in income tax states can use these securities to increase their after-state-income-tax returns.

Another conversion opportunity arises from the "passive" loss restrictions of the new tax code. The new rules allow deductions from passive activities only to the extent of income from other passive sources. (A passive activity definition, the code treats limited partnership interests and certain rental activities as passive activities.)

Losses from passive activities cannot be deducted from income such as salary, interest, dividends, or active business income. If you have passive losses that exceed passive income, you may want to convert some investments from, say, CDs, stocks or mutual funds, to a source of passive income. This would allow you to benefit from deducting the otherwise unusable passive losses.

One source of passive income might be limited partnerships that produce current income, such as real estate ventures that don't rely on debt or master limited partnerships. See Chapter 15 for more on these investments.

Deferrals

There are many options you can use to decide when tax payments will be made. By controlling the timing, you can postpone payments until you retire or to a later date when your tax bracket might be lower. Besides delaying taxes, many investments, such as annuities and IRA/Keogh plans, allow tax-deferred compounding of income.

NOTE: If you have large unrealized capital gains in certain assets, you need to consider the alternative minimum tax and should plan before you sell such assets in order to see if you can spread that non-recurring gain over several years to reduce the tax liability.

1. *Annuities.* Looking to build a retirement nest egg? Consider annuities. They offer the safety of an insurance contract but with tax-deferred compounding at prevailing interest rates (about 8% in 1986).
   Variable annuities increase your investment flexibility with the same tax advantages. These annuities allow you to invest in mutual funds with different investment objectives, e.g., high income or capital growth.
   BEWARE: Annuities must be considered long-term investments. The new tax code

is defined to include the conduct of any trade or business in which the taxpayer does not materially participate throughout the year. By imposes a 10% penalty (just like IRAs) if you withdraw money before age 59½. Refer to Chapter 7 for more on life insurance plans.

2. *IRA/Keogh Plans.* These retirement plans offer you a double tax advantage compared with other investments: Money placed in an IRA (if you qualify--see Chapter 18) or Keogh plan is deducted from current income, i.e., you invest *before-tax* money. This reduces your tax bill. For example, a $2,000 IRA for someone in the 28% marginal tax bracket will save $560 in taxes ($2,000 x 0.28).

In addition, income from your investment compounds tax-free until you withdraw it.

3. *Series EE Savings Bonds.* The interest income on Series EE bonds is exempt from state and local taxes because they're issued by the federal government. More importantly, no federal tax has to be paid until the bonds are redeemed. And there's much more--even at redemption, you can defer taxes once again by swapping the Series EE issues for Series HH bonds.

While interest on the HH bond is taxable each year, you still postpone payment of taxes on the Series EE bonds, and will be using tax-deferred dollars to earn interest on the Series HH bonds. (Refer to Chapter 6 for more.)

4. *Buy Put Options.* A tax strategy to defer gain recognition (and preserve your gain) is to buy a put option with an exercise price close to the stock's market price. A put option allows you to benefit from further stock appreciation because the put will be worthless (not exercised against you). If the stock price falls, you can always exercise your put and sell it at the exercise price. The main disadvantage is cost--it'll cost you up to 10% of the underlying stock value to buy the put. Refer to Chapter 14 for more on put options.

Deflections

Most investors buy securities in their own name and pay taxes on the earned income. Often these funds are going to be used for a certain purpose, such as a child's college tuition. By repositioning the assets so that a lower bracket taxpayer owns them, your taxes can be reduced.

1. *Uniform Gifts to Minors.* You and your spouse can each give $10,000 in cash or securities to each child each year, free of gift tax. For a child over 14 years old, any investment income is reported separately by the child and taxed at his/her lower tax rate. For a child under 14, only the first $1,000 of investment income is taxed at the child's rate. The excess is taxed at your rate. Investments to consider include growth mutual funds, zero coupon bonds or utility stocks. For a young child, consider a tax-deferred investment such as Series EE U.S. Savings Bonds with maturities that fall after the child's 14th birthday. The interest won't be taxed until the bonds mature.

2. *Clifford Trusts.* Under the old tax laws these trusts were often used to transfer income-producing assets to a child or other lower-bracket taxpayer. The Tax Reform Act of 1986 changed the rules-- any income from a newly created Clifford will be taxed to whoever sets up the trust. If you have already set up one, its tax treatment depends on when you did so. Income from trusts created before March 1, 1986, will be taxed at the beneficiary's rate. Income from trusts created after March 1, 1986 will be taxed at your rate.

For trusts that beat the March 1 deadline, load them with tax-deferred investments if the beneficiary is a young child. For trusts set up after the deadline, your best bet is probably tax-exempt municipal bonds.

3. *Charitable Remainder or Annuity Trusts.*
Gifts of highly appreciated securities can
be made through a Charitable Remainder
or Annuity Trust to a bona fide non-profit
organization. The benefits are:
- A tax-deductible charitable contribution
equal to the security's present value.
- If the trust is established properly, selling a security through the trust avoids
capital gains taxes.
- Income produced by the trust's assets
are available to the donor throughout
his/her life.

4. *Purchase of Parent's Residence.* Both you
and your parents can benefit from tax
breaks available when you buy their house
and rent it back to them.
- Parents' Benefit: If your parents are over
55, they claim the one-time $125,000
capital gains exclusion when the house
is sold to you.
- Your Benefit: You receive all the tax
benefits of a real estate investment (refer
to Chapter 15 on real estate
investments).

Your parents' sale proceeds can be invested in an annuity plan that pays monthly income to them and rent to you. For
more information, write:

Family Backed Mortgage Association
180 Grand Avenue
Oakland, CA 94612

Other Considerations

The new tax code provides for special exemptions which may be of interest to some investors.
For moderate income taxpayers, passive tax
losses arising from rental activities may be used
to offset up to $25,000 of wages and other
earned income. Chapter 15 discusses this in
more detail.

A special exemption also applies to investors
who own working interests in oil and gas properties. (A "working" interest is generally where
the investor bears a portion of the cost of
development and operation of the property.)

The new tax rules exempt these investments
from the passive loss limitations, thus losses can
be used to offset earned income.

AVOIDING AN I.R.S. AUDIT

Have you ever dreaded the thought of checking your mail and finding a letter from the I.R.S.
wanting to audit your tax report? (Exhibit 19-3
provides some tips on how to avoid an audit.)

Exhibit 19-3
How to Avoid an I.R.S. Audit

Ever wonder (worry about) how the I.R.S. decides
whom to audit?

The I.R.S. uses a computerized "Discriminant Function
System" that has built-in formulas that check your return
against different norms or standards. The greater your
return varies from the norm, the more likely it will be tagged
for closer scrutiny by an agent.

But what are these norms? No one's talking--it's a closely
guarded secret. However, a publicly-available manual used
by I.R.S agents to locate questionable items lends some
insight. For instance, it gives specific items to look out for
(see below).

The top items on the "1984 hit list" were (1) tax shelters
and (2) lawyers or accountants who are on a special list
of problem preparers.

To help you avoid the trauma of an I.R.S. audit, here's
a sampling of what agents give special scrutiny:

1. Itemized deductions in addition to the standard
deductions.
2. Interest payments made to individuals.
3. Real estate closing costs.
4. Large or unusual miscellaneous deductions.
5. Gains or losses on sales of rental property.
6. Pensions and annuities: Check whether lump sum
distributions are subject to the 3-year rule.
7. Rental properties, especially the treatment of repairs
and vacation homes.
8. Sale of residence.
9. Unreported income, especially interest on installment
sales, and business expenses without income.
10. Expenses for clubs, yachts, airplanes, etc.
11. Sales of assets without depreciation recapture.

As for tips on things to avoid,
- Don't skip any questions on the return.
- Avoid showing "miscellaneous" deductions in sizable
amounts.
- Don't turn in a sloppy/messy return.
- Avoid, if possible, filing amended returns requesting
additional refunds.

SOURCE: Reprinted by permission of Forbes magazine,
April 8, 1985. © Forbes, 1985.

Take heart, the chances are quite small that you'll be one of the unlucky ones (less than 1% of all returns get audited). Nevertheless, if your number turns up, your best defense: Good record keeping. Exhibit 19-4 describes the I.R.S. forms that you should be sure to save for your tax records. Failure to report the information contained in these forms is an open invitation for an I.R.S. letter.

TERMS TO KNOW

Average tax rate
Capital gain/loss
Charitable Remainder (Annuity) Trust
Clifford Trust
Conversions
Deductions
Deferrals
Deflections
Investment interest
Marginal tax rate
Passive activity
Personal exemption
Standard deduction
Uniform Gift to Minors

Exhibit 19-4

Common Forms Sent to I.R.S. and You—
Save Them for Your Tax Records

1099-B — Lists the gross proceeds of securities *sold* during the year.

1099-DIV — Reports dividends and any distributions from brokerage or mutual fund accounts.

1099-INT — Contains interest payments, including interest on CDs.

1099-R — Reports those receipts of total distributions from retirement plans or other individual retirement accounts. If you received a *total* distribution from a retirement account, you'll receive this form.

W-2P — Sent to recipients of annuities, pensions, retirement pay or IRA payments other than total distributions.

5498 — Reflects "rollover" or regular contributions made to IRA accounts during the last calendar year.

APPENDIX

Worksheet No. 1
Net Worth Statement

Date: _____

ASSETS (What You Own):

Cash or Liquid Assets

1.	Cash and Checking Account(s)	$ _____	
2.	Savings Accounts	_____	
3.	Money Market Funds	_____	
4.	Life Insurance Cash Values	_____	
5.	U.S. Savings Bonds	_____	
6.	Other	_____	
7.	Total Liquid Assets (Add Lines 1-6)		$ _____

Marketable Investments (Market Value)

8.	Common Stocks	$ _____	
9.	Preferred Stocks	_____	
10.	Bonds (Corporate & Municipal)	_____	
11.	Mutual Funds	_____	
12.	Other	_____	
13.	Total Marketable Investments (Add Lines 8-12)		$ _____

Nonmarketable Investments (Current or Estimated Value)

14.	Ownership in Business	$ _____	
15.	Vested Company Profit-Sharing or Pension Plan	_____	
16.	Real Estate Investments	_____	
17.	Notes Receivable (Loans to Others)	_____	
18.	Annuities	_____	
19.	IRAs or Keogh	_____	
20.	Total Nonmarketable Assets (Add Lines 14-19)		$ _____

Personal Assets (Current Value)

21.	Residence	$ _____	
22.	Automobiles	_____	
23.	Furniture	_____	
24.	Equipment	_____	
25.	Jewelry	_____	
26.	Collectibles	_____	
27.	Other	_____	
28.	Total Personal Assets (Add Lines 21-27)		$ _____

TOTAL ASSETS (Add Lines 7, 13, 20 and 28) $ _____

LIABILITIES (What You Owe):

Loans (Outstanding Balances)

29.	Charge/Credit Card Accounts	$ _____	
30.	Unpaid Bills	_____	
31.	Bank	_____	
32.	Margin	_____	
33.	Insurance	_____	
34.	Installment (e.g., car loan)	_____	
35.	Other	_____	
36.	Total Loans (Add Lines 29-35)		$ _____

Mortgages (Outstanding Balances)

37.	Personal Residence	$ _____	
38.	Other Real Estate	_____	
39.	Total Mortgages (Add Lines 37 and 38)		$ _____

TOTAL LIABILITIES (Add Lines 36 and 39) $ _____

NET WORTH (Total Assets Minus Total Liabilities) $ _____

A-1

Worksheet No. 2

Setting Your Personal Objectives By Their Relative Importance and Time Frame

OBJECTIVE	RELATIVE IMPORTANCE			TIME FRAME		
	Low	Medium	High	Short Term	Medium Term	Long Term
1. Reduce debt?						
2. Build cash reserves?						
3. Increase insurance coverage?						
4. Buy a house?						
5. Make home improvements?						
6. Buy a car?						
7. Make some other big purchase?						
8. Have children?						
9. Finance children's education?						
10. Increase your standard of living?						
11. Take an expensive vacation?						
12. Start your own business?						
13. Take early retirement?						
14. Live well after retirement?						
15. Other? _____						
_____						

SOURCE: Adapted from T. Mathesen, "Your Surest Route to Financial Security," 1984 Money Guide: Personal Finance, by special permission, © 1984, Time, Inc., all rights reserved.

Worksheet No. 3

Estimating Annual Cash Available for Investments

Annual Income and Expense Statement

Date: _____

INCOME:

1.	Salaries and Wages (Gross)	$_____
2.	Interest	_____
3.	Dividends	_____
4.	Social Security Income	_____
5.	Pension	_____
6.	Capital Gains/Losses	_____
7.	Other Income	_____
8.	TOTAL INCOME (Add Lines 1-7)	$_____

TAXES:

9.	Income Taxes	$_____
10.	Social Security Taxes	_____
11.	TOTAL TAXES (Add Lines 9-10)	$_____
12.	CASH AVAILABLE TO PAY EXPENSES (Subtract Line 11 from Line 8)	$_____

EXPENSES:

Fixed Expenses

13.	Rent or Mortgage	$_____
14.	Installment Debt (e.g., car loan)	_____
15.	Insurance Premiums	_____

Variable Expenses

16.	Food	$_____
17.	Transportation	_____
18.	Utilities	_____
19.	Home Repairs and Improvements	_____
20.	Clothing	_____
21.	Personal Care	_____
22.	Medical Care (Unreimbursed)	_____
23.	Interest Paid (Not Included in Lines 13-14)	_____
24.	Contributions/Donations	_____
25.	Recreation/Entertainment	_____
26.	Real Estate Taxes	_____
27.	Miscellaneous Expenses	_____
28.	TOTAL EXPENSES (Add Lines 13-27)	$_____

CASH AVAILABLE FOR SAVINGS AND INVESTMENTS
(Subtract Line 28 from Line 12) $_____

Worksheet No. 4

Practice on Calculating the Holding Period Yields for Different Types of Investments

(Original Investment = $1,000, Holding Period = 1 Year)

	6% Savings Accounts*	Treasury Bond	Common Stock	Real Estate
1. Current Income	(Interest)	(Interest)	(Dividends)	(Rent Less Expenses)
1st Quarter	$ 15.00	$ 0.00	$ 5.00	$ −20.00
2nd Quarter	15.22	60.00	5.00	−10.00
3rd Quarter	15.46	0.00	5.50	−15.00
4th Quarter	15.68	60.00	6.00	−15.00
Total =	$_____	$_____	$_____	$_____
2. Capital Gain (Loss)				
Ending Value	$ 1,000.00	$ 1,050.00	$ 850.00	$ 1,140.00
Beginning Value	1,000.00	1,000.00	1,000.00	1,000.00
Gain (Loss) =	$_____	$_____	$_____	$_____
3. Total Dollar Return =	$_____	$_____	$_____	$_____
4. Current Yield =	_____%	_____%	_____%	_____%
+ Capital Gain (Loss) Yield =	_____%	_____%	_____%	_____%
5. Holding Period Yield =	_____%	_____%	_____%	_____%

* Assume interest is paid quarterly and is left in the account to earn additional interest.

NOTE: For answers, see reverse side.

ANSWERS:

Practice on Calculating the Holding Period Yields for Different Types of Investments

(Original Investment = $1,000, Holding Period = 1 Year)

	6% Savings Accounts°	Treasury Bond	Common Stock	Real Estate
1. Current Income	(Interest)	(Interest)	(Dividends)	(Rent Less Expenses)
1st Quarter	$ 15.00	$ .00	$ 5.00	$ -20.00
2nd Quarter	15.22	60.00	5.00	-10.00
3rd Quarter	15.46	.00	5.50	-15.00
4th Quarter	15.68	60.00	6.00	-15.00
Total =	$ 61.36	$ 120.00	$ 21.50	$ -60.00
2. Capital Gain (Loss)				
Ending Value	$ 1,000.00	$ 1,050.00	$ 850.00	$ 1,140.00
Beginning Value	1,000.00	1,000.00	1,000.00	1,000.00
Gain (Loss) =	$ 0.00	$ 50.00	$ -150.00	$ 140.00
3. Total Dollar Return =	$ 61.36	$ 170.00	$ -128.50	$ 80.00
4. Current Yield =	6.14 %	12.00 %	2.15 %	-6.00 %
+ Capital Gain (Loss) Yield =	0.00 %	5.00 %	-15.00 %	14.00 %
5. Holding Period Yield =	6.14 %	17.00 %	-12.85 %	8.00 %

° Assume interest is paid quarterly and is left in the account to earn additional interest.

Worksheet No. 5

Annualizing Holding Period Yields

	HPY	Holding Period	Annualized Yield
1.	2.0%	1 Month	
2.	1.5%	4 Weeks	_____ %
3.	2.5%	3 Months	_____ %
4.	3.4%	16 Weeks	_____ %
5.	2.3%	125 Days	_____ %
6.	3.8%	6 Months	_____ %
7.	4.2%	26 Weeks	_____ %
8.	7.5%	10 Months	_____ %
9.	15.3%	18 Months	_____ %
10.	23.6%	24 Months	_____ %

NOTE: For answers, see reverse side.

ANSWERS:

	HPY	Holding Period	Annualized Yield
1.	2.0%	1 Month	24.0 %
2.	1.5%	4 Weeks	19.5 %
3.	2.5%	3 Months	10.0 %
4.	3.4%	16 Weeks	11.1 %
5.	2.3%	125 Days	6.7 %
6.	3.8%	6 Months	7.6 %
7.	4.2%	26 Weeks	8.4 %
8.	7.5%	10 Months	9.0 %
9.	15.3%	18 Months	10.2 %
10.	23.6%	24 Months	11.8 %

Worksheet No. 6

Estimating Your Life Insurance Needs

EXAMPLE: A man of 35 who earns $40,000 a year. His wife (also 35) stays home with two young children. Gross estate is $120,000.

	Your Family	Example: Wife and 2 Children
Step 1. Funeral expenses, estate taxes, etc.	$_____	$ 5,000
Step 2. Repay non-mortgage debt	_____	2,500
Step 3. Emergency funds	_____	5,000
Step 4. College funds	_____	76,800
Step 5. Expected living expenses:		
a. Average annual living expenses	_____	30,000
b. Minus: Spouse's average annual income	−_____	− 22,500
c. Minus: Annual Social Security benefits	−_____	− 5,000
d. Net annual living expenses	$_____	$ 2,500
e. [Years until spouse is 90]	[ ]	[55]
f. Investment rate factor *	×_____	× 22
g. Total living expenses [d x f]	$_____	$ 55,000
Step 6. Total monetary needs [Steps 1 + 2 + 3 + 4 + 5g]	$_____	144,300
Step 7. Minus: Total investments in hand	_____	− 10,000
Step 8. Life Insurance Needs [Step 6 minus Step 7]	$_____	**$ 134,300**

* **Investment Rate Factors:** Subtract your spouse's age from 90 and then look up the appropriate investment factor in the following table:

Years	25	30	35	40	45	50	**55**	60
Conservative Investments	20	22	25	27	30	31	33	35
More Agressive Investments	16	17	19	20	21	21	**22**	23

OVERVIEW: Using the worksheet, you first identify those sums to be paid at your death (Steps 1-4). Then calculate the gap between your family's potential income and living expenses (Steps 5a-5d). Next, you allow for additional money your spouse will receive from investing the proceeds from your life insurance (Steps 5d-5g). You get the total insurance need by adding the immediate and long-term expenses and subtracting the value of investment assets on hand (Steps 6-8).

(Continued)

Worksheet No. 6 (cont.)

EXAMPLE

Step 1: Use $2,200 if your gross estate (net worth and insurance proceeds) is under $20,000. Use $5,000 if it's between $20,000 and $200,000 and $10,000 if it's greater than $200,000. Our example falls in the second category.

Step 2: It'll take $2,500 to pay off their car loan and credit card debt.

Step 3: Use two months' take-home pay for a cash reserve. The man's take-home pay is $30,000 a year, or $5,000 for two months.

Step 4: This assumes $9,600 a year for a private college (based on the American Council on Education 1984-85 estimate for tuition, room and board). The estimate for a public school is $4,900.

Step 5a: This couple spends all its income, mostly on fixed expenses such as their mortgage payments.

Step 5b: The woman could probably go back to work today at an average salary of $22,500 after taxes.

Step 5c: For Social Security benefits, use $5,000 if you have two or more minor children, $4,000 for one child and $3,000 for no children.

Steps
5d-5g: You have two "investment rate factors" from which to choose. This factor helps determine the potential earnings from investing the insurance proceeds. A conservative portfolio assumes investments in bank accounts and bonds (2% real growth after inflation and taxes), while a more aggressive portfolio invests in stocks and real estate (4% real growth). This example assumes more aggressive investing.

Steps
6-7: The family has $10,000 in a mutual fund so after subtracting this from its total monetary needs, he needs $134,300 in insurance.

SOURCE: K. Slater. "Changing Life Insurance Needs Require Periodic Look at Your Family's Coverage," The Wall Street Journal, April 2, 1984, p. 29.

Worksheet No. 7

Stock Selection Format
(To Be Filled In By You or Your Broker)

NOTE: Except where indicated, this information is available in the S&P Stock Guide

Name of Stock _____ Ticker Symbol _____

Industry _____ Traded On: _____ NYSE _____ ASE _____ OTC

INITIAL SCREEN
Market Value:

Number of Shares Outstanding _____ × Price $_____ = $_____

Less than $200 million but more than $25 million?   Yes _____ No _____

Institutional Ownership:
Shares Owned by Institutions   _____

Total Shares Outstanding   ÷ _____

                                        = _____ %

Less than 10%?   Yes _____ No _____

NOTE: Continue if answers are "Yes" to both questions.

1. VALUE MEASURES

Current Price $_____   52-Week High-Low Prices $_____
Book Value Per Share $_____   Current P/E Ratio   _____

	Previous Year	Estimated for This Year**	Estimated for Next Year**
Earnings Per Share	$_____	$_____	$_____
Dividends Per Share	$_____	$_____	$_____

Current Dividend Yield   _____%
Dividends Paid Every Year Since 19____

2. PROFITABILITY MEASURES

Pre-Tax Profit Margin* _____   Return on Equity* _____%

3. RISK MEASURES

S&P Ranking _____
If Available,   Safety Rank* _____   Beta Value* _____
                                        Financial Strength Rating* _____

Current Ratio _____ (Current Assets ÷ Current Liabilities)
Debt Ratio   _____ (Debt ÷ Equity)
Debt Ratio Less than 35%?   Yes _____ No _____

(Continued)

A-10

Worksheet No. 7 (cont)

4. OTHER MEASURES

5-Year Historical Record:

	Rate	Increasing	Leveling Off	Decreasing
Sales Growth*	_____ %	_____	_____	_____
Earnings Growth*	_____ %	_____	_____	_____
Dividend Growth*	_____ %	_____	_____	_____
Average Pre-Tax Profit Margin	_____ %	_____	_____	_____
Average Return on Equity	_____ %	_____	_____	_____

Average P/E Ratio _____ Current P/E Below? _____ Above? _____

Highest-Lowest P/E Ratio: Highest _____ Lowest _____

Current P/E at: Lower end? _____ Upper end? _____

5. STOCK COMPARISONS

	Name	P/E Ratio	Dividend Yield
1.	_____	_____	_____
2.	_____	_____	_____
3.	_____	_____	_____
4.	_____	_____	_____

---

*   Available in the <u>Value Line Investment Survey</u> if the stock is covered by this advisory service.

** Obtain from your broker.

Worksheet No. 8

PERSONAL IRA LOG

We suggest that you turn to this personal log annually. This should be done between Feb. 1, by which time you should have received year-end IRA financial statements, and April 15, the normal tax-year deadline for contributions.

A special line is provided at the outset for recording any IRAs that you may already have. As the years pass, you will probably open accounts with two or more institutions; space is provided for four accounts.

Jotting down the rate of return on fixed-income IRAs—bank certificates, annuities, bonds—will alert you to investments that aren't earning as much as they might.

For mutual funds and stocks, and for some types of annuities and savings certificates, the rate of return is unpredictable. In that case, enter "variable," and at least once a year make a rough calculation of recent results to see whether you should switch investments. If you must pull money out, there's a column in the log for that too. As your total balance grows, so should your incentive to keep on contributing.

	Contributions	Where invested	Maturity date (if any)	Rate of return	Withdrawals	Balances at year-end
1982		Existing IRA:				
		New IRA:				
					TOTAL	
1983						
					TOTAL	
1984						
					TOTAL	
1985						
					TOTAL	
1986						
					TOTAL	
1987						
					TOTAL	

PERSONAL IRA LOG

	Contributions	Where invested	Maturity date (if any)	Rate of return	Withdrawals	Balances at year-end
1988						
					TOTAL	
1989						
					TOTAL	
1990						
					TOTAL	
1991						
					TOTAL	
1992						
					TOTAL	
1993						
					TOTAL	

Worksheet No. 9
Estimating Federal Income Taxes after Tax Reform

	1986	1987	1988
INCOME			
1. Wages, salaries, tips, etc.	$_____	$_____	$_____
2. Interest income	_____	_____	_____
3. Dividends*	_____	_____	_____
4. Taxable capital gains (or deductible losses)*	_____	_____	_____
5. Income (or deductible losses) from limited partnerships or rental property*	_____	_____	_____
6. All other income, including alimony	_____	_____	_____
7. **TOTAL INCOME** (add lines 1 through 6)	$_____	$_____	$_____
ADJUSTMENTS			
8. Employee business expenses*	$_____		
9. Two-earner deduction*	_____		
10. Alimony paid	_____	$_____	$_____
11. Keogh contributions	_____	_____	_____
12. Adjusted gross income before IRA contributions (add lines 8 through 11, then subtract sum from line 7)	_____	_____	_____
13. IRA contributions*			
14. **ADJUSTED GROSS INCOME** (subtract line 13 from line 12)	$_____	$_____	$_____
ITEMIZED DEDUCTIONS			
15. Medical expenses*	$_____	$_____	$_____
16. State and local income and property taxes	_____	_____	_____
17. State and local sales taxes*	_____		
18. Mortgage interest*	_____	_____	_____
19. Other deductible interest expenses*	_____	_____	_____
20. Charitable contributions	_____	_____	_____
21. Miscellaneous deductions and employee business expenses*	_____	_____	_____
22. Casualty and theft losses	_____	_____	_____
23. **TOTAL ITEMIZED DEDUCTIONS** (add lines 15 through 22)	$_____	$_____	$_____
TAXABLE INCOME			
24. For 1986 only, subtract $2,480 for singles or $3,670 for joint filers from line 23* (if the result is negative, write 0 and complete line 25; otherwise, fill in the amount and skip to line 27)	$_____		
25. Charitable contributions for those who don't itemize*	_____		
26. For 1987 and 1988 only, write in the amount on line 23 or your standard deduction, whichever is higher*		$_____	$_____
27. Exemptions*	_____	_____	_____
28. Total deductions and exemptions (add lines 24 through 27)	_____	_____	_____
29. **TAXABLE INCOME** (subtract line 28 from line 14)	$_____	$_____	$_____

(Continued)

* There is an explanation for this line in the accompanying text.

TAX BEFORE CREDITS

30.	Special capital-gains tax for 1987*		$_____	
31.	For 1987 only, taxable income minus capital gains (subtract line 4 from line 29)		_____	
32.	**TAX BEFORE CREDITS*** (see tax tables)	$_____	$_____	$_____

CREDITS

33.	Child-care credit	$_____	$_____	$_____
34.	Political contributions credit*	_____	_____	_____
35.	Total credits (add lines 33 and 34)	$_____	$_____	$_____
36.	**YOUR TAX** (subtract line 35 form line 32)	$_____	$_____	$_____

Line 3: Dividends

There is no dividend exclusion after 1986, so list your total anticipated dividend income for 1987 and 1988.

Line 4: Taxable Capital Gains (or Deductible Losses)

If you had a net long-term capital gain in 1986, put 40% of the total on line 4. But fill in the full amount of any net short-term gain. If you had a net short-term loss in 1986, put a minus sign in front of the total amount. You can't deduct more than $3,000 in net short- or long-term capital losses in any one year, however. For a net long-term loss, subtract half the loss up to $3,000 from your income.

Since it is difficult to predict gains or losses, use the amounts for 1986 as a rough estimate for 1987 and 1988. The distinction between short- and long-term investments disappear in 1987, so the amounts you fill in for 1987 and 1988 may be different from 1986. If you expect a net gain in these two years, write down the full amount regardless of how long you will have held the investments. But if you anticipate a net loss, deduct the full amount up to $3,000, even if it is long term.

Line 5: Income (or Deductible Losses) From Limited Partnerships or Rental Property

In 1986, you could deduct all your losses from tax shelters or rental-property investments. But in 1987, writeoffs from limited partnerships will start being phased out to the extent that they exceed income from passive investments. If you own a tax shelter, you will be able to subtract only 65% of any net losses in 1987 and 40% in 1988.

As a rental-property owner, after 1986 you can take deductions for mortgage interest, depreciation and other expenses up to $25,000--plus an amount equal to your rental income from the real estate--provided that your adjusted gross income in 1987 and 1988 is less than $100,000. You will also be able to deduct 65% of any additional losses from the property in 1987 and 40% in 1988. The $25,000 cap is gradually reduced for taxpayers with adjusted gross incomes above $100,000 until it disappears for those with incomes of $150,000 or more. To figure out the loss you will be able to deduct if you fall within this range, take half of each dollar of adjusted gross income above $100,000 and subtract the total from the $25,000 cap. The same 65% and 40% phaseout for any excess losses applies regardless of your income.

Line 8: Employee Business Expenses

After 1986, most of these adjustments to income will be considered miscellaneous deductions and deductible only to the extent that they exceed 2% of adjusted gross income on line 14. For 1986, put these adjustments on line 8; as for years 1987 and 1988, see line 21.

Line 9: Two-Earner Deduction

This write-off was eliminated after 1986. To compute it for 1986, see the tax return instructions.

Line 13: IRA Contributions

In 1986, taxpayers who work can deduct up to $2,000 for contributions to an Individual Retirement Account. If you have a nonworking spouse, you can deduct a total of $2,250.

(Continued)

Worksheet No. 9 (cont.)

In 1987 and 1988, you will still be able to write off the full amount of your IRA contributions if your income on line 12 is less than $40,000 for married couples and $25,000 for singles. No matter how much you earn, you will also be entitled to deduct your entire IRA contribution if you aren't covered by a company pension plan or a Keogh plan. But if the amount on line 12 is more than $50,000 for married couples or $35,000 for singles, and if you have a pension at work, whether or not you are vested, you will no longer be able to deduct your IRA contributions. Couples with earnings between $40,000 and $50,000 and singles with incomes between $25,000 and $35,000 will lose $200 of their IRA deduction for each $1,000 of additional income.

Line 15: Medical Expenses

In 1986, you can deduct such costs only to the extent that they exceed 5% of your adjusted gross income on line 14. In 1987 and 1988, that threshold will be 7.5%.

Line 17: State and Local Sales Taxes

The sales tax write-off was eliminated after 1986.

Line 18: Mortgage Interest

You can still deduct the mortgage interest that you pay for your primary residence and a second home after 1986. Interest on a second mortgage or home-equity loan can also be written off provided the value of these loans is no greater than the price you paid for the property, plus the cost of any improvements. Interest on mortgages that exceed that amount will be fully deductible only if you use the money to pay for educational or medical expenses. Otherwise, interest on second mortgages will be subject to the phaseout limitation explained under the next item.

Line 19: Other Deductible Interest Expenses

After 1986, the deduction for any interest you pay on car, college, credit-card or other consumer loans will be phased out. In 1987, you can write off only 65% of the interest; in 1988, 40%. Interest on borrowings that you use to invest, such as margin loans, will be deductible up to the amount of income you receive from investments. Any excess will be subject to the phaseout rule.

Line 21: Miscellaneous Deductions and Employee Business Expenses

After 1986, you will be able to write off miscellaneous deductions and employee business expenses only to the extent that the total exceeds 2% of your adjusted gross income on line 14. Only moving costs will be exempt from this limit. The instructions for the 1986 Form 1040 include a complete list of expenses that are deductible under this heading. Enter the totals on line 21 for 1987 and 1988.

Line 24: The Zero-Bracket Amount for 1986

If this figure, which is the maximum income on which you pay no tax, exceeds your total itemized deductions, then you will know that you can use the 1040 short form for your taxes in 1986. The zero-bracket amount is already in the 1986 tax tables, so people who don't itemize don't have to subtract it from their income. If you do itemize, subtract it from line 23.

Line 25: Charitable Deductions for Those Who Don't Itemize

Even if you fill out the short form in 1986, you can deduct all your charitable contributions, so write in the total on line 25. Only those who itemize will be allowed to write off their gifts to charity after 1986.

Line 26: Standard Deductions in 1987 and 1988

The new standard deductions will not be incorporated into the tax tables, so you must subtract the amount from the figure you wrote on line 14 unless your itemized deductions are greater than the standard deduction. In 1987, the standard deduction is $2,570 for singles and $3,800 for joint filers; in 1988, $3,000 for singles and $5,000 for married couples filing jointly. In both 1987 and 1988, taxpayers who are 65 or older or who are blind can use the more generous 1988 standard deductions, plus $750 if they are single or $600 for a spouse if they are married.

(Continued)

Worksheet No. 9 (cont.)

Line 27: Exemptions

In 1986, multiply the number of exemptions you can take by $1,080. In 1987 the personal exemption increases to $1,900 and then to $1,950 in 1988. You will, however, be able to take exemptions only for yourself, your spouse and your dependents.

Line 30: Special Capital-Gains Tax for 1987

Fill out this line only if your taxable income on line 29 exceeds $27,000 if you are single or $45,000 if you are married and filing jointly. In both cases, multiply any net long-term gains on line 4 by 28% and write the amount on line 30. This calculation is necessary because the maximum long-term-gains rate in 1987 will be 28%. If you anticipate a loss or a net short-term gain, skip to line 32.

Line 32: Tax Before Credits

For 1986 and 1988 use the amount on line 29 to compute your tax from the tax tables. (Note: The 1986 tables can be found in the instructions for Form 1040. See Chapter 18, Exhibit 18-1 for the 1987 and 1988 tables.)

In 1987, add your capital-gains tax on line 30 to the tax from the table that is appropriate for your income on line 31 and put the sum on line 32. In 1988, couples with dependent children whose taxable income exceeds $171,090 will be subject to the 33% rate on earnings up to 171,090 *plus* $10,920 per child. The new law phases out the benefits of any personal exemptions for upper-income taxpayers. Thus a couple with two children would be taxed at 33% on income of up to $192,930. Earnings above that amount would be taxed at 28%.

Line 34: Political Contributions Credit

This tax break, explained in the instructions for the 1986 Form 1040, was eliminated beginning in 1987.

SOURCE: Adapted from the 1986 October issue of <u>Money</u> magazine by special permission, copyright 1986 Time Inc., all rights reserved.

Appendix B

Model Portfolios

A frequently asked question is how one's portfolio should be split among different types of investments. It's also probably the question *least* frequently answered. *REASON:* It's a complex question that requires a unique answer because *your* investment portfolio will vary according to your personal objectives and circumstances such as age, income, family status, current financial resources, tax bracket and risk tolerance. This means no two individuals' portfolios will be identical and seldom are they alike.

While generalizations are hard to come by, certain guidelines can be suggested for developing your investment portfolio's mix of investments. Below, we present "model portfolios" for five "typical investors" at different stages in their life cycle. The focus of attention is on what your portfolio *proportions* should be and not on what individual securities or investments to hold. We also assume you have enough life and liability insurance (refer to Chapter 7).

1. PHASE OF LIFE CYCLE: EARLY YEARS

Family Status: Newlyweds   *Tax Bracket:* Low-to-moderate
Income: Low or moderate if both spouses work   *Risk Tolerance:* High
Investment Objective: Long-term aggressive growth with some liquidity
Portfolio Mix: 75% Common stocks and/or 2-3 mutual funds that emphasize long-term, maximum capital growth. You may also want to consider a mutual fund that specializes in shares of smaller companies.
           25% Savings or money market accounts and money market funds for safety and liquidity.

Comments: In the late 20s to early 30s, income is $25,000 to $45,000 if both spouses work and, probably, most of it is spent. Need to save for a downpayment on a home (a *must* first investment). Need to develop a savings habit, e.g., automatically set aside 10% of your income each month until 3-6 months of your salary has been accumulated. Place it in a *safe* place such as a money market account or fund. Since there's little need for current investment income and since you should feel comfortable assuming a higher risk posture (now's the time to take a big risk on a small amount), any other funds should be placed in long-term, aggressive growth investments. Use mutual funds until the *size* of your portfolio permits individual securities to be purchased. Alternatively, you can build this portion of your portfolio one stock or one fund at a time, slowly at first, and then more rapidly as your earnings rise later.

2. PHASE OF LIFE CYCLE: MID YEARS

Family Status: Married with children　　　　　　　*Tax Bracket:* Middle
Income: Moderate-to-high　　　　　　　　　　　*Risk Tolerance:* Moderate
Investment Objective: Long-term growth with some income, especially if children are preparing to enter college
Portfolio Mix: 35% Aggressive growth investments or mutual funds and perhaps real estate if in a high tax bracket
　　　　　　　30% Quality growth stocks or growth mutual funds
　　　　　　　20% Intermediate-to-long term debt securities or bond funds for income or reinvestment
　　　　　　　15% Savings and money market accounts or money funds for safety

Comments: In your late 30s to 40s, perhaps with 1-2 teenage children. Family income is $45,000-$60,000. Funds for the children's education fund should already be in place. Keep the money for the oldest child's first year in college easily available, e.g., in a money market fund. Also emphasis should be on longer term growth to build a retirement fund. Because your portfolio's size is larger now, you can diversify more widely.

3. PHASE OF LIFE CYCLE: MID YEARS

Family Status: Divorced with children　　　　　　*Tax Bracket:* Low-to-middle
Income: Moderate　　　　　　　　　　　　　　*Risk Tolerance:* Low
Investment Objective: Current income with some growth (conservative)
Portfolio Mix: 20% Long-term growth mutual funds
　　　　　　　30% Growth-income mutual funds
　　　　　　　25% Bond mutual funds
　　　　　　　25% Savings and money market accounts or mutual funds for safety and liquidity

Comments: A divorced mother or father aged 35-45 and has custody of 1-2 children. With salary and child-support payments, income ranges $20,000-$35,000. Biggest needs are (1) to be able to obtain funds quickly in case of an emergency (liquidity) and (2) to supplement current salary with additional income. May or may not be able to establish an education fund for the children. Allocate any money from a divorce settlement according to the percentages indicated above. Our suggestion is to stay with mutual funds primarily because you probably don't have time to actively manage your investments.

4. PHASE OF LIFE CYCLE: LATER YEARS

Family Status: Married, children gone   *Tax Bracket:* High
Income: High   *Risk Tolerance:* Low-to-moderate
Investment Objective: Conservative growth
Portfolio Mix: 65% Quality common stocks or growth mutual funds (deemphasize income stocks) and tax-sheltered investments such as real estate
            25% Tax-exempt municipal bonds or bond funds and short- and intermediate- term discount bonds whose maturities match up with when you need the money to live on
            10% Savings and money market accounts or money market funds for safety and liquidity

Comments: In your 50s and planning for retirement in 10-15 years. Now in your peak earnings years with fewer needs to be met, current salary is $45,000-$65,000 (or more if both spouses are working) so current income is not important. Time to invest every dollar you can. Because you're in a high tax bracket, emphasis is on growth and tax-advantaged investments. You want to maximize your growth potential in the shortest time, *but* with the least risk. That is, you'll want to be able to supplement your retirement income from your pension and Social Security, yet you also must be careful to preserve what you have. As retirement approaches, begin to roll your growth investments into money market and shorter-term debt or income mutual funds.

5. PHASE OF LIFE CYCLE: RETIREMENT

Family Status: Married or Widowed   *Tax Bracket:* Low
Income: Low   *Risk Tolerance:* Very low
Investment Objective: Current income and safety (very conservative)
Portfolio Mix: 25% Quality, high income stocks or income-growth mutual funds
            55% Short- to intermediate-term fixed-income securities or bond mutual funds for current income. Consider tax-exempt municipals if still in a high tax bracket
            20% Savings and money market accounts or money market funds for safety and liquidity

Comments: If you're a male and 65, you can expect to live 15-20 years more--even more if you're female. Your peak earnings period is behind you, and you're looking at living on 50%-75% of your former income. Safety (capital preservation) is of foremost importance --if you lose your investment funds, you can't go and earn it back. Given the outlook for inflation (your worst enemy now), don't be *too* conservative. If you can afford it, put a small percentage of your funds into growth-oriented stocks or mutual funds. *ONE SUGGESTION:* Keep only enough money for the next year in money market funds. *ANOTHER SUGGESTION:* Keep 80% of your money safe in money funds and invest 20% in aggressive growth funds. This diversified approach takes advantage of money market rates and risky stock prices tending to move in opposite directions.

Appendix

C

HOW TO READ AN ANNUAL REPORT

Chapter Objectives

1. To Discuss the Major Sections of an Annual Report and How to Read Them
2. To Describe the Content of Other Important Financial Reports and Other Sources of Company Information

---

Reading a financial report is like going to the dentist---you know you should *but* you dread the prospect of doing it. Nonetheless, financial reports published by companies are "must" reading for the smart investor because no one knows more about a particular company than the company itself. This is why they are the single best source of information you can get.

As you'll learn below, the three best areas to look for *vital* information are in (1) the footnotes, (2) management's discussion and analysis of operations and (3) the auditor's opinion. While we'll touch on all the major sections of the annual reports, the emphasis will be on these three areas. In addition, Exhibit C-1 gives a description of other important financial reports that you'll want to keep tabs on.

Just remember, executives apparently still believe that there's no merit to dwelling on bad news, so they downplay it. And, alert investors aren't misled by the thickness and glossiness of annual reports---this has little to do with the good fortunes of a company.

HOW ANNUAL REPORTS ARE ORGANIZED

A typical annual report is laid out in the following manner:

- Letter to the Shareholders
- Description of Operations
- Financial Statements
- Footnotes to the Financial Statements

Exhibit C-1
Description of Other Important Financial Reports

S.E.C. 10-K Report
The drier, more numbers-oriented, counterpart to the Stockholders' Annual Report that is filed with the S.E.C. Besides a much more detailed account of the firm's operating results and financial position, this report also provides an extensive breakdown of expenses and sales by product lines. You must specifically request copies from the firm.

Quarterly Report
A report automatically sent to stockholders that summarizes a firm's performance for the past three months. They usually contain a short description of significant events as well as abbreviated versions of the financial statements. While limited in scope compared to the annual report, they do provide an idea about a firm's sales and earnings for the quarter and the year earlier quarter. NOTE: Quarterly reports are *unaudited* and may be restated later.

S.E.C. 10-Q Report
The counterpart to the Stockholders' Quarterly Report that is filed with the S.E.C. In fact, the Quarterly Report is a *summary* of the 10-Q. And, like the 10-K, it's a more detailed report of the firm's financial situation. It also must be requested from the firm.

Prospectus
Another S.E.C. document that is issued whenever a new public issue or repurchase of stock or bonds is made, a major acquisition or divesture is proposed, or any other major financial event occurs which requires stockholder approval. Because all relevant information about the proposal must be disclosed, the prospectus is often an important source of information. Current stockholders automatically receive a copy. Outsiders, on the other hand, need to ask their broker to get a copy for them.

Proxy Materials
Usually issued in conjunction with the annual stockholders' meeting, where members are elected to the board of directors, an independent auditor is approved and other matters requiring stockholder approval are voted on. Proxy materials are composed of a *proxy* (ballot) and a *proxy statement* which describes the issues to be considered. Other information such as principal stockholders and executives' compensation is also included.

News Releases
Official announcements issued occasionally. They contain noteworthy information concerning new products, merger activity, dividend payments, and management changes. These releases often form the basis for articles found in newspapers such as The Wall Street Journal.

- Management's Discussion and Analysis of Operations
- Auditor's Opinion
- Ten-Year Summary of Comparative Results

Now this may also look like a perfectly logical way to read through an annual report. Wrong! The best way is actually to begin *at the back* of the report and read forward. While we'll discuss each section in the order presented above, keep in mind that the wise investor usually takes them in *reverse* order. Let's see why.

LETTER TO THE SHAREHOLDERS

This is the first thing you see but is the *last* thing you should read. Written by the president or C.E.O. (Chief Executive Officer), this letter highlights the year's events and perhaps gives a forecast of what to expect next year.

It usually boils down to largely a public relations job that can border on self-promotion. After all, management needs to convince you that it has the skills to succeed in its business. *RESULT:* Expect management to put its best foot forward. *OUR SUGGESTION:* You best spend your time elsewhere in the annual report.

DESCRIPTION OF OPERATIONS

After the shareholders' letter, the annual report may describe in words and pictures the various segments of the business. You'll see nice, glossy photos of products, places and smiling people (especially of the officers). Enjoy the pictures and, if you're not very familiar with the company, brief yourself. Otherwise, more serious reading lies ahead.

THE FINANCIAL STATEMENTS

After the descriptive material comes the first substantive information---the financial statements. This will include the *balance sheet,*

income statement and statement of changes in financial condition.
- *Balance Sheet*---Lists what assets a firm owns and how these assets are financed (liabilities) *at a point in time.*
- *Income (or Profit and Loss) Statement*---reports a firm's activities or performance by measuring revenues, expenses, taxes and profits (losses) *over a period of time.*
- *Statement of Changes in Financial Condition*---Summarizes what funds were provided by internal and external sources and the uses to which these funds were put.

"Reading the numbers" contained in these statements can be intimidating at times. Most of us haven't studied accounting, which is a must to interpret properly what insights lie within the statements. Fortunately, alot can be learned from reading the *remaining* sections of the annual report, and they don't require you to be a C.P.A.

If you are the inquisitive type, however, one of the best guides to understanding financial statements is a brochure published by Merrill Lynch entitled "How to Read a Financial Report." We think it would be well worth your time to pick up a copy and study it. It was written with the average (non-accountant) investor in mind.

THE FOOTNOTES

Referred to as "Notes to The Financial Statements," *footnotes* expand on items in the financial statements, or give additional information on factors that have or could have a significant effect on a company's performance.

To most, footnotes may seem unintelligible. (Your broker can help you on the tough ones.) Nevertheless, they are a valuable source of information. For example,
- Did the firm receive a *qualified* auditor's opinion (see below)?
- Was their a surprising jump (drop) in earnings?
- Did the annual report tell a different story from the one given by the unaudited quarterly reports?

The footnotes may hold the key to why these things happened, so let's look at a sample of footnotes that might contain significant information.

Contingent Liabilities

The number one cause of qualified opinions, *legal claims* or *pending lawsuits* may materially affect a firm's financial results. Even with well-publicized lawsuits, you'll need to refer to the footnotes for the important details---amount of damages claimed or the length of time lawsuits have been pending. (Unfortunately, disclosure of such information is at management's discretion unless it's "material" in nature.) Moreover, until such matters are settled, it's difficult to assess how they will affect the company---*but* these disclosures bear close monitoring.

Changes in Accounting Methods

Accounting changes are always something to look for. They can temporarily distort successive years' balance sheets and reported income. For instance, a change in inventory valuation or depreciation methods can give a boost to earnings, but don't expect that easy profit again next year.

Non-Recurring or Extraordinary Gains/Losses

These are one-time events that should be excluded from figuring earnings per share. Substantial *gains* arise from selling real estate or other large assets. The question you need to ask yourself is: Is management simply capitalizing on a good opportunity *OR* is it trying to make up for lower operating income? The latter is a "red flag" that could spell trouble.

Unusual charges or losses (referred to as "adjustments") are extraordinary if they aren't expected to happen again. They reduce net income, so you should examine the financial statements to see what they would have looked like without them.

Write-Offs and Write-Downs

Similar to non-recurring items, *write-offs* of

assets relate directly to a certain event or project. For instance, a company eventually ends up with a money loser. Getting rid of it, as "discontinued operations," is usually good news. Just make sure it's not a regular habit.

Write-downs are used to revalue assets to be more in tune with economic realities, i.e., their *actual* rather than *book* value.

Stock Transactions

Check this footnote to see if the firm repurchased its own stock. This will reduce shares outstanding and give a one-time shot-in-the-arm to earnings per share, but that's all.

MANAGEMENT DISCUSSION AND ANALYSIS OF OPERATIONS

Simply put, this section explains
- how the company did over the prior year
- how it got where it is
- where it expects to go in the future.

It's perhaps the most revealing part of an annual report. (This is the first thing I turn to when an annual report has been stuffed into my mailbox.) Here, management must, by law, accurately and truthfully inform you of both favorable and unfavorable events that have significantly affected last year's operations.

Things to watch for are discussions of:
- growth (slowdown) in sales and income
- changes in profitability, i.e., profit margins and return on equity
- factors that contributed to earnings increase/decrease, especially whether they were industry or company related, e.g., cost overruns on a major contract
- liquidity position
- major events that may affect future results, such as a contract renewal with a major customer or supplier, inability to arrange bank financing or large pension (unfunded) liabilities.

Exhibit C-2 lists other items you'll want to look for.

AUDITOR'S OPINION

One of the first things to check out is the *auditor's opinion,* which appears as a letter at the end of the annual report. This statement serves as a "stamp of approval" by outside, independent accountants. It gives assurance that the financial statements are fairly presented "in conformity with generally accepted accounting principles." (Of course, this is NOT a guarantee that the books have not been "cooked"---even experienced auditors can be misled.)

The opinion *normally* contains two paragraphs. If this is the case, you're looking at an *unqualified opinion* which, of itself, conveys very little information--but that's good.

However, if it contains *three or more paragraphs,* you probably have a *qualified opinion* that needs to be read carefully. Check out the middle paragraph(s) for factors that could modify the interpretation of the financial statements. It may just describe a legitimate change in accounting policy.

If these paragraphs contain *caveats* or *exceptions* about the company's future performance, e.g., its ability to repay debt, it's safest to take your money and run.

RULE OF THUMB: If the opinion is short and sweet, that's good. If not, look for "subject to" or "except for" phrases that tip you off that it's not a standard report. There may be a major uncertainty that could materially affect the company's future. And, the longer the opinion is, the more reservations the auditors have. This means a careful analysis of the annual report is in order, especially the footnotes and management's discussion and analysis.

NOTE: Auditors don't pass judgment on how wise management's decisions have been or assess the risk associated with buying the firm's stock---just on the accounting practices used.

TEN-YEAR SUMMARY OF COMPARATIVE RESULTS

To be really useful, financial reports must be *compared*-- compared with other companies in their industry or compared with a company's different reports over time. In this regard, more and more firms are starting to report a 10-year summary of financial highlights.

This provides a long-term perspective on performance. Important trends to make note of, as well as to their consistency, are
* sales and earning, especially in relation to fluctuations in the general economy
* net earnings as a percentage of sales (profit margin)
* returns on assets and equity
* earnings and dividends per share.

Other items to examine are changes in net worth (stockholders' equity), book value per share, capital expenditures for plant and equipment and long-term debt.

In short, one year's results can't tell you much. You need to compare them to competitors and year-to-year. This is important because you're not only interested in how a company is doing but how it will do.

A FINAL WORD

The key is to really read an annual report; don't just look at or toss it in the trash. Annual reports are required by law for a good reason-- to help you get an *informed* picture of a company's financial situation.

Warning signals often appear in annual reports that will tip you off to actual or potential problems. AND, don't expect them to appear on the first few pages---you'll have to hunt for them. So, no matter whether you read an annual report back-to-front or front-to-back, give it your attention.

Exhibit C-3 has three other valuable sources of information used by professionals. You'll want to familiarize yourself with them.

TERMS TO KNOW
Annual report
Auditor's opinion
Balance sheet
C.E.O.
Contingent liabilities
Footnotes to financial statements
Income statement
Letter to the shareholders
News release
Non-recurring or extraordinary gains/losses
Prospectus
Proxy
Proxy statement
Quarterly report
Statement of changes in financial condition
Write-downs
Write-offs
10-K Report
10-Q Report

Exhibit C-3
Other Valuable Sources of Company Information

Standard & Poor's Stock Guide
An excellent publication that contains information on every stock listed on the exchanges, including price history (past 2 years and the range for the past 10 years), P/E ratio, dividend record, condensed financial position, number of shares outstanding, annual earnings per share (the past 4 years plus the current year's) and the interim earnings for the current fiscal year. Your broker may provide you with one free of charge--just ask for it.

Standard & Poor's Stock Reports
This "tear sheet" service offers a great deal of historical and factual information on actively-traded stocks. It provides a brief summary of the company's business and its product lines, recent developments, a 10-year statistical table of income statements and balance sheets (including the most recent quarterly sales and earnings reports) and a comparison of key financial ratios.

Value Line Investment Survey
This service contains information similar to the S & P Stock Reports but in far greater detail. In addition, Value Line contains *stock recommendations* (updated weekly) and *earnings forecasts* (updated quarterly).
NOTE: Access to these materials is fairly easy. Your local brokerage firm and most public libraries will have subscriptions to them.

SOURCE: From STREET SMART INVESTING, by George B. Clairmont and Kiril Sokoloff. Copyright © 1983 by George B. Clairmont and Kiril Sokoloff. Reprinted by permission of Random House, Inc.

BIBLIOGRAPHY

General Reading

F. Amling and W. G. Droms, The Dow Jones-Irwin Guide to Personal Financial Planning, Dow Jones-Irwin, 1982.

P. Beadle. Investing in the Eighties, Harcourt, Brace Jovanovich, 1981.

L. A. Berstein, Analysis of Financial Statements (Revised), Dow Jones-Irwin, 1984

S. Blotnick, Winning: The Pyschology of Successful Investing, McGraw Hill, 1978.

B. Branch. Investments: A Practical Approach. Longman Financial Services Publishing, Inc., 1985.

R. Bridwell, The Battle for Financial Security, Times Books, 1980.

H. Browne, Inflation-Proofing Your Investments, Morrow, 1980.

D. M. Brownstone and J. Sartisky, Personal Financial Survival, John Wiley, 1981.

I. Cobleigh, Double Your Dollars, Crown, 1979.

J. B. Cohen, E. D. Zinbarg and A. Zeikel. Investment Analysis and Portfolio Manage-, ment, Richard D. Irwin, 1982.

A. S. Donnelly. The Three Rs of Investing: Return, Risk and Relativity, Dow Jones-Irwin, 1985.

L. Dunton, Your Book of Financial Planning: The Consumer's Guide to a Better Financial Future, Reston Publishing Co., 1983.

W. J. Grace, The ABCs of IRAs, Dell Trade Paperbacks, 1983.

V. L. Hampton, K. A. Kitt and S. A. Greninger. Personal and Family Finance (2nd ed.), Burgess Publishing Co., 1982.

C. C. Hardy, ABCs of Investing Your Retirement Funds, Medical Economics, 1982.

C. C. Hardy. Dun & Bradstreet's Guide to Your Investments. Harper & Row, 1985.

C. C. Hardy, Funk & Wagnall's Guide to Personal Money Management, Funk & Wagnalls, 1976.

T. Herzfeld and R. F. Brach, High Return, Low Risk Investment, Putnam, 1981.

G. A. Hirt and S. B. Block, Fundamentals of Investment Management and Strategy, Richard D. Irwin, 1983.

D. King and K. Levine, The Best Way in the World for a Woman to Make Money, Ravson, Wade, 1980.

R. Kinsman, Low Risk Profits in High Risk Times, Dow Jones-Irwin, 1983.

G. Krefetz, The Smart Investor's Guide, A & W Publishers, 1982.

R. T. LeClair, S. R. Leimburg and H. Chasman, Money and Retirement: How to Plan for Lifetime Financial Security, Addison-Wesley, 1982.

B. G. Malkiel, A Random Wall Down Wall Street (2nd edition), Norton, 1981.

B. G. Malkiel, Winning Investment Strategies, Norton, 1982.

R. Nemet, Investment Tips for Today's Woman, Norton, 1981.

D. R. Nichols, Starting Small Investing Smart: What to Do With $5 to $5,000, Dow Jones-Irwin, 1984.

T. C. Noddings. Low-Risk Strategies for the High-Performance Investor, Probus Publishing Co., 1985.

A. H. Pessin and J. A. Ross, Words of Wall Street: 2,000 Investment Terms Defined, Dow Jones-Irwin, 1982.

S. Porter, <u>New Money Book</u>, Avon, 1980.
M. J. and N. Rogers. <u>Women and Money</u>, McGraw-Hill, 1978.

M. Schulman. <u>How to Invest Your Money and Profit from Inflation</u>, Random House, 1980.

D. V. Shane, <u>The Reston Guide to No-Load Financial Planning</u>, Reston Publishing Co., 1984.

C. W. Smith, <u>The Mind of the Market</u>, Rowman and Littlefield, 1981.

A. Tobias. <u>The Only Investment Guide You'll Ever Need</u>, Bantam Books, Revised 1983.

M. Whitman and M. Shubik, <u>The Agressive Conservative Investor</u>, Random House, 1979.

W. W. Widicus and T.E. Stitzel, <u>Personal Investing</u>, Dow Jones-Irwin, 1982.

Fixed Income Securities

H. M. Berlin, <u>The Dow Jones-Irwin Guide to Buying and Selling Treasury Securities</u>, Dow Jones-Irwin, 1984.

D. M. Darst, <u>The Complete Bond Books</u>, McGraw-Hill, 1980.

G. Diller, <u>Investor's Guide to Fixed Income Securities</u>, Van Nostrand Reinhold, 1983.

F. J. Fabozzi (ed.). <u>The Handbook of Mortgage-Backed Securities</u>, Probus, 1984.

F. J. Fabozzi and I. M. Pollack (Eds). <u>The Handbook of Fixed Income Securities</u>, Dow Jones-Irwin, 1983.

R. L. Holt, <u>The Complete Book of Bonds</u>, Harcourt, Brace Jovanovich, 1981.

R. Lamb and S. P. Rappaport, <u>Municipal Bonds</u> McGraw-Hill 1980.

L. R. Rosen. <u>The Dow Jones-Irwin Guide to Interest</u>, Dow Jones-Irwin, 1983.

H. C. Sherwood, <u>How to Invest in Bonds</u>, McGraw-Hill, 1983.

M. L. Stigum, <u>The Money Market</u> (revised), Dow Jones-Irwin, 1983.

Common Stock

W. M. Bowen, IV and F. P. Ganucheau III, <u>The Investor's Equation: Creating Wealth Through Undervalued Stocks</u>, Probus Publishing, 1984.

D. Dreman. <u>The New Contrarian Investment Strategy</u>, Random House, 1982.

E. S. Emory, <u>When to Sell Stocks</u>, Exposition Press, 1980.

L. Engel. <u>How to Buy Stocks</u>, Bantam Books, 1967.

K. L. Fisher. <u>Super Stocks</u>. Dow Jones-Irwin, 1984.

P. E. Jessup. <u>Competing for Stock Market Project</u>, John Wiley, 1974.

C. Moder and R. Hagin, <u>The Dow Jones-Irwin Guide to Common Stocks</u>, Dow Jones-Irwin, 1980.

L. Miller, <u>The Perfect Investment</u>, E. P. Dutton, 1983.

W. H. Pike, <u>Why Stocks Go Up (and Down)</u>, Dow Jones-Irwin, 1983.

C. N. Rosenberg, <u>The Common Sense Way to Stock Market Profits</u>, New American Library, 1978.

D. R. Sargent, <u>Stock Market Profits and Higher Income for You</u>, Simon and Schuster, 1978.

R. J. Teweles and E. S. Bradley, <u>The Stock Market</u> (4th edition), John Wiley, 1982.

Mutual Funds

A. Corrigan and P. C. Kaufman, <u>No-Nonsense Financial Guide to Understanding Money Market Funds</u>, Longmeadow Press, 1984.

W. E. Donoghue, <u>Complete Money Market Guide</u>, Harper & Row, 1980.

Handbook for No-Load Fund Investors, The No-Load Fund Investor, Inc., P.O. Box 283, Hastings-on-Hudson, NY 10706.

Investment Company Institute, 1775 K Street, N.W. Washington, DC 20006.

No-Load Mutual Fund Association, 11 Penn Plaza, New York, NY 10001.

G. W. Perritt and L. K. Shannon, The Individual Investor's Guide to No-Load Mutual Funds, American Association of Individual Investors, 1985.

W. Proctor. The Templeton Touch, Doubleday, 1983.

D. D. Rugg and N. B. Hale, The Dow Jones-Irwin Guide to Mutual Funds, Dow Jones-Irwin, 1983.

B. Seligman, Money Market Funds. Praeger, 1983.

United Mutual Fund Selector, 210 Newbury Street, Boston, MA 02116.

Wiesenberger Services, Investment Companies, 19_____, 870 Seventh Avenue, New York, NY 10019.

Real Estate

R. G. Allen, Creating Wealth, Simon and Schuster, 1983.

R. Bruss, The Smart Investor's Guide to Real Estate, Crown Publishers, 1982.

C. Hall, Real Estate Investing, Holt, Rinehart & Winston, 1982.

C. Mader and J Bortz, The Dow Jones-Irwin Guide to Real Estate Investing (revised), Dow Jones-Irwin, 1984.

D. A. Miller, How to Invest in Real Estate Syndicates, Dow Jones-Irwin, 1978.

D. W. Walters, The Intelligent Investor's Guide to Real Estate, John Wiley, 1981.

B. H. Zick, How to Make Your Real Estate Fortune, Real Estate Investor's Training, P.O. Box 12085, Overland Park, KS 66212.

Stock Options

H. K. Clasing, Jr. The Dow Jones-Irwin Guide to Put and Call Options, Dow Jones-Irwin, 1984.

G. L. Gastineau, The Stock Options Manual, McGraw-Hill, 1979.

T. Lin, Complete Investor's Guide to Listed Options, Prentice-Hall, 1981.

L. G. McMillan, Options as a Strategic Investment, Prentice-Hall, 1980.

J. A. Wilson, Investing in Call Options, Praeger, 1982.

Sources of Information

American Association of Individual Investors (AAII) Journal, 612 N. Michigan Avenue, Suite 317, Chicago, IL 60611.

*Barron's Financial Weekly, 200 Burnett Rd., Chicopee, MA 01021.

Business Week, 1221 Avenue of the Americas, New York, NY 10020.

Changing Times, 179 H St., N.W., Washington D.C. 20006

Financial World, 1250 Broadway, New York, NY 10021

*Forbes, 60 Fifth Avenue, New York, NY 10011

*Fortune, 541 North Fairbanks Court, Chicago, IL 60611.

*Investors Daily, 1941 Armacost Avenue, Los Angeles, CA 90025

M. B. Lehmann, The Dow Jones-Irwin Guide to Using the Wall Street Journal, Dow Jones-Irwin, 1984.

*Money, 1271 Avenue of the Americas, New York, NY 10020.

*Moody's Investors Service, Inc., 99 Church t., New York, NY 10007

*Personal Investor, 4300 Campus Dr., Newport Beach, CA 92660.

*Standard & Poor's, Publishers, 25 Broadway, New York, NY 10004.

*Value Line, 711 Third Avenue, New York, NY 10017.

*The Wall Street Journal, 200 Burnett Rd., Chicopee, MA 01021.

---

* Have been found to be of special interest.

GLOSSARY OF INVESTMENT TERMS

A

Accelerated Depreciation. Depreciation methods that involve writing off the cost of an asset at a faster rate than the write-off under the straight-line method.

Advance-Decline line. See Breadth of Market.

Agency Bonds. Bonds issued by political subdivisions of the U.S. government, but without direct obligation of the Treasury. The two types of agency bonds are government sponsored and federal agency bonds.

AMEX. A popular name for the American Stock Exchange.

Annual Report. The formal financial statement issued yearly by a corporation. The annual report shows assets, liabilities, earnings--how the company stood at the close of the business year, how it fared profitwise during the year and other information of interest to shareholders.

Annual Stockholders' Meeting. Meeting to present major policy items for discussion or vote-annual report, future prospects, election of the board of directions, special issues.

Annuity. A contract between an insurance company and an individual in which the company agrees to provide an income, which may be fixed or variable in amount, for a specified period in exchange for a stipulated amount of money.

Appreciate. To increase or grow in value.

Arrearage. Overdue payment; frequently, omitted dividend on preferred stocks.

Assets. Everything a corporation owns or due to it: Cash, investments, money due it, materials, and inventories, which are called current assets; buildings and machinery, which are known as fixed assets.

Ask Price. The lowest price at which a given security is offered for sale.

At-the-Money Option. A put or call is at-the-money when the underlying stock sells at the same price as the exercise price of the option.

Auction Market. The system of trading securities through brokers or agents on an exchange such as the New York Stock Exchange. Buyers compete with other buyers while sellers compete with other sellers for the most advantageous price. Most transactions are executed with public customers on both sides since the specialist buys or sells for his own account primarily to offset imbalances in public supply and demand.

Automatic Reinvestment Plan. System by which dividends or capital gains are automatically plowed back to buy additional shares.

Average Tax Rate. Total taxes paid stated as a percentage of total taxable income. The average tax rate is always less than the marginal tax rate in a progressive tax system.

Averages. Various ways of measuring the trend of securities prices, one of the most popular of which is the Dow Jones average of 30 industrial stocks listed on the New York Stock Exchange.

B

Back-End Load. A 1 or 2 percent commission on the sale of mutual fund shares.

Balance Sheet. An condensed financial statement showing the nature and amount of a company's assets, liabilities, and capital on a given date. In dollar amounts, the balance sheet shows what the company owned, what it owed, and the ownership interest in the company of its stockholders.

Balanced Fund. An investment company with the policy of investing its assets proportionately in bonds, preferred stocks and common stocks. The proportions vary depending on market conditions for stocks and bonds. Such funds are generally conservative in investment policy, choosing less volatile securities and providing a high quarterly income.

Banker's Acceptance. A check ordering a bank to pay money for a borrower. When the bank signs a banker's acceptance on behalf of its customer in order to help the customer pay a bill, the banker's acceptance becomes a money-market security that the bank can sell to another investor if it wishes.

Bankruptcy. A company or person is bankrupt when a bankruptcy court judges that the company or person is unable to meet financial obligations; the court then orders any remaining assets to be auctioned off to pay debts.

Bear. Someone who believes the market will decline

in price.

Bear Market. A period of time, usually measured in months, during which the market indexes and the market prices of most securities in a given market decline, and pessimism prevails over optimism among investors. Usually, the volume of shares traded is also low during bearish periods.

Bearer Bond. A bond which does not have the owner's name registered on the books of the issuing company and which is payable to the holder. (See: Coupon Bond, Registered Bond)

Beta. A measure of volatility, or relative systematic risk, for stock or portfolio returns. Typically found by regressing stock (or portfolio) returns on a market index such as the S&P 500.

Bid and Asked. Often referred to as a quotation or quote. The bid is the highest price anyone has declared that he wants to pay for a security at a given time, the asked is the lowest price anyone will sell at the same time.

Big Board. A popular name for the New York Stock Exchange.

Block. A large holding or transaction of stock—usually considered to be 10,000 shares or more.

Blue Chip. A company known nationally for the quality and wide acceptance of its products or services, and for its ability to make money and pay dividends.

Blue Chip Stock. Stocks that are unsurpassed in quality and have a long record of earnings and dividends; the strongest and stablest on the market.

Bond. Basically an IOU or promissory note of a corporation, usually issued in multiples of $1,000 or $5,000, although $100 and $500 denominations are not unknown. A bond is evidence of debt on which the issuing company usually promises to pay the bondholders a specific amount of interest for a specified length of time, and to repay the loan on the expiration date. In every case a bond represents debt-- its holder is a creditor of the corporation and not a part owner as is the shareholder. In some cases, bonds are secured by a mortgage.

Bond Fund. A mutual fund with a portfolio consisting primarily of bonds. The emphasis of such funds is normally on income rather than growth.

Bond Quality Ratings. Alphabetic designations (AAA, AA, A, BBB, BB, etc.) used by financial services (e.g., Standard & Poor's and Moody's) to rate bonds. The ratings are essentially estimates of the probability of default.

Bond Yield. An annual rate of return; a measure of the return an investor would receive on a bond if it were held to maturity.

Book Value. An accounting term. Book value of a stock is determined from a company's records, by adding all assets (generally excluding such intangibles as goodwill), then deducting all debts and other liabilities, plus the liquidation price of any preferred issues. The sum arrived at is divided by the number of common shares outstanding and the result is book value per common share. Book value of the assets of a company or a security may have little or no significant relationship to market value.

Book Value Per Share. A measure that represents the difference between total assets and total liabilities.

$$\text{Book Value Per Share} = \frac{\text{Stockholder's equity}}{\text{No. common shares outstanding}}$$

Broker. An agent who handles the public's orders to buy and sell securities, options, or other property. For this service a commission is charged.

Brokers' Loans. Money borrowed by brokers from banks for a variety of uses. It may be used by specialists and odd-lot dealers to help finance inventories of stock they deal in; by brokerage firms to finance the underwriting of new issues of corporate and municipal securities; to help finance a firm's own investments; and to help finance the purchase of securities for customers who prefer to use the broker's credit when they buy securities.

Budget. A schedule of income and expenditures commonly broken into monthly intervals and covering a one-year period.

Bull. One who believes the market will rise in price.

Bull Market. A period of months or years during which the market indexes and the prices of most securities in a given market rise, and optimism prevails over pessimism.

Business Activity. An overall measure of the employment rate, manufacturing activity, the rate at which plant and equipment are being utilized, and other related factors.

Business Cycle. A period of time of from one to 12 years during which the general business activity expands for a while, then contracts.

Business Risk. The degree of uncertainty associated with an investment's earnings and ability to pay interest, dividends, and other returns owed investors.

C

Call. (1) an option to buy (or "call") a share of stock at a specific price within a specified period; (2) the process of redeeming a bond or preferred stock issue before its normal maturity.

Call Premium. Payment made to holders of securities that is an excess over the face value of the securities when the corporation redeems the security before its maturity. Call premium may be constant at a stipulated amount over the entire life of the security, or it may decline as maturity approaches.

Callable. A bond issue, all or part of which may be redeemed by the issuing corporation under conditions before maturity. The term also applies to preferred shares that may be redeemed by the issuing corporation.

Capital. Generally, the money or property used in a business. The term is also used to apply to cash in reserve, savings, or other property of value. In financial reports, it is the total of all assets less the total of all liabilities.

Capital Gain or Loss. Profit or loss from the sale of a capital asset. A capital gain, under current federal income tax laws, may be either short term (six months or less) or long term (more than six months). A short-term capital gain is taxed at the reporting individual's full income tax rate. A long-term capital gain is subject to a lower tax.

Capital Gains Distributions. Payments to mutual fund shareholders of gains realized on the sale of the fund's portfolio securities. These amounts usually are paid once a year.

Capital Growth. An increase in the market value of a mutual fund's securities which is reflected in the net asset value of fund shares. This is a specific long-term objective of many mutual funds.

Capital Stock. All shares representing ownership of a business, including preferred and common.

Capital Structure. The permanent long-term financing of the firm represented by long-term debt, preferred stock, and net worth (net worth consists of common stock, paid in capital and retained earn-

ings). Capital structure is distinguished from financial structure, which includes short-term debt.

Capitalization. Total amount of the various securities issued by a corporation. Capitalization may include bonds, preferred and common stock. Bonds and debentures are usually carried on the books of the issuing company in terms of their par or face value. Preferred value may be an arbitrary figure decided upon by the directors or may represent the amount received by the company from the sale of securities at the time of issuance.

Cash Dividends. Cash payments (usually paid quarterly) to stockholders. Many corporations pay about half of their earnings in cash dividends.

Cash Value Insurance. Insurance policies with built-in "savings account" features, e.g., whole life.

Certificate. The actual piece of paper that is evidence of ownership of stock in a corporation. Watermarked paper is finely engraved with delicate etchings to discourage forgery. Loss of a certificate may at the least cause a great deal of inconvenience-- at the worst, financial loss.

Certificate of Deposit. (1) If negotiable, a marketable short-term deposit liability of the issuer that pays principal (a minimum of $100,000) plus interest at maturity; (2) if non-negotiable, savings certificates with varying maturities and interest rates.

Checkwriting Privilege. Mutual fund feature that allows an investor to redeem his/her shares by writing a check on the fund.

Chicago Board Options Exchange (CBOE). An exchange that has promoted the organized trading of options.

Collateral. Securities or other property pledged by a borrower to secure repayment of a loan.

Commercial Paper. A short-term promissory note maturing in 270 days or less and sold by a major corporation to obtain a loan.

Commission. The broker's basic fee for purchasing or selling securities or property as an agent.

Commission Broker. An agent who executes the public's orders for the purchase or sale of securities or commodities.

Common Stock. Securities that represent an ownership interest in a corporation. If the company has also issued preferred stock, both common and preferred have ownership rights. The preferred normally is limited to a fixed dividend but has prior claim on dividends and, in the event of liquidation, assets. Claims of both common and preferred stockholders are junior to claims of bondholders or other creditors of the company. Common stockholders assume the greater risk, but generally exercise the greater control.

Common Stock Fund. A mutual fund with a portfolio consisting primarily of common stocks. The emphasis of such funds is usually on growth.

Compound Interest. An interest rate that is applicable when interest in succeeding periods is earned not only the initial principal but also on the accumulated interest of previous periods. Compound interest is in contrast to simple interest, in which returns are not earned on interest received.

Compounding. The arithmetic process determining the final value of a payment or series of payments when compound interest is applied.

Consumer Price Index (CPI). A general cost-of-living index prepared monthly by the U.S. government's Bureau of Labor Statistics. The CPI is based on the cost of a representative market basket of goods.

Contrary Opinion. The idea of trading opposite those investors who supposedly always lose--to go against the crowd.

Contribution to Savings or Investment. The difference between total income and total expenses during a given period of time.

Conversion Privilege (Exchange Privilege). Enables a mutual fund shareholder to transfer his investment from one fund to another within the same fund group if his/her needs or objectives change, sometimes with a small transaction charge.

Corporate Bonds. Nongovernmental bonds from corporate sources: industries, banks and financial institutions, rail/transportation, and public utilities.

Coupon Bond. Bond with interest coupons attached. The coupons are clipped as they come due and are presented by the holder for payment of interest.

Covenant. Specific clauses that are contained in bond indentures.

Coverage of Fixed Charges. The number of times available pre-tax earnings would cover bond interest and related charges.

Covered Call Writer. The writer of a call who owns the shares of stock on which he/she has written a call.

Covered Put Writer. The writer of a put who holds an identical put on the same class of stock, and one in which the exercise, or strike price, of the put held is equal to or greater than that of the written put.

Credit Union. Cooperative association where the members' pooled savings are available for loans.

Cumulative Preferred. A stock having a provision that if one or more dividends are omitted, the omitted dividends must be paid before dividends may be paid on the company's common stock.

Curb Exchange. Former name of the American Stock Exchange, second largest exchange in the country. The term comes from the market's origin on a street in downtown New York.

Current Assets. Those assets of a company that are reasonably expected to be realized in cash, or sold, or consumed during the normal operating cycle of the business. These include cash, U.S. government bonds, receivables and money due usually within one year, and inventories.

Current Income. Income received periodically from an investment; may be interest, dividends, or rent, and is either cash or easily converted to liquid assets.

Current Liabilities. Money owed and payable by a company, usually within one year.

Current Ratio. The most commonly cited of all financial ratios. It is computed as follows:

$$\text{Current ratio} = \frac{\text{Current assets}}{\text{Current liabilities}}$$

Current Yield. A stock or bond's cashflow to investors in the form of cash dividends or interest, stated as a percentage of the security's current market price.

Custodian. For mutual funds, a qualified bank otherwise unconnected with the fund. It holds the cash and securities of the fund and performs a variety of clerical services for the fund related to the securities held.

Cyclical Industries. Industries that usually do well when the economy prospers and are likely to be hurt when it falters.

D

Dealer. An individual or firm in the securities

business acting as a principal rather than as an agent. Typically, a dealer buys for his own account and sells to a customer from his inventory of the stock.

Debenture. A promissory note backed by the general credit of a company and usually not secured by a mortgage or lien on any specific property.

Debit Balance. Portion of purchase price stock, bonds or commodities covered by credit extended by a broker to margin customers.

Deduction. An item that may be subtracted from taxable income, the taxable estate, or taxable gifts, thereby lowering the amount subject to taxes.

Default Risk. Risk arising from the chance that a company issuing securities might fail to pay its fixed obligations and possibly go bankrupt.

Defensive Industries. Industries least affected by recessions and economic adversity.

Deferred Annuity. Benefits begin after a given number of years or at optional ages specified in a contract purchased with a single premium or annual premiums.

Denomination. Standard principal amounts into which issues are broken to facilitate the marketing of bonds.

Depreciation. Normally, charges against earnings to write off the cost, less salvage value, of an asset over its estimated useful life. It is a bookkeeping entry and does not represent any cash outlay nor are any funds earmarked for this purpose.

Discount. The amount by which a preferred stock or bond may sell below its par value. Also used as a verb to mean "takes into account" as the price of the stock has discounted the expected dividend cut.

Discount Bond. Issues with a market value lower than par.

Discount Broker. Brokers with low overhead operations who will make transactions at lower commissions than a full-service broker.

Director. Person elected by shareholders to establish company policies. The directors appoint the president, vice-presidents, and all other operating officers. Directors decide, among other matters, if and when dividends shall be paid.

Discretionary Account. An account in which the customer gives the broker or someone else discretion, which may be complete or within specific limits, as to the purchases and sales of securities or com-

modities including selection, timing, amount, and price to be paid or received.

Diversifiable Risk. Risk arising from the characteristics of individual assets. A diversified portfolio averages individual differences out to zero, thus eliminating this type of risk. Also called "unsystematic risk."

Diversification. Spreading investments among different companies in different fields. Another type of diversification is also offered by the securities of many individual companies because of the wide range of their activities.

Dividend. The payment designated by the Board of Directors to be distributed pro rata among the shares outstanding. On preferred shares, it is generally a fixed amount. On common shares, the dividend varies with the fortunes of the company and the amount of cash on hand, and may be omitted if business if poor or the directors determine to withhold earnings to invest in plant and equipment. Sometimes a company will pay a dividend out of past earnings even if it is not currently operating at a profit.

Dividend Arrears. An outstanding unfulfilled preferred dividend obligation.

Dividend Yield. The ratio of the level of current income from dividends to the most recent share price.

$$\text{Dividend yield} \quad = \quad \frac{\text{Annual dividend income}}{\text{Stock price}}$$

Dividends Per Share. A method of translating total aggregate (dollar) dividends paid by the company into a per share figure.

$$\text{Dividends per share} \quad = \quad \frac{\text{Annual dividends paid}}{\text{Number of common shares outstanding}}$$

Double Taxation. Short for double taxation of dividends. The federal government taxes corporate profits once as corporate income; any part of the remaining profits distributed as dividends may be taxed again as income to the recipient stockholder.

Dow. Usually refers to the Dow Jones Industrial Average, the most commonly used stock market index.

Dow Jones Averages. Four stock averages prepared by Dow Jones, publisher of The Wall Street Journal. They are the Dow Jones Industrial Average (DJIA), the transportation, the public utility, and the composite averages.

Dow Jones Industrial Average (DJIA). See Dow Jones averages.

Dow Theory. A theory of market analysis based upon the performance of the Dow Jones industrial and transportation stock price averages. The theory says that the market is in a basic upward trend if one of these averages advances above a previous important high, accompanied or followed by a similar advance in the other. When the averages both dip below previous important lows, this is regarded as confirmation of a basic downward trend. The theory does not attempt to predict how long either trend will continue, although it is widely misinterpreted as a method of forecasting future action.

Down Tick. (See: Up Tick)

E

Earnings Multiplier. (See: Price-Earnings Ratio)

Earnings Per Share. A corporation's total earnings divided by the number of shares of common stock outstanding: an estimate of the earning power behind each share.

Earnings Report. A statement also called an income statement--issued by a company showing its earnings or losses over a given period. The earnings report lists the income earned, expenses and the net result.

Economic Analysis. The study of the general state of the economy and its potential effects on security returns.

Economic Forecasts. Projections of macroeconomic variables (e.g., a country's gross national product, aggregate corporate profits, changes in the stage of the business cycle, and other factors). Economic consultants sell such predictions.

Equity. The ownership interest of common and preferred stockholders in a company. Also refers to excess of value of securities over the debit balance in a margin account.

Equity Kicker. A provision in a loan entitling the lender to a portion of the borrower's profits from the project.

Estate Planning. Process of planning assets, bequest, and estate disposition to assure liquidity, provide for family needs, minimize confusion, and avoid unnecessary taxes and forced sales.

Eurodollar Loans. U.S. dollars deposited in a bank located outside of the United States and loaned to borrowers.

Eurodollars. Deposits of U.S. dollars in foreign branches of U.S. banks. Eurodollar CDs are time deposits denominated in dollars that are issued by foreign branches of U.S. banks. Euro-instruments are not FDIC insured and Federal Reserve requirements do not apply to Eurodollar deposits.

Ex-dividend. A synonym for "without dividend." The buyer of a stock selling ex-dividend does not receive the recently declared dividend. Every dividend is payable on a fixed date to all shareholders recorded on the books of the company as of a previous date of record. For example, a dividend may be declared as payable to holders of record on the books of the company on a given Friday. Since five business days are allowed for delivery of stock in a "regular way" transaction on the New York Stock Exchange, the exchange would declare the stock "ex-dividend" as of the opening of the market on the preceding Monday. That means anyone who bought it on and after Monday would not be entitled to that dividend. When stocks go ex-dividend, the stock tables include the symbol "X" following the name.

Exercise Price. Also the Strike Price. The price at which the holder may purchase (in the case of call options) or sell (in the case of put options), the underlying stock.

Expenses. A business outlay chargeable against revenues for a specific period.

Expiration Date. The last date on which an option may be exercised at the strike or exercise price.

Extra. The short form of "extra dividend." A dividend in the form of stock or cash in addition to the regular or usual dividend the company has been paying.

F

Face Amount. This amount is stated on the face of the policy. This is the amount of a policy that is paid at death or at contract maturity, less any policy loans or withdrawals made.

Face Value. The value of a bond that appears on the face of the bond, unless the value is otherwise specified by the issuing company. Face value is ordinarily the amount the issuing company promises to pay at maturity. Face value is not an indication of market value. Sometimes referred to as par value.

Federal Agency Bonds. Bonds issued by an agency of the U.S. government (for example, the Federal Home Loan Bank).

Financial Assets. Pieces of paper evidencing a claim on some issuer.

Financial Market. A forum in which suppliers and demanders of funds are brought together.

Financial Leverage. The use of borrowed funds to acquire an asset; the use of debt financing.

Financial Planner. One who helps individuals in an ongoing process to arrange and coordinate their personal and financial affairs to enable the individuals to achieve their objectives.

Financial Risk. Risk arising from the use of debt in financing the assets of a firm.

Financial Risk. (See: Default Risk)

Financial Statements. The major financial data provided by a corporation, primarily the balance sheet and the income statement.

Fiscal Policy. Government tax and spending policy that affects the economy.

Fiscal Year. A corporation's accounting year. Due to the nature of their particular business, some companies do not use the calendar year for their bookkeeping. A typical example is the department store which finds December 31 too early a date to close its books after the Christmas rush. For that reason, many such stores wind up their accounting year January 31. Their fiscal year, therefore, runs from February 1 of one year through January 31 of the next. The fiscal year of other companies may run from July 1 through the following June 30. Most companies, though, operate on a calendar year basis.

Fixed Charges. A company's fixed expenses, such as bond interest, that it has agreed to pay whether or not earned, and that are deducted from income before earnings on equity capital are computed.

Fixed-Income Securities. Securities with specified payment dates and amounts, primarily bonds and preferred stock.

Fixed Payout Ratio. A way of keeping payments of dividends at a constant ratio equal to the distributed funds divided by earnings.

Floor. The huge trading area--about two-thirds the size of a football field--where stocks and bonds are bought and sold, e.g., on the New York Stock Exchange.

Floor Broker. A member of a stock exchange who executes orders on the floor of the exchange to buy or sell listed securities.

Flower Bond. Purchase of an older government bond at a discount and used to pay estate taxes at par when the holder dies.

Form 10-K. A statement filed with the SEC by firms that have securities listed on an organized exchange or traded in the OTC market.

Fundamental Analysis. Analysis of industries and companies based on such factors as sales, assets, earnings, products or services, markets, and management. As applied to the economy, fundamental research includes consideration of gross national product, interest rates, unemployment, inventories, savings, etc.

Funded Debt. Usually interest-bearing bonds or debentures of a company. Could include long-term bank loans. Does not include short-term loans, preferred or common stock.

G

GNMA (Ginnie Mae) Pass-Throughs. Obligations of Government National Mortgage Association, representing an undivided interest in a pool of federally insured mortgages. Coupons carry interest rates related to the mortgage market.

General Mortgage Bond. A bond that is secured by a blanket mortgage on the company's property, but which may be outranked by one or more other mortgages.

General Obligation (GO) Bond. A municipal bond backed by the full faith and credit of a municipality, rather than by the revenues from a specific project.

General Partner. The managing partner who accepts all liability and makes all decisions.

Generally Accepted Accounting Principles (GAAPs). A standard set of rules developed by the account profession for the preparation of financial statements.

Good 'Til Cancelled Order (GTC) or Open Order. An order to buy or sell that remains in effect until it is either executed or cancelled.

Government Bonds. Obligations of the U.S.

government, regarded as the highest grade issues in existence.

Gross National Product (GNP). The market value of all goods and services produced by a country over the period of a year.

Growth Fund. A mutual fund with the primary investment objective of growth of capital. Invests principally in common stocks with growth potential.

Growth-Income Fund. A mutual fund with the aim of providing for a degree of both income and long-term growth.

Growth Industries. Industries whose earnings are expected to be significantly above the average of all industries.

Growth Stock. Stock of a company with a record of growth in earnings at a relatively rapid rate.

H

Hybrid Securities. Securities possessing features of both common stocks and bonds.

Hedge (Option Hedging). Combining two or more securities into a single investment position to reduce risk.

I

Inactive Stock. An issue traded on an exchange or in the over-the-counter market in which there is a relatively low volume of transactions. Volume may be no more than a few hundred shares a week or even less.

Income. Items that represent cash received during a given period; includes wages, salaries, bonuses, commissions, dividends, rents and interest earned.

Income Bond. Generally income bonds promise to repay principal but to pay interest only when earned. In some cases, unpaid interest on an income bond may accumulate as a claim against the corporation when the bond becomes due. An income bond may also be issued in lieu of preferred stock.

Income Fund. A mutual fund with the primary investment objective of current income rather than growth of capital. It invests in stocks and bonds that normally pay the highest dividends and interest.

Income Statement. Description of the financial activities that have taken place during a specified period of time, which is typically one year, for a given firm.

Income Stocks. Issues having a long, sustained record of regularly paying higher than average dividends. Many income stocks are also blue chips.

Indenture. A written agreement under which bonds and debentures are issued, setting forth maturity date, interest rate, and other terms.

Index. Measurement of the current price behavior of a representative group of stocks in relation to a base value set at an earlier point in time.

Index Funds. Mutual funds holding portfolios that attempt to duplicate a market average such as the S&P 500.

Individual Retirement Accounts (IRAs). Tax-sheltered accounts available to all income earners. IRA funds can be invested in a wide range of assets.

Industry Analysis. Study of the industry within which a particular company operates and the outlook for that industry.

Inflation. An increase in the general price level; though a few prices may fall, the overall cost of living and cost of doing business rise.

Inflation Hedge. An asset whose market price rises as fast as or faster than the rate of inflation; thus, the owner of the asset suffers no loss of purchasing power.

Inflation Rate. The percentage change per year (or over some other time period and then annualized) in an index of general price levels, such as the Consumer Price Index.

Initial Margin. The equity required to finance a security transaction, with the remainder borrowed from a broker. The margin requirement is set by the Federal Reserve System.

Insider. The directors, officers, other executives, and technicians (e.g., outside consultants and auditors) who have access to confidential information about a company and are therefore legally restricted in their investment activities involving that company.

Insolvency. A state of financial distress in which an individual or a corporation cannot meet its maturing debt obligations.

Institutional Investor. An organization whose primary purpose is to invest its own assets or those held in trust by it for others. Includes pension funds, investment companies, insurance companies, universities, and banks.

Insurance. A mechanism that allows people to reduce risk by sharing in the losses associated with the occurrence of uncertain events.

In-The-Money Option. An option is in the money when it has intrinsic value. A call is in the money when the underlying stock's price is greater than the option's exercise price. A put is in the money when the underlying stock's price is lower than the option's exercise price.

Interest. Payments a borrower pays a lender for the use of his money. For example, a corporation pays interest on its bonds to its bondholders.

Interest Rate Risk. The change in the price of a security resulting from a change in market interest rates.

Interest-Sensitive Industries. Industries particularly sensitive to expectations about changes in interest rates.

Intrinsic Value. The true economic worth of a share of stock, calculated by finding the discounted present value of all the share's future income. Fundamental analysts estimate the intrinsic value in order to see if a stock's current market price is too high or too low.

Investment. The process of evaluating, selecting, and monitoring the use of funds to make more money; to gain income, to increase capital value or both. Safety of principal is an important consideration. (See; Speculation)

Investment Advisor. The organization that a mutual fund pays for investment advice and, usually, general business management. The adviser is often the sponsor and promoter of the fund. Also, one whose principal business consists of acting as investment counsel, and a substantial part of his business consists of rendering investment supervisory services.

Investment Banker. Also known as an underwriter. He is the middleman between the corporation issuing new securities and the public. The usual practice is for one or more investment bankers to buy outright from a corporation a new issue of stocks or bonds. The group forms a syndicate to sell the securities to individuals and institutions. Investment bankers also distribute very large blocks of stocks or bonds--perhaps held by an estate. Thereafter, the market in the security may be over the counter, on a regional stock exchange, the American Exchange or the New York Stock Exchange.

Investment Company. A company or trust that uses it capital to invest in other companies. There are two principal types: the closed end and the open end, or mutual fund. Shares in closed-end investment companies, some of which are listed on the New York Stock Exchange, are readily transferable in the open market and are bought and sold like other shares. Capitalization of these companies remains the same unless action is taken to change, which is seldom. Open-end funds sell their new shares to investors, stand ready to buy back their old shares, and are not listed. Open-end funds are so called because their capitalization is not fixed; they issue more shares as people want them.

Investment Letter. A publication that provides analyses, conclusions, and recommendations on securities and the general market and may provide opinions of various experts on different aspects of security investment.

Investment Objective. The goal (e.g., long-term capital growth, current income, etc.) that an investor or a mutual fund pursues.

Investment Value. An indication of the worth placed in a stock--what the public thinks the stock should be traded for. (See: Intrinsic Value)

Issue. Any of a company's securities, or the act of distributing such securities.

K

Keogh Plan. A retirement program for self-employed individuals and their employees based on tax-saving provisions. An individual can contribute 15 percent of income to a maximum of $15,000. A Keogh plan may be funded with mutual fund shares.

L

Leading and Lagging Indicators. Certain economic factors (such as stock market indexes, money supply, unemployment, etc.) that tend to anticipate (i.e., lead) changes in the general level of business activity. Other variable factors (such as inflation) that tend to follow (i.e., lag behind) changes in the general level of business activity.

Leverage. The effect on the per-share earnings of the common stock of a company when large sums must be paid for bond interest or preferred stock dividends, or both, before the common stock is entitled to share in earnings. Leverage may be advantageous for the common stock when earnings are good but may work against the common when earnings decline. Example: Company A has 1,000,000 shares of common stock outstanding, no other securities. Earnings drop from $1,000,000 to $800,000 or from $1 to 80 cents a share, a decline of 20 percent. Company B has 1,000,000 shares of common but must pay $500,000 annually in bond interest. If earnings amount to $1,000,000, there is $500,000 available for the common or 50 cents a share. But earnings drop to $800,000 so there is only $300,000 available for the common, or 30 cents a share--a drop of 40 percent. Or suppose earnings of the company with only common stock increased from $1,000,000 to $1,500,000--earnings per share would go from $1 to $1.50, or an increase of 50 percent. But if earnings of the company that had to pay $500,000 in bond interest increased that much-- earnings per common share would jump from 50 cents to $1 a share, or 100 percent. When a company has common stock only, no leverage exists because all earnings are available for the common, although relatively large fixed charges payable for lease of substantial plant assets may have an effect similar to that of a bond issue.

Leverage Ratios. Financial ratios used to measure a firm's use of borrowed money (e.g., the debt-to-equity ratio).

Liabilities. All the claims against a corporation. Liabilities include accounts and wages payable, dividends declared payable, accrued taxes payable, and fixed or long-term liabilities such as mortgage bonds, debentures and bank loans.

Limit Order or Limited Price Order. An order to buy or sell a stated amount of a security at a specified price, or at a better price, if obtainable after the order is represented in the trading crowd.

Limited Liability. Common stock owners are not responsible for the debts of their corporation; hence, their liability is limited to the amount of their capital paid in.

Limited Partner. A passive investor who supplies most of the capital and has liability limited only to the amount of his or her investment.

Limited Partnership. A business organization form under which certain partners are designated as limited partners--that is, their liability is limited to their investment.

Liquid Asset Fund. A money market fund; a mutual fund that invests only in money-market securities.

Liquid Investment. An investment that can be converted easily into cash, without penalty.

Liquidation. The process of converting securities or other property into cash. The dissolution of a company, with cash remaining after sale of its assets and payment of all indebtedness being distributed to the shareholders.

Liquidity. The ability of the market in a particular security to absorb a reasonable amount of buying or selling at reasonable price changes. Liquidity is one of the most important characteristics of a good market.

Listed Stock. The stock of a company that is traded on a securities exchange, and for which a listing application and a registration statement, giving detailed information about the company and its operations, have been filed with the Securities and Exchange Commission (unless otherwise exempted) and the exchange itself. The various stock exchanges have different standards for listing. Some of the guides used by the New York Stock Exchange for an original listing are national interest in the company, a minimum of 1 million shares publicly held among not less than 2000 round-lot stockholders. The publicly held common shares should have a minimum aggregate market value of $16 million. The company should have net income in the latest year of over $2.5 million before federal income tax and $2 million in each of the preceding two years.

Listing Requirements. The requirements that an organized securities exchange imposes on an issue of securities before it will make a market in (i.e., list) the securities.

Load. The portion of the offering price of shares of open-end investment companies that covers sales commissions and all other costs of distribution. The load is usually incurred only on purchase, there being, in most cases, no charge when the shares are sold (redeemed).

Load Funds. Mutual funds with a sales charge.

Long. Signifies ownership of securities: "I am long 100 U.S. Steel" means 100 shares are owned.

Long Position. Buying and holding an asset in hopes of profiting from its cash dividends, interest, price increase, or other benefits.

Long-Term Asset. An asset that is expected to last (or to be held) for more than one year.

Long-Term Debt. Debt that becomes due after more than one year.

M

Maintenance Margin. The amount, established by brokers and exchanges, below which an investor's equity as a percentage of total portfolio value cannot fall.

Management. The Board of Directors, elected by the stockholders, and the officers of the corporation, appointed by the Board of Directors.

Management Company. The business entity that begins, promotes and manages a fund or funds, each of which is a separate corporation with its own board of directors.

Management Fee. The fee charged by all investment companies for managing the portfolio. A typical fee is 0.5% of the net assets.

Margin. The amount borrowed by the customer when he uses his broker's credit to buy a security. Under federal reserve regulations, the initial margin of equity required in the past 20 years has ranged from 50 percent of the purchase price all the way to 100 percent.

Margin Account. A special account set up with a broker to handle all margin transactions regardless of the type of security being margined. This amount is opened with a minimum of $2,000 in equity, in cash or deposited securities.

Margin Call. A demand upon a customer to put up money or securities with the broker. The call is made when a purchase is made; also if a customer's equity in a margin account declines below a minimum standard (maintenance margin) set by the exchange or by the firm.

Margin Loan. Financial leverage or use of borrowed funds to get increased capital gains.

Margin Purchase. A security purchase that is not made on a 100% cash basis; borrowed funds are used.

Margin Trading. Buying securities with borrowed money to magnify returns; margin refers to the equity in the investment.

Marginal Tax Rate. The percentage that must be paid in taxes on the next one dollar income. With a progressively graduated tax system, as income increases, the marginal tax rate increases. (See: Average Tax Rate)

Market Average. An arithmetic average of the prices for the sample of securities being used.

Market Data. Primarily stock price and volume data.

Market Index. Measures the current price behavior of a sample of securities in relation to a base value established for a previous time period.

Market Maker. A securities dealer who earns the bid-asked spread for facilitating trading in a security (e.g., a NYSE specialist).

Market Order. An order to buy or sell a stated amount of a security at the most advantageous price obtainable after the order is represented in the trading crowd. (See: Good 'Til Cancelled Order, Limit Order, Stop Order)

Market Price. In the case of a security, market price is usually considered the last reported price at which the security sold.

Market Return. Measure usually calculated by the average return on all (or a large sample of) securities, such as Standard and Poor's 500 Stock Composite Index.

Market Risk. Risk that results from life-style changes, preferences, or behavior of investors in the marketplace. Risk arising from the alternation of bull and bear market conditions.

Market Value. The prevailing market price of an issue; an indication of how the market as a whole has assessed a security's worth.

Marketability Risk. The risk of illiquidity; inability to liquidate an investment conveniently and reasonably.

Marketable Securities. Financial assets that are easily and inexpensively traded among investors.

Maturity. The date on which a loan, bond or debenture comes due and is to be paid off.

Member Corporation. A securities brokerage firm,

organized as a corporation, with at least one member of the New York Stock Exchange, Inc. who is a director and a holder of voting stock in the corporation.

Member Firm. A securities brokerage firm organized as a partnership or corporation and having at least one general partner who is a member of the New York Stock Exchange, Inc. (See: Member Corporation)

Merger. The formation of one company from two or more previously existing companies.

Monetary Assets. Assets that are denominated in dollars--such as cash, bonds, and savings accounts-- and thus tend to make poor inflation hedges.

Monetary Policy. Government policy affecting the economy through impact on money supply. The Federal Reserve influences the money supply through its control of bank reserves and required reserves.

Money Fund. A money market fund.

Money Market. The collection of institutions and organizations that facilitate purchase and sale of short-term debt instruments such as Treasury bills, commercial paper, bankers' acceptances, certificates of deposit, etc. Typically, the maturity of the the debt instruments that are traded in money markets is less than one year.

Money Market (Cash Management) Fund. A mutual fund that invests primarily in short-term instruments, such as instruments issued or guaranteed by the U.S. government or its agencies and instrumentalities, bank certificates of deposit, banker's acceptances, and commercial paper. The fund's primary objective is current income.

Money Market Certificate (MMC). A special type of certificate of deposit issued by banks, savings and loans, mutual savings banks, and credit unions. Also called money market time deposits.

Mortgage Bond. A bond secured by a mortgage on a property. The value of the property may or may not equal the value of the so-called mortgage bonds issued against it. (See: Bond, Debenture)

Municipal Bond. A bond issued by a state or a political subdivision, such as county, city, town, or village. The term also designates bonds issued by state agencies and authorities. In general, interest paid on municipal bonds is exempt from federal income taxes and state and local income taxes within the state of issue.

Municipal Bond Fund. A mutual fund that invests in a broad range of tax-exempt bonds issued by states, cities, and other local governments. The interest obtained from these bonds is passed through to the shareowners free of federal tax. The fund's primary objective is current income.

Municipality. A state, city, town, hospital, toll bridge, or other local, public service, nonprofit incorporation.

Mutual Fund. (See: Investment Company)

N

NASD. The National Association of Securities Dealers. An association of brokers and dealers in the over-the-counter securities business. The Association has the power to expel members who have been declared guilty of unethical practices. NASD is dedicated to--among other objectives--"adopt, administer, and enforce rules of fair practice and rules to prevent fraudulent and manipulative acts and practices, and in general to promote just and equitable principles of trade for the protection of investors."

NASDAQ. An automated information network that provides brokers and dealers with price quotations on securities traded over the counter. NASDAQ is an acronym for National Association of Securities Dealers Automated Quotations.

NASDAQ Indexes. Indexes that reflect over-the-counter market activity; calculated like the S&P and NYSE indexes, based on a value of 100 set February 5, 1971.

NYSE Common Stock Index. A composite index covering price movements of all common stocks listed on the "Big Board." It is based on the close of the market December 31, 1965 as 50.00 and is weighted according to the number of shares listed for each issue. The index is computed continuously and printed on the ticker tape each half hour. Point changes in the index are converted to dollars and cents so as to provide a meaningful measure of changes in the average price of listed stocks. The composite index is supplemented by separate indexes for four industry groups: industrials, transportation, utilities, and finances.

Naked Option Writer. Options written on stock

not owned by the writer.

Negotiable. Refers to a security, title to which is transferable by delivery.

Negotiated Market. A market involving dealers, such as the OTC.

Net Asset Value. A term usually used in connection with investment companies, meaning net asset value per share. It is common practice for an investment company to compute its assets daily, or even twice daily, by totaling the market value of all securities owned. All liabilities are deducted, and the balance divided by the number of shares outstanding. The resulting figure is the net asset value per share.

Net Change. The change in the price of a security from the closing price on one day and the closing price on the following day on which the stock is traded. The net change is ordinarily the last figure on the stock price list. The mark + 1 1/8 means up $1.125 a share from the last sale on the previous day the stock traded.

Net Investment Income Per Share. Dividends and interest earned during an accounting period (such as a year) on a fund's portfolio, less operating expenses, divided by number of shares outstanding.

Net Realized Capital Gain Per Share. The amount of capital gain realized on sale of a fund's portfolio holdings during an accounting period (such as a year), less losses realized on such transactions, divided by number of shares outstanding.

Net Worth. The ownership position or amount or wealth, or equity, in the assets owned.

New Issue. A stock or bond sold by a corporation for the first time. Proceeds may be issued to retire outstanding securities of the company, for new plant or equipment of for additional working capital.

New York Stock Exchange (NYSE) The key exchange for stock and bond transactions, accounting for about 65 percent of the total annual volume of shares traded.

No-Load Fund. A mutual fund selling its shares at net asset value without the addition of sales charges.

Nominal Interest Rates. Money interest rates advertised in newspapers; they have an inflation allowance built into them.

Noncallable Bond. A bond that cannot be retired before maturity.

Noncumulative. A preferred stock on which unpaid dividends do not accrue. Omitted dividends are, as a rule, gone forever.

Nondiversifiable (Systematic) Risk. Risk attributed to forces affecting all investments and therefore not unique to a given vehicle, such as war, inflation, and political events; the risk possessed by every investment vehicle.

NOW Account: Negotiable Order of Withdrawal. A special type of savings account that draws interest and allows the depositor to write checks on his funds. All depository institutions can offer such accounts to customers.

O

Odd Lot. An amount of stock less than the established 100-share unit or 10-share unit of trading: from 1 to 99 shares for the great majority of issues. 1 to 9 for so-called inactive stocks.

Off-Board. This term may refer to transactions over the counter in unlisted securities, or to a transaction involving listed shares which was not executed on a national securities exchange.

Offer. The price at which a person is ready to sell. Opposed to bid, the price at which one is ready to buy.

Open-End Investment Company. An investment company (mutual fund) which continually issues shares of stock. Such shares are usually sold and redeemed on the basis of the net asset value which is computed at the market close each day. (See: Investment Company)

Open Order. (See: Good 'Til Cancelled Order)

Opportunity Cost. The annual rate of return that could be earned on a similar investment.

Option. A right to buy (call) or sell (put) a fixed amount of a given stock at a specified price within a limited period of time. The purchaser hopes that the stock's price will go up (if he bought a call) or down (if he bought a put) by an amount sufficient to provide a profit greater than the cost of the contract and the commission and other fees required to exercise the contract. If the stock price holds steady or moves in the opposite direction, the price paid for the option is lost entirely. There are several other types of options available to the public but these are basically combinations of puts and calls. Individuals may write (sell) as well as purchase options and are thereby obliged to deliver or buy the stock at the specified price. There are also listed call option markets on the Chicago Board Options Exchange and the American and PBW Stock Exchanges. These differ from the over-the-counter market in that trading is limited to selected issues, expiration of contracts is standardized at four dates during the year, exercise prices are set at multiples of 5, and option prices are determined through a continuous competitive auction market system.

Option Income Fund. The investment objective of these funds is to seek a high current return by investment primarily in dividend-paying common stocks on which call options are traded on national securities exchanges. Current return generally consists of dividends, premiums from expired call options, net gains from sales of portfolio securities or exercises of options or otherwise, and any profits from closing purchase transactions.

Option Premium. The price that a buyer of a put or call option must pay to purchase the option. Also called the option's "price."

Options Clearing Corp. The actual issuer of options. Moreover, in the event of an exercise, it is the corporation, as the ultimate obligor, that becomes the source of securities for buyers.

Ordinary Income. Income from all sources such as salaries, dividends, interest, income from investments, and earnings from incorporated businesses (sole proprietorships or partnerships).

Organized Exchange. A formal organization that conducts orderly markets for the securities in which it chooses to make markets. The NYSE is an example of an organized securities exchange.

Out-of-the-Money Option. An option with no intrinsic value. A call is out of the money when the exercise price is higher than the underlying stock's price. A put is out of the money when the exercise price is lower than the current market value of the stock.

Over-the-Counter. A market for securities made up of securities dealers who may or may not be members of a securities exchange. Over-the-counter is mainly a market made over the telephone. Thousands of companies have insufficient shares outstanding, stockholders, or earnings to warrant application for listing on the New York Stock Exchange. Securities of these companies are traded in the over-the-counter market between dealers who act either as principals or as brokers for customers. The over-the-counter market is the principal market of U.S. government and municipal bonds.

Overbought. An opinion as to price levels. May refer to a security that has had a sharp rise or to the market as a whole after a period of vigorous buying that, it may be argued, has left prices "too high."

Oversold. An opinion--the reverse of overbought. A single security or a market that, it is believed, has declined to an unreasonable level.

P

Paper Profit. An unrealized profit on a security still held. Paper profits become realized profits only when the security is sold.

Par. In the case of a common share, par means a dollar amount assigned to the share by the company's charter. Par value may also be used to compute the dollar amount of the common shares on the balance sheet. Par value has little significance so far as market value of common stock is concerned. Many companies today issue no-par stock but give a stated per share value on the balance sheet. In the case of preferred shares and bonds, however, par is important. It often signifies the dollar value upon which dividends on preferred stocks, and interest on bonds, are figured. The issuer of a 6 percent bond promises to pay that percentage of the bond's par value annually.

Participating Preferred. A preferred stock that is entitled to its stated dividend and, also, to additional dividends on a specified basis upon payment of dividends on the common stock.

Passed Dividend. Omission of a regular or scheduled dividend.

Payment Date. The actual date on which the company will mail dividend checks to the holders of record.

Payout Ratio. A indication of the amount of earnings paid out to stockholders in the form of dividends.

$$\text{Payout ratio} = \frac{\text{Dividends per share}}{\text{Earnings per share}}$$

Peaks and Troughs. A peak of business activity occurs when general business activity is at its highest level. Peaks separate the end of an expansion in business activity from the start of a recession. Troughs occur when general business activity is at its lowest level. Troughs separate the end of a recession from the start of an expansion.

Penny Stocks. Low-priced issues often highly speculative, selling at less than $1 a share. Frequently used as a term of disparagement, although a few penny stocks have developed into investment-caliber issues.

Permanent or Whole Life Insurance. This is any type of insurance, other than term, which has the following characteristics: A cash value that can be borrowed, used as collateral, or withdrawn by surrendering the policy; and a lump sum benefit payable at death.

Point. In the case of shares of stock, a point means $1. If ABC shares rise 3 points, each share has risen $3. In the case of bonds a point means $10, since a bond is quoted as a percentage of $1000. A bond which rises 3 points gains 3 percent of $1000, or $30 in value. An advance from 87 to 90 would mean an advance in dollar value from $870 to $900 for each $1000 bond. In the case of market averages, the word point means merely that and no more. If, for example, the Dow Jones Industrial average rises from 870.25 to 871.25, it has risen a point . A point in this average, however, is not equivalent to $1.

Portfolio. Holdings of securities by an individual or institution. A portfolio may contain bonds, preferred stocks, and common stocks of various types of enterprises.

Portfolio Manager. An individual who makes decisions regarding buying, selling, or holding securities for an investment organization.

Portfolio Turnover. A measure of how much security trading went on within a portfolio during a given time period. Generally given in percentage of total assets in a year; 80% of the dollar value of a portfolio's holdings, for example, were changed in a year.

Preferred (Quality) Ratings. Ratings of preferred stocks that show yield and potential price behavior.

Preferred Stock. A class of stock with a claim on the company's earnings before payment may be made on the common stock and usually entitled to priority over common stock if the company li-

quidates. Usually entitled to dividends at a specified rate--when declared by the Board of Directors and before payment of a dividend on the common stock-- depending on the terms of the issue.

Premium. The amount by which a preferred stock or bond may sell above its par value. In the case of a new issue of bonds or stocks, premium is the amount the market price rises over the original selling price. Also refers to a charge sometimes made when a stock is borrowed to make the delivery on a short sale. May refer, also, to redemption price of a bond or preferred stock if it is higher than face value.

Pre-tax (Net) Profit Margin. The rate of profit from sales and other revenues.

$$\text{Net profit margin} = \frac{\text{Net profit before taxes}}{\text{Total revenues}}$$

Price-Earnings (P/E) Ratio. The current market price divided by the previous year's per share earnings.

$$P/E = \frac{\text{Market price of common stock}}{\text{Earnings per share}}$$

Price Risk. That part of interest rate risk involving the inverse relationship between bond prices and required rates of return.

Primary Distribution. Also called primary offering. The original sale of a company's securities. (See: Investment Banker)

Primary Market. The market for new issues of securities, typically involving investment bankers.

Principal. The term "principal" refers to a person's capital or to the face amount of a bond.

Private Placement. The sale of an issue of securities to an institutional investor.

Profit-Taking. Selling stock which has appreciated in value since purchase, in order to realize the profit which has been made possible. The term is often used to explain a downturn in the market following a period of rising prices.

Profitability Ratio. A ratio used as a relative measure of success; relates the returns (profits) of a company to sales, assets, or equity.

Progressive Tax. A graduated tax; taxpayers with larger income pay a larger percent in taxes.

Promised Yield. Indication of the fully compounded rate of return available to the investor, assuming the obligation is held to maturity. Also called yield-to-maturity.

Prospectus. A document describing in detail the

key aspects of the issuer, its management and financial position, and the security to be issued; explains in detail the operations of a fund, its investment objectives, and other key financial matters.

Proxy. A written authorization that a shareholder can sign to give voting rights to another party.

Public Offering. An offering in which a dealer offers new securities for sale to the public by registering the issue with the Securities and Exchange Commission and disseminating prospectuses to all potential investors.

Publicly Traded Issues. Shares that are rapidly available to the general public and are bought and sold on the open market.

Purchasing-Power Risk. Risk arising from inflation.

Put Bond. A bond that has its market price supported by a provision in the bond issue's indenture allowing bond investors to sell (or put) the bond back to the issuer at a specified price.

Puts and Calls. (See: Option)

Q

Quotation. Often shortened to "quote." The highest bid to buy and the lowest offer to sell a security in a given market at a given time. If you ask your broker for a "quote" on a stock, he may come back with something like "45¼ to 45½." This means that $45.25 is the highest price any buyer wanted to pay at the time the quote was given on the floor of the exchange and that $45.50 was the lowest price which any seller would take at the same time. (See: Bid and Asked)

R

Rally. A brisk rise following a decline in the general price level of the market, or in an individual stock.

Real Assets. Physical assets, such as gold or real estate.

Real Property. Land, buildings, and that which is permanently affixed to the land.

Realized Yield. The return actually earned on a bond as opposed to the yield to maturity, which is a promised yield.

Recession. A period of time (several months to a few years) during which general business activity contracts.

Record Date. The date on which you must be registered as a shareholder in the stock book of a company in order to receive a declared dividend or, among other things, to vote on company affairs. (See: Ex-dividend)

Redemption Price. The price at which a mutual fund's shares are redeemed (bought back) by the fund. The bid or redemption price usually means the net asset value per share.

Redemption Price. The price at which a bond may be redeemed before maturity, at the option of the issuing company. Redemption value also applies to the price the company must pay to call in certain types of preferred stock. (See: Callable)

Refinancing. Same as refunding. New securities are sold by a company and the money is used to retire existing securities. Object may be to save interest costs, extend the maturity of the loan, or both.

Registered Bond. A bond which is registered on the books of the issuing company in the name of the owner. It can be transferred only when endorsed by the registered owner. (See: Bearer Bond, Coupon Bond)

Registered Investment Adviser. A person who provides advice to the public concerning the purchase or sale of securities is required, by the Securities and Exchange Commission and the Investment Advisers Act, to be registered with the SEC as an advisor.

Registered Representative. In a New York Stock Exchange Member Organization, a registered representative is a full-time employee who has met the requirements of the exchange as to background and knowledge of the securities business. Also known as an account executive or customer's broker.

Registration. Before a public offering may be made of new securities by a company, or of outstanding securities by controlling stockholders--through the mails or in interstate commerce--the securities must be registered under the Securities Act of 1933. Registration statement is filed with the SEC by the issuer. It must disclose pertinent information relating to the company's operations, securities, management, and purpose of the public offering. Securities of railroads under jurisdiction of the Interstate Commerce Commission, and certain other types of securities, are exempted. On security offerings involving less than

$300,000, less information is required. Before a security may be admitted to dealings on a national securities exchange, it must be registered under the Securities Exchange Act of 1934. The application for registration must be filed with the exchange and the SEC by the company issuing the securities. It must disclose pertinent information relating to the company's operations, securities, and management.

Registration of an Issue. The filing of a prospectus and other information with the Securities and Exchange Commission, as required by the Securities Act of 1933; it provides full disclosure of information to investors.

Regular Dividend. The payment of fixed dollar increments on a quarterly basis.

Regular-Extra Dividend. A dividend paid whenever the level of earnings is higher than normal and the firm has an extra pool of funds from which to pay dividends.

Reinvestment Privilege. A service provided by most mutual funds for the automatic reinvestment of dividends and capital gains distributions into additional fund shares.

REIT. Real Estate Investment Trust, an organization similar to an investment company in some respects but concentrating its holdings in real estate investments. The yield is generally liberal since REITs are required to distribute as much as 90 percent of their income.

Relative Strength. A technical trading strategy that maintains today's strongest performing stocks relative to a market index will also be tomorrow's strongest performing stocks.

Renewable Term. Term life insurance which may be renewed at the rate for the attained age without evidence of insurability.

Rental Property. A property that provides rental income to its owners.

Repurchase Agreement (Repos). These agreements consist of three component transactions. One is the purchase of U.S. Government securities by an investor. The second is an agreement by a second investor to purchase them temporarily with a promise that the original investor, in the third step, will repurchase these securities on a specified date at a specified price. Retail repos are secured short-term loans with T-Bills as collateral.

Required Rate of Return. The minimum expected return on an asset that an investor requires before investing.

Residential Properties. Rental units with permanent occupants.

Residual Claim. The claim with the lowest priority (e.g., common stockholders have a residual claim on their corporation's income and assets.)

Retained Earnings. The amount of past and current earnings not paid out as dividends, and left to accumulate in the firm to finance the operations of the company.

Retention Rate. 1.0 minus the payout ratio.

Return. (See: Yield)

Return on Equity (ROE). The rate of return on stockholders' equity, equal to net income divided by equity.

Risk. The chance that the actual return on an investment will be different from the expected return.

Risk Premium. The additional compensation demanded by investors, above the risk-free rate of return, for assuming risk--the larger the risk, the larger the risk premium.

Risk-Return Tradeoff. The inverse relationship between the risk associated with a given investment and its expected return.

Round Lot. A unit of trading or a multiple thereof. On the NYSE the unit of trading is generally 100 shares in stocks and $1000 par value in the case of bonds. In some inactive stocks, the unit of trading is 10 shares.

Round Trip Commission. The commission costs on both ends of a transaction, buying and selling.

S

SEC. The Securities and Exchange Commission, established by Congress to help protect investors. The SEC administers the Securities Act of 1933, the Securities Exchange Act of 1934, the Securities Act Amendments of 1975, the Trust Indenture Act, the Investment Company Act, the Investment Advisers Act, and the Public Utility Holding Company Act.

SIPC. Securities Investor Protection Corporation that provides funds for use, if necessary, to protect customers' cash and securities that may be on deposit with a SIPC member firm in the event the firm fails and is liquidated under the provisions of the SIPC

Act. Protection is limited to $100,000 per customer account of which no more than $40,000 may be used for cash claims. SIPC is not a government agency. It is a nonprofit membership corporation created, however, by an act of Congress.

Sales Charge. An amount charged to purchase shares in most mutual funds. Typically the charge is 8.5 percent of the initial investment. The charge is added to the net asset value per share in determining the offering price.

Savings Account. A deposit made to a financial institution which then pays a stated rate of interest on the funds.

Savings and Loan Association (S&L). A financial institution that accepts time deposits and uses this money primarily for financing home mortgages. Some S&Ls are stock corporations. These are usually chartered and regulated on the state level. Many S&L's are mutually owned by their depositors, who receive dividends from the association's profits.

Savings Plan. A systematic savings and capital accumulation program in which the investor agrees to add to a mutual fund regularly (monthly or quarterly); the money is used to purchase added shares.

Seat. A traditional figure of speech for a membership on an exchange. Price and admission requirements vary.

Secondary Market. A market (e.g., the NYSE or the OTC market) where previously issued securities are traded. The issuer of the security receives no cash flow from secondary market trades among investors.

Security. An investment of money in a common enterprise with the expectation of profit from the effort of others.

Serial Bonds. Bonds that mature at specified stated intervals.

Simple Interest. Interest paid only on the principal and computed only on the principal. See Compound Interest for comparison.

Sinking Fund. Money regularly set aside by a company to redeem its bonds, debentures, or preferred stock from time to time as specified in the indenture or charter.

Specialist. A member of the New York Stock Exchange who has two functions: first, to maintain an orderly market, insofar as reasonably practicable, in the stocks in which he or she is registered as a specialist. In order to maintain an orderly market, the exchange expects the specialist to buy or sell for his own account, to a reasonable degree, when there is a temporary disparity between supply and demand. Second, the specialist acts as a broker's broker. When a commission broker on the exchange floor receives a limit order, say to buy at $50 a stock then selling at $60--he cannot wait at the post where the stock is traded to see if the price reaches the specified level. So he leaves the order with the specialist, who will try to execute it in the market if and when the stock declines to the specified price. At all times the specialist must put his customers' interest above his own. There are about 350 specialists on the NYSE.

Specialty Fund. Concentrated holdings in one industry, or group of related industries, geographical area, or specialty. Electronics, metals, chemicals, health fields, and foreign specialties (Japanese stocks, South African gold) are all examples of specialty funds.

Speculation. The employment of funds by a speculator for short-term profit. Safety of principal is a secondary factor.

Speculative Stock. Shares offering little more than hope that their prices will go up. Imperfect records of success, uncertain earnings, and high instability are all qualities of speculative stock.

Speculator. One who is willing to assume a relatively large risk in the hope of gain. The speculator may buy and sell the same day or speculate in an enterprise that he does not expect to be profitable for some time.

Split. The division of the outstanding shares of a corporation into a larger number of shares. A 3-for-1 split by a company with 1 million shares outstanding results in 3 million shares outstanding. Each holder of 100 shares before the 3-for-1 split would have 300 shares, although his proportionate equity in the company would remain the same; 100 parts of 1 million are the equivalent of 300 parts of 3 million. Ordinarily splits must be voted by directors and approved by shareholders. (See: Stock Dividends)

Standard and Poor's (S&P) Corporation. A large financial publisher that provides information on specific industries and companies on a subscription basis.

Standard Deviation. A statistic that measures the dispersion of outcomes around their expected (or mean) value; it is used to measure total risk.

Stock Dividend. A dividend paid in securities rather than cash. The dividend may be additional shares of the issuing company, or shares of another company (usually a subsidiary) held by the company. (See: Ex-dividend, Split)

Stockholder of Record. A stockholder whose name is registered on the books of the issuing corporation.

Stockholder's Report. A source of operating data on an individual firm published annually by most publicly held corporations. It contains a wide range of information, including financial statements for the most recent period of operation, along with summarized statements for several prior years. (See: Annual Report)

Stop-Loss. Order to sell a stock when its market price reaches or drops below a specified level; used primarily to protect the investor against rapid declines in prices and to limit losses.

Stop Order. An order to buy at a price above or sell at a price below the current market. Stop buy orders are generally used to limit losses or protect unrealized profits on a short sale. Stop sell orders are generally used to protect unrealized profits or limit losses.

Street. The New York financial community in the Wall Street area.

Street Name. Securities held in the name of a broker instead of his customer's name are said to be carried in a "street name." This occurs when the securities have been bought on margin or when the customer wishes the security to be held by the broker.

Strike Price. The Exercise Price, or the price at which the holder of an option may purchase (a call) or sell (a put) an underlying stock.

Super NOW Account. An unrestricted checking account paying money market rates.

Syndicate. A group of investment bankers who together underwrite and distribute a new issue of securities or a large block of an outstanding issue. (See: Investment Banker)

Systematic Risk. See Nondiversifiable Risk.

T

Take-Over. The acquiring of one corporation by another--usually in a friendly merger but sometimes marked by a "proxy fight." In "unfriendly" take-over attempts, the potential buying company may offer a price well above current market values including new securities and other inducements to stockholders. The management of the subject company might ask for a better price, fight the take-over, or attempt to merge with another company.

Tax Credit. Provision of Internal Revenue Service regulations allowing a taxpayer to claim a credit on taxes due under certain specified conditions.

Tax Deductible. Expenses that reduce the amount of taxable income, for example, medical expenses, charitable deductions, and interest paid.

Tax-Deferred Income. Cash flow on which no tax is payable, generally because the depreciation deduction is at least as large as the cash flow and debt service.

Tax-Free Rollovers. A transfer of funds from a company pension plan, IRA or other tax-sheltered plans into an IRA, completed within 60 days after funds are available.

Tax Selling. Sales made to realize gains or losses for income tax purposes.

Tax Shelter. Certain forms of investment that can lower ordinary taxable income.

Tax-Sheltered Retirement Plans. Contributions to individual retirement accounts, Keogh plans, tax-sheltered annuities, and appropriately administered company pension plans that are tax deductible.

Technical Analysis. Analysis of the market and stocks based on supply and demand. The technician studies price movements, volume, trends and patterns that are revealed by charting these factors, and attempts to assess the possible effect of current market action on future supply and demand for securities and individual issues. (See: Fundamental Analysis)

Tender Offer. An offer made by a corporation to purchase the stock of another firm from its stockholders at a specifically announced price. Typically, the tender price is higher than the prevailing market price of the stock.

Term Life Insurance. This type of insurance covers a limited specific period of time. In the event of death, benefit will be paid only if death occurs during the period the policy is in force. There is a type of term insurance, called convertible term, which can be guaranteed to be exchanged for other types of insurance even if the policyholder would not otherwise qualify.

Term to Maturity. The remaining life of a bond.

Thin Market. A market in which there are comparatively few bids to buy or offers to sell or both. The phrase may apply to a single security or to the entire stock market. In a thin market, price fluctuations between transactions are usually larger than they are when the market is liquid. A thin market in a particular stock may reflect lack of interest in that issue or a limited supply of or demand for stock in the market.

Ticker. The instrument that prints prices and volume of security transactions in cities and towns throughout the U.S. and Canada within minutes after each trade on the floor.

Time Value of Money. Money has time value because a dollar can grow to a dollar plus interest income as time passes.

Tips. Supposedly "inside" information on corporate affairs.

Total Risk. Total variability of the investor's returns due to diversifiable plus undiversifiable risk.

Trader. One who buys and sells for his own account for short-term profit.

Trading Floor. (See: Floor)

Trading Post. One of 23 trading locations on the floor of the New York Stock Exchange at which stocks assigned to that location are bought and sold. About 75 stocks are traded at each post.

Treasury Bill. A short-term money market instrument sold at discount by the U.S. government.

Treasury Bond. Long-term bonds sold by the U.S. government.

Treasury Note. U.S. securities with maturities of 1 to 10 years.

Turnover Ratio. A measure of the purchase and sale activity of a mutual fund. It is calculated by dividing the lesser of purchases or sales for the fiscal year by the monthly average value of the securities owned by the fund during the year. However, securities with maturities of less than one year are excluded from the calculation. A portfolio turnover of 100 percent implies a complete turnover of fund assets.

12b-1 Plan. Named for an SEC ruling, the plan provides that a mutual fund may assess a fee against the assets of the fund to cover marketing and distribution expenses. This plan is in addition to the advisor's management fee agreement (which is not allowed to include fees for these purposes). To adopt the 12b-1 plan, the shareholders must vote approval unless it is included in the charter at inception of the fund. This information must be provided in the prospectus.

U

Underwriter. (See: Investment Banker)

Unit Investment Trust. A limited portfolio of bonds or other securities in which investors may purchase shares. It differs from a mutual fund in that no new securities will be added to the portfolio.

U.S. Savings Bond. A security readily available to the individual investor issued by the U.S. Treasury.

Universal Life. An interest-sensitive form of life insurance indexed to money market yields, offering variable cash values and mobility between permanent and term life insurance plans.

Unlisted. A security not listed on a stock exchange. (See: Over-the-Counter)

Unsystematic Risk. Also called nonmarket risk or diversifiable risk. It is risk attributable to factors unique to the security.

Up Tick. A term used to designate a transaction made at a price higher than the preceding transaction. Also called a "plus" tick. A stock may be sold short only on an up tick, or on a "zero-plus" tick. A "zero-plus" tick is a term used for a transaction at the same price as the preceding trade but higher than the preceding different price. Conversely, a down tick, or "minus" tick, is a term used to designate a transaction made at a price lower than he preceding trade. A "zero-minus" tick is a transaction made at the same price as the preceding sale but lower than the preceding different price.

V

Valuation. A procedure for estimating the true worth of an investment vehicle.

Value Line Investment Survey. One of the most popular subscription services used by individual investors; published weekly and covering more than 1,700 companies and their stocks.

Variability. Dispersion in the likely outcome.

Variable Life Insurance. An equity-based life insurance policy in which the reserves may be invested in common stocks. The death benefit is guaranteed never to fall below the face value, but it could increase if the value of the securities increases. There may be no guaranteed cash surrender value under this kind of policy.

Variable Rate Note. An unusual form of debt with two unique features: (1) after the first 6 to 18 months of the issue, the coupon "floats" so that every 6 months it is pegged at a certain amount (usually 1 percent) above prevailing Treasury bill or bond rates; (2) the notes are redeemable--at par at the holder's option--every 6 months, after the first year.

Volatility. Fluctuations in a security's or portfolio's return.

Volume. The number of shares traded in a security or an entire market during a given period. Volume is usually considered on a daily basis and a daily average is computed for longer periods.

Voluntary Plan. An accumulation plan without any stated duration or specific requirements other than the minimum amounts that may be invested at one time. Sales charges are applicable individually to each purchase made.

Voting Right. The stockholder's right to vote his stock in the affairs of his company. Most common shares have one vote each. Preferred stock usually has the right to vote when preferred dividends are in default for a specified period. The right to vote may be delegated by the stockholder to another person. (See: Cumulative Voting, Proxy)

W

The Wall Street Journal. The most popular and comprehensive source of financial news. The WSJ is published daily.

Wealth. The sum of current income and the present value of all future income.

Whipsawing. Situation in which a stock temporarily drops in price and then bounces back up.

Whole Life Insurance. Insurance coverage over the entire life of an insured.

Withdrawal Plan. Investment funds that offer shareholders the opportunity to receive payments regularly on a monthly or a quarterly basis.

Yearly Renewal Term. Term policies written for one-year periods and renewable each year without evidence of insurability.

Yield. Also known as return. The dividends or interest paid by a company expressed as a percentage of the current price. A stock with a current market value of $40.00 a share paying dividends at the rate of $2.00 is said to return 5 percent ($2.00 ÷ $40.00). The current return on a bond is figured the same way. A 3 percent $1000 bond selling at $600 offers a current yield return of 5 percent ($30 ÷ $600). (See: Dividend, Interest)

Yield to Maturity. The yield of a bond to maturity takes into account the price discount from or premium over the face amount. It is greater than the current yield when the bond is selling at a discount and less than the current yield when the bond is selling at a premium.

Z

Zero Coupon Bond. A bond sold with no coupons. It is purchased at a discount and redeemed for face value at maturity.

INDEX

N

NASDAQ—NASD Automated Quotation
    System, 5-4
NASDAQ OTC Composite Index, 13-3
NOW account, 6-3
NYSE Composite Index, 13-3
Naked writer (option), 14-5
National Association of Securities Dealers
    (NASD), 5-4
National OTC market, 5-4
National unit trust, 8-9
Negotiable certificates of deposit (CDs), 2-2
Negotiated market, 5-3
Net asset value, 2-5, 16-1
Net current asset value per share, 12-6
Net income available to stockholders, 10-2
Net worth, 1-1
New York Stock Exchange (NYSE), 5-3
News release, C-1
No load fund, 16-3
Non-discretionary account, 17-5
Non-governmental purpose municipal bond, 8-6
Non-recurring or extraordinary gains/losses, C-3
Noncumulative preferred, 9-1
Nondiversifiable risk, 3-8
Nonparticipating insurance, 7-6
Nonparticipating preferred, 9-1

O

Odd-lot order, 5-8
Odd-lot short sales, 13-5
Open-end investment company, 16-1
Option buyer (holder), 14-2
Option premium, 14-2
Option seller (writer), 14-2
Organized (listed) exchange, 5-1
Out-of-favor stocks, 12-5
Out-of-the-money option, 14-3

P

Par value, 8-1, 9-1, 11-2
Participating insurance, 7-7
Participating mortgage REIT, 15-6
Participating preferred, 9-1
Passbook account, 6-2
Passive income/losses, 15-1, 19-2
Payable date (dividend), 10-5
Personal exemption, 19-1
"Pink sheet" stocks, 5-4
Preferred dividend, 9-1

Preferred stock rating system, 9-3
Preferred stock, 2-4, 9-1
Premium bond, 8-8
Price-earnings (P/E) ratio, 11-6
Primary (new issue) market, 5-1
Principal, 8-1
Product-oriented IRA plan, 18-5
Profit margin, 11-5
Prospectus, C-1
Proxy statement, C-1
Proxy, C-1
Public-purpose municipal bond, 8-6
Pure risk protection, 7-1
Put option, 2-5, 14-1

Q

Quarterly report, C-1

R

Range of returns, 3-4
Real estate earnings-based account, 6-3
Real estate investment trust (REIT), 15-5
Real estate limited partnership (RELP), 15-6
Realized returns, 3-3
Record date (dividend), 10-5
Redemption or surrender fee, 16-4
Registered bond, 8-2
Regular OTC market, 5-4
Regular dividend, 10-6
Regular-extra dividend, 10-6
Rehabilitated real estate, 15-10
Renewable and convertible term insurance, 7-3
Repurchase agreement (repo), 2-2
Retail repos, 2-2
Retained earnings, 10-2
Return on equity, 11-5
Return, 1-3
Revenue bond, 2-3
Rollover IRA, 18-7
Round-lot order, 5-8

S

S&P 500 Composite Index, 13-2
S.E.C. 10-K Report, C-1
S.E.C. 10-Q Report, C-1
Safety of principal, 1-2
Seasoned bond, 8-8
Secondary (used issue) market, 5-1
Sector fund, 16-5
Secured bond, 2-4
Securities & Exchange Commission (SEC), 5-10

Self-directed IRA Plan, 18-5
Short interest, 13-5
Short sale, 5-6
Simple interest, 6-2
Single-premium whole life policy, 7-5
Single-state municipal fund or state unit trust, 8-9
Sinking fund provision, 8-8, 9-1
"Sleeping Beauty" stocks, 12-5
Specialist, 5-1
Speculative stock, 11-2
Standard deduction, 19-1
Standard deviation, 3-5
Stated (or nominal) interest rate, 6-2
Statement of changes in financial condition, C-2
Stock dividend, 10-4
Stock option, 2-5
Stock split, 10-4
"Stop-loss" order, 5-8
Straight term insurance, 7-3
"Street-name" account, 5-6
Strike price, 14-2
SuperNOW account, 6-3

T

Taxable municipal bond, 8-6
Technical (market) analysis, 11-7, 13-1
Term life insurance, 7-2
The "Big Board" exchange, 5-3
The "Curb" exchange, 5-3
Theory of Contrary Opinion, 13-5
Ticker symbol, 5-9
Time value of an option, 14-3
Tombstone, 5-1
Top down approach, 11-4

Total return, 1-3
Triple-net lease, 15-10
12b-1 plan, 16-4

U

U.S. Treasury bill, 2-1, 8-3
U.S. Treasury bond, 2-2, 8-3
U.S. Treasury note, 2-2, 8-3
Underwriter, 5-1
Underwriter syndicate, 5-1
Uniform Gift to Minors, 19-8
Unit investment trust, 8-7
Universal life insurance, 7-4
Universal variable insurance, 7-4
Unleveraged RELP, 15-10
Unsecured bond, 2-4

V

Variability, 3-5
Variable annuity, 7-6
Variable life insurance, 7-4
Volatility, 3-6
Volume, 11-3
Voting rights, 9-1

W

Whole (ordinary or permanent) life insurance, 7-3
Withdrawal procedure, 6-4
Write-downs, C-3
Write-offs, C-3

Y

Yield pick-up swap, 8-8
Yield-to-maturity, 8-3

ABOUT THE AUTHOR

Andrew J. Senchack, Jr. is a Professor of Finance at The University of Texas at Austin. He received his B.S. degree in Industrial Engineering and his M.B.A. from Texas Tech. He performed graduate work in finance and investments at the Harvard Business School and received his Ph.D. in Finance (with distinction) from U.C.L.A.

Dr. Senchack is the author of over 40 articles on securities investments and portfolio management. He is a former Associate Editor of the Journal of Financial Research, and Referee for Journal of Financial and Quantitative Analysis, Management Science, Journal of Business Research, Journal of Economics and Business and Journal of Risk and Insurance.

He has served as a financial consultant and expert witness in stockholder class action suits, regulatory hearings, and personal liability suits. He is a co-founder and former president of Mentor Systems, Inc., a microcomputer software development company for the financial industry. He also participates in the U.T. Management Development Program and the Texas S&L League Management Development Program. He has also been a private investor for over 15 years.